T0254879

Lecture Notes of the Institute for Computer Sciences, Social Informatics and Telecommunications Engineering 260

More information about this series at http://www.springer.com/series/8197

Rafik Zitouni · Max Agueh (Eds.)

Emerging Technologies for Developing Countries

Second EAI International Conference, AFRICATEK 2018
Cotonou, Benin, May 29–30, 2018
Proceedings

 Springer

Editors
Rafik Zitouni
ECE Paris, VEDECOM
Paris, France

Max Agueh
ECE Paris
Paris, France

ISSN 1867-8211   ISSN 1867-822X (electronic)
Lecture Notes of the Institute for Computer Sciences, Social Informatics
and Telecommunications Engineering
ISBN 978-3-030-05197-6   ISBN 978-3-030-05198-3 (eBook)
https://doi.org/10.1007/978-3-030-05198-3

Library of Congress Control Number: 2018963117

This Springer imprint is published by the registered company Springer Nature Switzerland AG
The registered company address is: Gewerbestrasse 11, 6330 Cham, Switzerland

Preface

We are delighted to introduce the proceedings of the second edition of the 2018 European Alliance for Innovation (EAI) International Conference on Emerging Technologies for Developing countries (Africatek 2018). This conference targets the use of new technologies such as cloud computing, IoT, data analytics, green computing, etc. Building innovative solutions and services based on cutting-edge technologies is very challenging in developing countries for several reasons. The limited IT infrastructure and Internet penetration are two of the key hindering barriers. The goal is to bring together researchers and practitioners from academia and industry to share their results and ideas on how to benefit the developing world from the technologies' advances despite the existing limitations.

The technical program of Africatek 2018 consisted of 12 full papers, including four short papers in oral presentation sessions at the main conference tracks. The conference tracks were: Track 1 – Intelligent Transportation Systems (ITS) and Security; Track 2 – Applications and IT Services; Track 3 – Gaming and User Experience; Track 4 – Augmented Reality and Data Analytics. Aside from the high-quality technical paper presentations, the technical program also featured two keynote speeches and two invited talks. The first keynote speaker was Dr. Patrick Valduriez from Inria Sophia Antipolis, France. The second speaker was Dr. Martial Ahyi from Accenture/L'Oréal, France. The invited talks were presented by Her Excellency Mrs. Marie-Odile Attanasso, Minister of Education, Benin, Her Excellency Mrs. Aurelie Adam Soule Zoumarou, Minister of Digital Economy, Benin.

We would like to express our gratitude and thanks to many people who contributed to the organization of this first edition. Without their support and dedicated efforts, the conference would not have been possible. Coordination with the steering chairs, Max Agueh, Fatna Belqasmi, Henoc Soude, was essential for the success of the conference. We sincerely appreciate their constant support and guidance. It was also a great pleasure to work with such an excellent Organizing Committee team for their hard work in organizing and supporting the conference. In particular, the Technical Program Committee, led by our TPC co-chairs, Dr. Rafik Zitouni, Dr. Taha Ridene, and Dr. Pélagie Houngue, who completed the peer review of the technical papers and made a high-quality technical program. We are also grateful to the conference manager, Eliska Vlckova, for her support and all the authors who submitted their papers to the Africatek 2018 conference.

We strongly believe that the Africatek conference provides a good forum for all researchers, developers, and practitioners to discuss all technical and scientific aspects for innovation. We also expect that the future Africatek conferences will be as successful and stimulating, as indicated by the contributions presented in this volume.

November 2018   Rafik Zitouni
                                                                      Max Agueh

Organization

Steering Committee

Imrich Chlamtac   University of Trento, Italy/EAI

Steering Committee Member

Fatna Belqasmi   CTI, Zayed University, UAE

Organizing Committee

General Chair

Max Agueh   ECE Paris, France

General Co-chairs

Fatna Belqasmi   CTI, Zayed University, UAE
Henoc Soude   IMSP, Benin

Technical Program Committee Chair and Co-chairs

Pélagie Houngue   IMSP, UAC, Benin
Taha Ridene   U2IS-ENSTA ParisTech, France
Rafik Zitouni   ECE Paris, VEDECOM, France

Web Chair

Alemayehu Addisu Desta   ESIEE Paris, France

Publicity and Social Media Co-chairs

Martial Ahyi   L'Oreal, Paris, France
Max Olivier Loko   BearingPoint, France
Antoine Bagula   University of the Western Cape, South Africa

Workshops Chair

Fabien Houeto   SLB, USA

Sponsorship and Exhibits Chairs

Gilles Ahouanmenou   Deloitte, Benin
Martial Ahyi   L'Oreal, France
Max Olivier Loko   BearingPoint, France

Publications Chairs

Rafik Zitouni   ECE Paris, VEDECOM, France
Laurent George   University of Paris-Est Creteil, France

Panels Chair

Christelle Agossou   SES Broadband Service, Benin

Tutorials Co-chairs

Jean-François Diouris   IRESTE, France
Stefan Ataman   ELI-NP, Romania

Demos Co-chairs

Fabrizio Delage   Valeur Tech, France
Pierre Poullain   Valeur Tech, France
Pierre Courbin   ESILV, France

Posters and PhD Track Chair

Alemayehu Addisu Desta   ESIEE Paris, France

Local Co-chairs

Sem Marie-Odile Attanasso   MESRS, Benin
Henoc Soude   IMSP, UAC, Benin
Pelagie Houngue   IMSP, UAC, Benin

Technical Program Committee

Alemayehu Desta   ECE Paris, France
Marco Zennaro   ICTP, Italy
Eugene C. Ezin   University of Abomey Calavi, Benin
Christian Attiogbe   University of Nantes, France
Jonathan Ouoba   VTT Technical Research Centre, Finland
Karl Jonas   Hochschule Bonn-Rhein-Sieg University, Germany
Patrick Valduriez   Inria, France
Pierre Courbin   ESILV, France
Tayeb Lemlouma   IRISA/IUT of Lannion, France
Aurel Randolph   Polytechnique Montréal, Canada
Ouzzif Mohamed   ESTC, Morocco
Eleanna Kafeza   Zayed Universty, UAE
Elhadj Benkhelifa   Staffordshire University, UK
May El Barachi   University of Wollongong, Dubai
Mehdi Kaddouri   Université Mohamed Premier-Oujda, Morocco
Mohamed Adel Serhani   UAE University, UAE
Mohamed Bakhouya   UIR, Morocco

Mohammed Erradi	ENSIAS, Morocco
Pierre de Saqui-Sannes	ISAE SUPAERO, France
Radouane Mrabet	University Mohammed V, Morocco
Saiqa Aleem	Zayed University, UAE
Slimane Bah	EMI, Morocco
Tounwendyam F. Ouedraogo	Universite de Koudougou, Burkina Faso
Zahi Jarir	Cadi Ayyad University, Morocco
Abdellah Boulouz	Univesity UIZ Agadir, Morocco
Abdeslam Ennouaary	INPT, Morocco
Mostafa Belkasmi	University Mohammed V, Morocco
Nadir Bouchama	CERIST Research Center, Algeria
Ahmed Soua	VEDECOM, France
Hakim Badis	LIGM, France
Frédéric Fauberteau	ESILV, France
Mohamed Anane	ESI, Algeria
Sihem Zitouni	Bejaia University, Algeria
Houda Chihi	SupCom, Tunisia
Federico Mele	ECE Paris, France
Ahcene Bendjoudi	CERIST Research Center, Algeria

Contents

Short Paper Session

Gaming and User Experience

ITS and Security

Internet of Things-Based Framework for Public Transportation Fleet Management in Non-smart City

Muthoni Masinde[1(✉)], Ahmed Shoman[1],
and Mohamed Hassan Mostafa[2]

[1] Unit for Research on Informatics for Droughts in Africa (URIDA),
Central University of Technology, Free State,
Private Bag X20539, Bloemfontein 9300, South Africa
muthonimasinde@gmail.com, admsho@gmail.com
[2] Sustainable, Urban, Roads and Transportation (SURT),
Central University of Technology, Free State,
Private Bag X20539, Bloemfontein 9300, South Africa
mmostafa@cut.ac.za

Abstract. The notable increase in location-based applications especially in smart cities realm is driven by the emergence of miniaturized, cheaper and readily available location-based internet of things' devices. The backbone of the internet of things is a well-orchestrated electronic infrastructure, telecommunication and information technology. Such a backbone is the precursor for the success of internet of things applications that have mushroomed in the public transportation sectors of the developed world. The developing countries such as South Africa have not kept pace with the development of these electronic infrastructures. Implementation of smart city concepts such as intelligent public transportation system in these countries therefore requires novel approaches. As one of the solutions to this, we present an internet of things framework that enables the integration of multiple cost-effective internet of things technologies through which public transport-related information can be obtained in cost-effective and robust ways. The framework was designed and evaluated using a system prototype for the Free State province (South Africa) public transport system case.

Keywords: Intelligent public transport system · Internet of things framework
Free State province · South Africa

1 Introduction

1.1 Background Information

Since the birth of the Internet of Things (IoT) concept at MIT in 1999 [1], tens of other definitions have emerged – mostly depending on the application context. Conceptualization of IoT in terms of the 4As vision (anytime, anyplace, anyone and anything) by ITU in 2005 expanded this definition and closely tied it with ubiquitous computing [2]. In the definition used in the Cluster of European Research projects on the Internet of

© ICST Institute for Computer Sciences, Social Informatics and Telecommunications Engineering 2019
Published by Springer Nature Switzerland AG 2019. All Rights Reserved
R. Zitouni and M. Agueh (Eds.): AFRICATEK 2018, LNICST 260, pp. 3–17, 2019.
https://doi.org/10.1007/978-3-030-05198-3_1

Things (CERP-IoT), the ITU's 4As vision has been extended to 6As by including Any path/network and Any service representing any type of location or network and any available service respectively. The IoT definition in CERP-IoT is adopted in this paper [3]:

> *"a dynamic global network infrastructure with self-capabilities based on standard and inter-operable communication protocols where physical and virtual "things" have identities, physical attributes, virtual personalities and use intelligent interfaces, and are seamlessly integrated into the information network"*

The basic concept behind IoT is the interlinking of physical, social and cyber worlds. This has resulted in huge impacts on society and humans as well as social networks. The driver for this impact is the ability of IoT to turn traditional systems into smart systems, for example, smart mobility services that provide citizens with tools to accurately plan their journeys with public transportation [4]. IoT brings tangible benefits, primarily to physical industries such as agriculture, manufacturing, energy, transportation and health care.

Key generic requirements for IoT application include ability to manage heterogeneity, support for dynamism, scalable, support for interoperable communication protocols, cost effective, self-configuration (including self-organization, self-adaptation, self-reaction to events and stimuli, self-discovering of entities and services and self-processing of Big Data), flexibility in dynamic management/reprogramming of devices or group of devices, Quality of Service (QoS), Quality of Experience (QoE), context awareness, intelligent decision making capability and adherence to secure environments [4, 5].

Over the last five years, the number of IoT applications has grown exponentially. Figure 1 below shows the main domain areas under which these applications fall.

Close to half of the application scenarios shown in Fig. 1 below fall under the Smart City domain. The core challenges of this domain are urban sensing and data acquisition, computing with heterogeneous data, and hybrid systems blending the physical and virtual worlds [6]. Of interest to this paper is the transport and mobility aspect of a smart city. Examples of applications in this realm include a system that automatically records public vehicle positioning data [7] and OnRoute – an information services for passengers [8]. Others are cooperative intelligence transport system [9] and internet of vehicles by Kaiwartya et al. [10]. Datta et al. [11] looks at the five challenges around connected vehicles while Rakotonirainy et al. [12] tackle a more complex solution of managing driver's behaviour by incorporating Quantified Self and Artificial Intelligence.

Researchers have proposed various object (the 'things') federation architectures to ensure that the myriad components that are part of the IoT can operate in harmony. Borga [4] presents this in form of three phases: data collection phase, transmission phase and process, management and utilization phase (see Fig. 2 below). Similar architecture for the implementation of low-power applications is presented by Yelmarthi and Khattab [13] while a middleware designed around *inlining* approach is describe in Mhlaba and Masinde [14]. A semantic-based framework that integrates machine learning is found in [15] - here five layers are included: physical entities, abstract entities, data stream, fusion and utility layer.

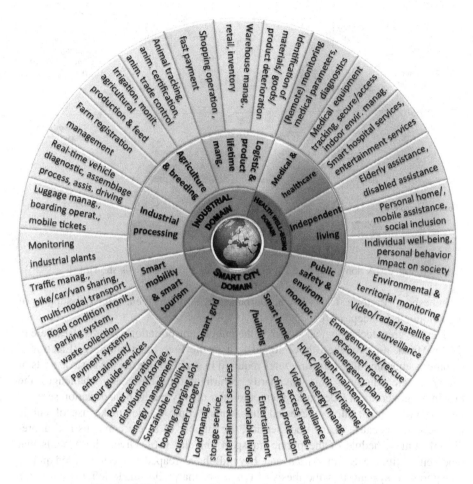

Fig. 1. IoT application domains and related applications [4]

Public transportation is an important area that governments constantly must pay attention to because of the large number of people that depend on it on a daily basis. The South African government established a department of transport to deal with all transport related matters, including the public transportation environment. The Department of Transport, over a period of 10 years has carried out many surveys as part of the initiative to improve the service level of public transportation in South Africa. Some of the results of these surveys indicate that about 19% of the public is willing to make use of public transportation if their service requirements are met [16]. Developments in this field is ongoing in order to improve the service and to meet the requirements of the public [16].

The Internet of Things-technology has already been used to improve the quality of service in the field of public transportation in the country. Cape Town uses the Transport for Cape Town (TCT) application (app) [17] and Johannesburg uses i-Traffic [18]. Uber has also been widely used in the larger South African cities such as

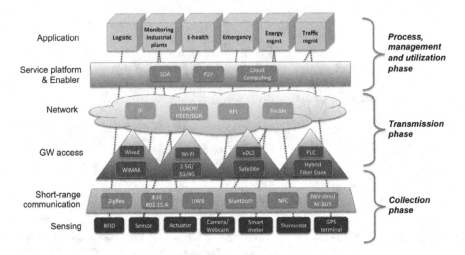

Fig. 2. A non-exhaustive list of technologies and protocols is shown [4]

Johannesburg, Pretoria, Cape Town, Durban, and Port Elizabeth with full support of the ubiquitous concept [19].

Despite great technological strides in the public transportation systems elsewhere in South Africa, none of these have found root in the Free State province. Electronic, communication and ICT infrastructures required in supporting even the basic aspects of smartness are missing. This has partly contributed to the many challenges the provincial government faces in its attempt to offer quality public transportation services [20]. A government survey revealed that many people do not make use of public transportation because of the poor service, the number of safety concerns and unpredictably time schedule of the public transport vehicles [16]. Given the benefits that other cities (in the South Africa and beyond) have reaped from IoT-based public transportation system, it is the thesis of this paper that, tailor-made IoT system is the solution to the problems in the Free State's public transportation system [21].

1.2 Research Objectives

The aim of this research was to develop a framework that would allow the integration of a number of technologies within the Internet of Things (IoT) paradigm in order to provide efficient and effective way of managing public transportation in a resource-challenged environment such as the Free State province in South Africa. This aim was achieved through two sub-objectives: (1) a detailed investigation of the technological challenges facing the public transportation sector in the province and identification IoT technologies that are applicable to the province's context; and (2) the development of an IoT integration framework, consisting of five IoT components – a system prototype was then developed and used to evaluate the working of this framework.

2 Methodology

2.1 Data Collection Methods

Three data collection methods were employed, namely, observation, interview and questionnaires. In order to experience the challenges faced by the stakeholders of the public transportation sector, the researcher visited a number of the public transport hubs in the city of Bloemfontein (the capital of Free State province). Observation data collection method [22] was then applied and the challenges experienced first-hand recorded. Selected stakeholders of the public transportation sector were interviewed. The findings from these interviews, together with information elicited from literature reviews and the observations, was used to design questionnaires for three categories of the sector's stakeholders. The three questionnaires were targeted to all of the three different participants, namely; passengers who make use of the public transportation, the owners of the public transportation vehicles and the drivers who are employed to drive these vehicles. The order in which these data collection methods were executed is shown in Fig. 3 below.

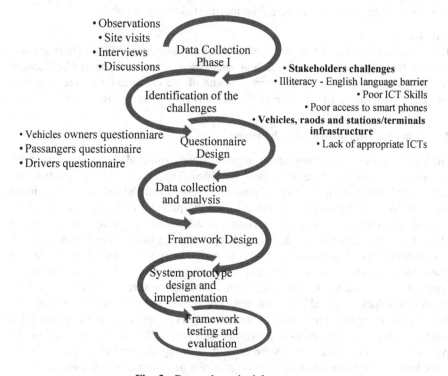

Fig. 3. Research methodology steps

As depicted in the flowchart in Fig. 3, the study was divided into the following five phases: (1) data collection phase 1 (observations and interviews), (2) identification of challenges facing the public transportation sector, (3) design and administration of questionnaires, (4) data analysis and (5) designed, implementation (through prototyping) and evaluation of an IoT integration framework. These phases are discussed in detail below.

2.2   Data Collection Phase 1 - Observation and Interviews

During this phase, the data for the research study was collected by means of observations and interviews. The researcher aimed to gather as much information as possible about the case study of the Free State public transportation management system. This provided the much-needed understanding of the Sector.

Observation

During this phase, the researcher visited the research sites of interest and just observed how the public transportation business was conducted. The sites visited consisted of two public transport terminals in the Free State; Bloemfontein and Thaba Nchu. The researcher also commuted between these two stations by means of public transportation to experience first-hand what the public transportation was all about.

Interviews

The researcher interviewed members of the Public Transportation Committees and took note of their opinions, complaints and suggestions. Some of the public transport vehicles' owners as well as members of some of the organizations were also interviewed in an effort to identify the challenges that they were facing.

2.3   Phase 2 - Identification Challenges

From the interviews and observations in phase 1, the main challenges facing the public transportation sector in Free State were identified. These were divided into two categories: (1) infrastructural limitation in the Free State terminals/stations, and (2) infrastructural needs of the people that make use of the public sector. It also emerged that both of these categories of limitations could be addressed by appropriate employment of Information and Communication Technologies (ICTs), this is especially at the public transportation terminals/stations. It was also discovered that the main key players (passenger, drivers, and owners) had such diverse needs and one-solution-fit-all approach would not work. For instance, the passengers were in need of prior information on vehicles' arrival times and real-time notifications of specific (of interest to them) vehicle arrival. The needs of the passengers differed from one passenger to another– this is due differences in general literacy levels, ICT-literacy, age and gender. As for the drivers, their needs were around ensuring the quality of service to the passengers. Such included prior knowledge of the next stop at which passengers need to disembark. On the other hand, all the vehicle owners needed most was the ability to manage and monitor their vehicles on real-time basis.

2.4 Phase 3 - Questionnaire Administration

In order to gather information on opinions on various stakeholders as well as the of the proposed system, questionnaires designed and administered to passengers, drivers and vehicle owners. All the three questionnaires (for passengers, drivers and vehicle owners) focused on three areas: current infrastructure/ICT/services/management, quality of transportation service, and anticipated/expected improvements in efficiency of the transportation system emanating from the proposed IoT framework. The data collected frm using these questionnaires was analysed and reports compiled in Excel. The results of analysing this data is discussed in Sect. 2.5 below.

2.5 Phase 4 - Data Analysis

Each of the three questionnaires were analysed separately. For demonstration purposes, only data for the passenger questionnaire is presented here.

The participants who completed the passenger questionnaire consisted of 45% males and 55% females. The age of the participants ranged from 18–35 years. The majority of school learners younger than 18 years of age made use of taxis (minibuses) rather than other public transportation vehicles such as buses. The passengers rated the average waiting time for a vehicle as 7 out of 10, where 1 is not having to wait at all, and 10 having to wait for a long time. Approximately 55% of passengers preferred to do shopping while they are waiting at the public transport station, which results in 40% of them indicated that they missed their awaited transport. More than a third of the passengers complained that they never disembarked where they were supposed to as, most of the time, the driver dropped them further down the route. This is due to the method used to notify the driver of a disembarking passenger, which is either by shouting, asking someone to notify the driver, knocking on the window or, in some cases, using a buzz button. However, most of the vehicles were not equipped with buzz buttons, and if they were, the driver is notified too late, not allowing him enough time to prepare to stop the vehicle. The remainder of the passengers, who did not experience these problems, are passengers on long distance routes outside the city, or passengers who drive from one station to another that allows them to avoid stopping between the two main points. The study shows that the majority of the passengers, more than 70%, own smartphones and it is seldom that one finds a passenger without any kind of cell phone.

2.6 Phase 5 - Framework Development

Borrowing from the cross-cutting elements of IoT frameworks presented in [4] and supported by Yelmarthi and Khattab [13] and Mhlaba and Masinde [14], a framework for integrating IoT into the Free State public sector was designed. As discussed in Sect. 3, the framework consists of 5 layers: storage layer, service layer, communication layer, sensor/devices layer and application layer.

2.7 System Prototype Development and Testing

In line with the framework, a system prototype was developed using four IoT 'things': Radio Frequency Identifier (RFID), Global Positioning System (GPS), Infra-Red (IR), and Global General Packet Radio Service (GPRS). Mobile phones were incorporated – they played the role of a sensing (camera, motion and GPS sensors) devices, a computing device for the mobile application and finally as input/out device for the resulting system. A mobile application and an integrated web portal were also designed to provide for friendly user input/output interface.

3   IoT Framework for Public Transport System

3.1   Framework Layers

As depicted in Fig. 4, the framework consists of five main layers. The layers interact with each other through the different channels.

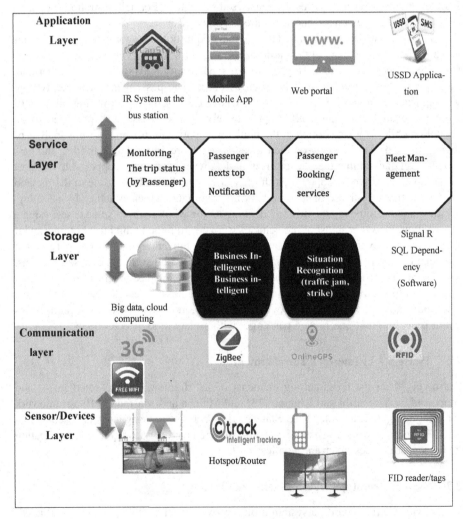

Fig. 4. IoT framework for public transport application

Application Layer

The top layer is the application layer; different user interacts with the system through this layer. In order to achieve this, the layer supports different user interfaces that offer different services to the different users such as monitoring, visualising, analysing, reporting, notifications, guiding, and managing information. It is through this layer that ubiquity (access by anyone, at any time, from anywhere and using any of the supported devices) of the framework is implemented. As currently implemented, the framework is designed to offer an Unstructured Supplementary Service Data (USSD) application for non-smart phones users and an Android mobile phone application for smartphone users. The web portal ensures availability of the system online for all users who have access to the internet.

Device/Sensor Layer

The device layer is where all the IoT devices are located. This layer is responsible for generating data from the sensors and sending it to the server for processing. This layer is currently implemented to support four sensing devices: RFID, GPS, IR and GPRS.

RFID tags are supposed to be attached to each vehicle to identify the vehicle, while the RFID reader is installed at the station/terminal entrance to notify the users of the arrival of vehicles. RFID sensors are linked to a server (Gateway) that transmits its data to the online database.

Each vehicle participating in the system is fitted with a GPS sensor to enable real-time tracking. Together with the GPRS, the GPS transmits the GPS coordinates of the location of the vehicle to the online database.

An IR sensor is used for counting the number of passengers boarding or leaving the vehicle. Each vehicle uses two IR sensors; one of these is located at the gate (the point where the passenger leaves/enters the vehicle) to determine the direction of the passenger. If the outside IR is activated first then the inside IR will indicate that the passenger is getting into the vehicle, conversely, if it is the other way around, it will mean that the passenger is disembarking. The IR sensor is linked to a smart chip that is programmed to count the number of passengers (according to this method), and this information transmit it via GPRS to the online database.

Communication Layer

The next layer is the communication layer, which establishes different types of communication technology (3G, GPS, RFID, Bluetooth, Zigbee and IR-Light Emitting Diode) between the devices, sensors, servers and users. As currently implemented, this layer uses three different types of communication signals. The RFID reader at the gate of the bus station uses a computer that is connected to the internet via Local Area Network (LAN), Wi-Fi or a 3G modem. Both GPS and IR sensors on the vehicles will uses GPRS communication. Users at the station access the station's Wi-Fi. Users outside the station use the 3G connection on their smartphones, or the general cellular connection for the USSD application in the case of non-smart phones.

Service Layer

The other layer is the service layer; here, several communication services are offered to first layer objects (passengers, owners, drivers, vehicles, stations) [5]. Station administration/vehicle owners are provided with fleet management service, and vehicles are equipped with real-time tracking equipment so that the station can be notified when a vehicle is arriving or leaving. Vehicle owners will be able to receive a real-time location for their vehicles, and keeping records of number of passengers used their vehicle. The passenger can make a booking for the next trip and will be notified of the arrival of the vehicle.

The driver application offers services such as an update on the current number of passengers who have registered for a specific trip and advance notification of the next location where passengers will be disembarking.

Storage Layer

The storage layer is the layer where database engines, such as the Oracle engine or Microsoft SQL, manage and control the database. The database engine is responsible for the following: storing, querying, managing and clouding big data. This layer will be further discussed in the next section. Future extension to the framework will include the ability to support big data, cloud computing, situation recognition and business intelligence (BI) analytics.

3.2   Framework Implementation

The actual implementation of the framework is in form of a working system prototype whose system architecture is presented in Fig. 5 below.

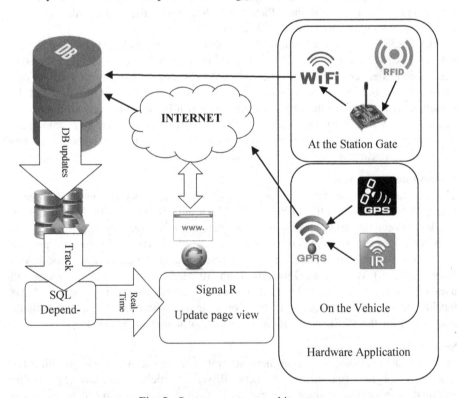

Fig. 5. System prototype architecture

A system prototype was implemented to mimic the working of the framework. Firstly, a GPS sensor was used to determine coordinates of the vehicles' location; these coordinates were published through the internet. Secondly, an RFID sensor was used to identify vehicles that were arriving at and departing from the bus station(s)/terminals. Thirdly, Waspmote sensors[1], that communicate via Zigbee, were used to complement both RFID and GPS sensors. Fourthly, GPRS was used to transmit GPS data to the server. Fifthly, Wi-Fi was used to transmit the received data from Zigbee to the server and used in the station to connect the public monitor and other users. Sixthly, 3G communication was used on a smartphone to register, monitor and manage data by different users. Seventhly, the general cellular signal was used, for non-smartphones, to send the USSD code and to receive SMS for notifications. Finally, the web page was used to register, monitor and manage all the data relating to the entire system. By making use of all of these integrated sub-systems, the successful implementation of the IoT framework was made possible.

3.3 System Prototype Testing

Mobile Application
This application (app) to be viewed. It serves the three main user-types, namely; passengers, vehicle owners and drivers. Although the main page of the app is visible to all users, it distinguishes between the different types of users. After determining the user type, the application page navigates to the next applicable page where the user is able to perform user-specific functions. For instance, a vehicle owner or driver has to complete a login page to navigate to the next page. However, the passenger page will navigate

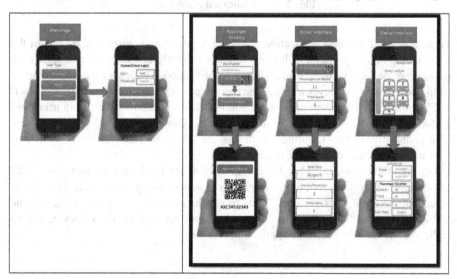

Fig. 6. Mobile application main page

---

[1] http://www.libelium.com/products/waspmote/.

directly to the next passenger page without having to login or sign-up. If the driver/owner is not yet registered, he/she will have to sign up first, and can only be able to use the system once the administrator (admin) user has approved his registration (Fig. 6).

Web Application
Users can browse the web application online from anywhere and using any smart device, e.g. smartphones, tablets, laptops and computers. Module Viewer Controller (MVC) was used in the development of this application; C#.net was the main programming language. It consists of a Login Page visible to all users (passengers, drivers, owners and administrator). The system distinguishes between the different user levels to enable navigation to the relevant page for a specific kind of user. From the login page (Fig. 7).

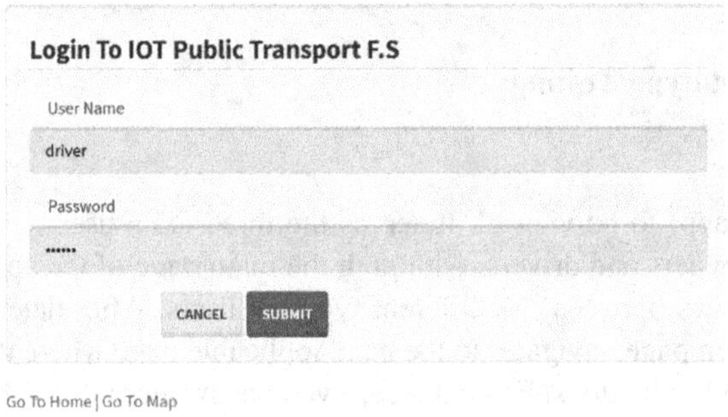

Fig. 7. We application login page

The next page of the web application is the home page that is displayed on one of the public monitors in the station. It lists all vehicles currently at the station and shows the arrival time for each vehicle. It also displays notifications (with a visual pop-up and a sound notification) whenever a vehicle arrives or leaves the station. (see Fig. 8 below)[2]

The other important web page is the administration (admin where admin users will be able to create the credentials for different users. The admin user also registers new vehicles and trips (routes). Further, from this, the admin user assigns every vehicle to all of the drivers, the owner and a route.

On the other hand, the Map Page displays on one of the public monitors at the station real-time tracking for all of the vehicles in transit. Using Signal-R and Database-Dependency with SQL-Dependency, this page offers a real-time update trigger on the database and pages. This acts as an intermediate tool between the GPS tracking sensor on the vehicle and the software application (Fig. 9).

[2] https://docs.oracle.com.

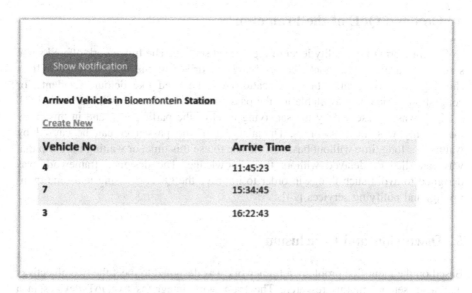

Fig. 8. Web application home page

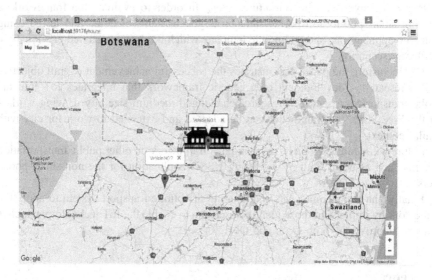

Fig. 9. Web application map page

4 QoS and QoE of the Framework

QoS is measuring the quality level of the offered service. The framework offered some services to achieve this goal like notifying the driver of the next stop, as well as showing the driver, and other notifications can be used like detour, accidents, or congestion, which also available for the passengers to be notified with the delay [23].

QoE was represented by the satisfying level of the participants, and in this study that mainly was the passengers. Dissatisfying of the passenger can be caused by waiting for long time without having a chance to use this time, or waiting for a trip that was cancelled or delayed without their knowledge. The designed framework was designed to avoid such things in order to improve the QOE by using real-time monitoring, and notifying services [24].

5 Discussion and Conclusion

Based on the identified problem, a framework was designed to meet the two objectives that were set out in this research. The framework integrates five IoT devices in a generic fashion such that it is scalable to help using it in any other places. This was made possible by the layered approach that was used; the framework has different layers that serve at different levels (application layer, devices layer, communication layer, service layer, and infrastructure layer). In order to evaluate the framework, a working smart public transport system prototype was implemented and tested using both web applications, and the mobile template which has been discussed previously in a different scenario.

In conclusion, the paper demonstrates the successful achievement overall objective of this research – development of a generic framework that integrates IoT into the public transportation sector of resource-challenged medium size city. Having worked for the Free State, the framework can be adapted and extended to work for city with similar context.

Future work can be made by applying this framework on other public transportation systems such as trains, and by activating USSD application for the non-smart phone users.

Finally, the short comes was encouraging the public transport system to apply the framework by implement those identified sensors to enable the IoT technology which is going to improve the both QoS, and QoE.

References

1. Gama, K., Touseaui, L., Donsez, D.: Combining heterogeneous service technologies for building an internet of things middleware. Comput. Commun. **35**(4), 405–417 (2012)
2. International Telecommunication Union: ITU Internet Report 2005: The Internet of Things. International Telecommunication Union, Geneva (2005)

3. Jain, A.K., Hong, L., Pankanti, S.: Internet of things - strategic research roadmap. Technical report, Cluster of European Research projects on the Internet of Things, September 2009. http://www.internet-of-things-research.eu/pdf/IoT_Cluster_Strategic_Research_Agenda_2011.pdf
4. Borgia, E.: The internet of things vision: key features, applications and open issues. Comput. Commun. **54**, 1–31 (2014)
5. Ray, P.P.: A survey on internet of things architectures. J. King Saud Univ.-Comput. Inf. Sci. **30** (2016)
6. Behrendt, F.: Why cycling matters for smart cities. Internet of bicycles for intelligent transport. J. Transp. Geogr. **56**, 157–164 (2016)
7. Padrón, G., García, C.R., Quesada-Arencibia, A., Alayón, F., Pérez, R.: Using massive vehicle positioning data to improve control and planning of public road transport. Sensors **14**(4), 7342–7358 (2014)
8. García, C.R., Pérez, R., Lorenzo, Á., Quesada-Arencibia, A., Alayón, F., Padrón, G.: Architecture of a framework for providing information services for public transport. Sensors **12**(5), 5290–5309 (2012)
9. Neisse, R., Baldini, G., Steri, G., Mahieu, V.: Informed consent in internet of things: the case study of cooperative intelligent transport systems. In: 2016 23rd International Conference on Telecommunications (ICT), pp. 1–5. IEEE, May 2016
10. Kaiwartya, O., et al.: Internet of vehicles: motivation, layered architecture, network model, challenges, and future aspects. IEEE Access **4**, 5356–5373 (2016)
11. Datta, S.K., Da Costa, R.P.F., Härri, J., Bonnet, C.: Integrating connected vehicles in internet of things ecosystems: challenges and solutions. In: 2016 IEEE 17th International Symposium on A World of Wireless, Mobile and Multimedia Networks (WoWMoM), pp. 1–6. IEEE, June 2016
12. Rakotonirainy, A., Orfila, O., Gruyer, D.: Reducing driver's behavioural uncertainties using an interdisciplinary approach: convergence of quantified self, automated vehicles, internet of things and artificial intelligence. IFAC-PapersOnLine **49**(32), 78–82 (2016)
13. Yelmarthi, K., Abdelgawad, A., Khattab, A.: An architectural framework for low-power IoT applications. In: 2016 28th International Conference on Microelectronics (ICM), pp. 373–376. IEEE, December 2016
14. Mhlaba, A., Masinde, M.: Implementation of middleware for internet of things in asset tracking applications: in-lining approach. In: 2015 IEEE 13th International Conference on Industrial Informatics (INDIN), pp. 460–469. IEEE (2015)
15. Zhang, N., Chen, H., Chen, X., Chen, J.: Semantic framework of internet of things for smart cities: case studies. Sensors **16**(9), 1501 (2016)
16. van Ryneveld, P.: 15 Year Review of Public Transport in South Africa with emphasis on metropolitan areas. Hunter van Ryneveld (Pty) (2008)
17. Berg, R.: Cape Town launches mobile transport app. BDlive, 20 October 2014. https://www.techcentral.co.za/cape-town-launches-transport-app/51895/
18. Sanral: Cameras. Sanral, South Africa (2017)
19. Uber: Uber Cities (2017). https://www.uber.com/en-ZA/cities/. Accessed 29 Nov 2017
20. National Household: Statistics South Africa (2014)
21. Avenri, E.: A cumulative prospect theory approach to passengers behavior modeling: waiting time paradox revisited. Taylor and Francis (2004)
22. Johnson, B., Turner, L.A.: Data collection strategies in mixed methods research. In: Handbook of Mixed Methods in Social and Behavioral Research, pp. 297–319 (2003)
23. Singh, J., Singh, K.: Congestion control in vehicular ad hoc network: a review. In: Lobiyal, D.K., Mansotra, V., Singh, U. (eds.) Next-Generation Networks. AISC, vol. 638, pp. 489–496. Springer, Singapore (2018). https://doi.org/10.1007/978-981-10-6005-2_49
24. Hoßfeld, T., et al.: The memory effect and its implications on web QoE modeling. In: Teletraffic Congress (ITC), 6–9 September 2011, pp. 103–110 (2011)

A Middleware for Cyber Physical Systems in an Internet of Things Environment: Case of for Mobile Asset Tracking

Muthoni Masinde[✉] and Admire Mhlaba

Unit for Research on Informatics for Droughts in Africa(URIDA),
Central University of Technology, Free State, Private Bag X20539,
Bloemfontein 9300, South Africa
muthonimasinde@gmail.com, yaddly@gmail.com

Abstract. The upsurge in Cyber Physical Systems (CPSs) has made researchers conclude that these systems have the potential of rivalling the contribution of the Internet. Driving this wave is the emergence of miniaturized, cheaper and readily available location-based hardware devices. One of the main applications of CPSs is mobile asset tracking system whose roles are to monitor movements of a mobile asset and to track the object's current position. Localization accuracy of these systems is one of the key performance indicators. This is usually maximised through the introduction of extra hardware devices. The drawbacks with this approach include restriction of the system's application only to one domain, introduction of extra cost to the overall system and introduction of a single point of failure. Conversely, the Internet of Things (IoT) paradigm facilitates coalescing of diverse technologies through which locus data can be extracted in cost-effective and robust way. The challenge is the lack of a dependable and responsive middleware that is capable of handling and servicing such devices. We present a solution to this problem; a middleware designed around In-lining approach that acts as an insulator for hiding the internal workings of the system by providing homogenous and abstract environment to the higher layers. The evaluation of laptop tracking and monitoring system prototype was carried out through implementation of a middleware that integrates diverse IoT components in a university environment.

Keywords: Cyber Physical Systems (CPSs)
Mobile Asset Management (MAM) · Internet of Things (IoT) · Middleware
Laptop monitoring and tracking system (LMTS)

1 Introduction

1.1 Background Information

The concept behind Cyber Physical Systems (CPSs) is the incorporation of information and data communication technologies with the physical and real worlds, especially engineering operations and tasks [1]. Although invented back in 2006 [2], there is noticeable increase in CPSs applications which is driven by the emergence of miniaturized, cheaper and readily available location-based hardware devices. This draws

© ICST Institute for Computer Sciences, Social Informatics and Telecommunications Engineering 2019
Published by Springer Nature Switzerland AG 2019. All Rights Reserved
R. Zitouni and M. Agueh (Eds.): AFRICATEK 2018, LNICST 260, pp. 18–31, 2019.
https://doi.org/10.1007/978-3-030-05198-3_2

parallels with other related technological advancements such as Internet of Things (IoT), Machine-to-Machine (M2 M) communication and Wireless sensor networks (WSNs). Figure 1 below shows the evolution of CPSs and their correlation with these technologies [3]. There are possibilities that CPSs may even surpass the massive contributions made by internet [2].

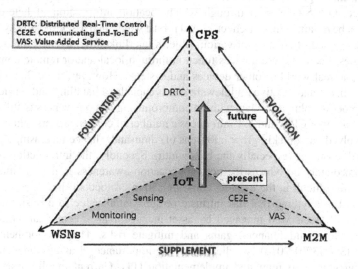

Fig. 1. IoT application range of CPSs [3]

Application areas of CPSs include smart transportation, smart cities, precision agriculture and entertainment [4]. Over the last decade, CPSs frameworks have been developed to address the following aspects: complexity, adaptability, safety, reliability and maintainability. In [4, 5] for instance, the focus is on adaptability. One area where CPSs have attained some maturity is in mobile asset tracking systems or mobile asset management systems (MAMs). Their application domains include patient monitoring, equipment management and emergency management [6]. MAMs implantation involve attaching a node to a mobile object to monitor the object's movement and current location real-time [7]. This is achieved through location-based services.

The requirements for location-based systems introduce opposing performance metrics such as localization accuracy, precision, complicity, cost effectiveness, low power consumption and tiny size, portability across domains, robustness and scalability (variable number of nodes) [8]. In particular, accuracy factor is inversely proportional to the number of nodes that can be supported simultaneously [9]. Despite this, when it comes to tracking our valuable assets, localization accuracy ranks high because it increases chances of recovering the asset.

Most implementers of asset tracking systems tend to achieve this accuracy by introducing extra hardware [10]. Global Positioning System (GPS), General Packet Radio Service (GPRS) and Radio Frequency Identifier (RFID) technology provide such devices; however, the drawback with this approach is that the cost of the solution is considerably increased and the application domain is highly restricted. Besides, such applications introduce a single point of failure or bottleneck; for instance, GPS devices tend to fail when indoors and their high demand for power makes them inappropriate for use for small mobile assets and battery powered devices.

On the contrary, CPSs and Internet of Things (IoT) enables the unification of multiple technologies (the Internet, mobile phones, RFID readers/tags, Bluetooth, Wi-Fi, ZigBee, GPRS/GPS etc.) through which location information of heterogeneous objects can be obtained in cost-effective and robust way. Such asset tracking systems are usually composed of an array of various objects interlinked by diverse communication technologies. Each of these devices function through local and/or remote communication with the real world or other devices and systems. However, the difficult of maintaining a reliable and reactive middleware that is capable of handling and servicing such devices, process volumes of data without compromising responsiveness is still eminent. The very nature of CPSs and IoT introduces a number of challenges: first, the number of nodes involved can quickly grow into (tens of) thousands, hence increasing contention for limited resources (especially the bandwidth). Secondly, the introduction of mobile nodes immediately introduces the need for location-awareness in the communication, which is still difficult in the existing communication protocols [9].

An asset is anything that has intrinsic or substantial value to a business or individual entity. Assets well managed by asset management systems, can among other things lead to sound financial gains and mitigate risks. The development of ISO standard (ISO 55001:2014) is indicative of the importance of asset management systems along with their regulated implementation [11]. Current mobile asset tracking systems are expensive and inefficient – this is especially due to the cost transferring huge amounts of data that is required in tracking assets' position and velocity [12].

The intensified use of mobile devices such as smartphones and tablets has workers around the globe increasingly becoming mobile - they to do their work at the office, at home, and while travelling. This has resulted to the anytime, anywhere information workers - those who use three or more devices, working from multiple locations, and use many applications [13]. Consequently, the traditional asset management and tracking systems have to be re-designed to cater for this as well as for the "bring your own device" (BYOD) concept. In the meantime, the availability of these devices has led to an increase in their (devices) loss through theft. This increase in larceny is somewhat motivated by the fact that laptops (including iPads and tablets) are miniature and easy to conceal and pocket away. In addition, filched devices carry a remarkable resale value on the informal market and are conveniently disposed of online, using platforms such as Gumtree, cheaply and anonymously. The difficulties in tracking and tracing the physical location of stolen mobile devices can be attributed as the primary reason for the surge in theft. In an attempt to annihilate this growing calamity, many solutions have been developed, however several small and medium-sized organizations are compelled to do with one due high cost of ownership. Regardless of improvements in electronic engineering and availability of miniature GPS and GPRS hardware, there remains a gap that portable computing device manufacturers need to fill with regards to the integration of tracking technologies to combat this menace.

1.2 Research Objectives

The main objective of this research was to develop a generic IoT architecture that innovatively and intelligently integrates wireless sensors, RFID tags (and readers), fingerprint readers, and mobile phones. The operation of this middleware was then evaluated using an asset monitoring and tracking application capable of dispelling laptop theft. This research was aimed at investigating a solution to the following question: How to design a middleware that ensures an effective and efficient integration (of biometrics, mobile phones, RFIDs and mobile phones) and for use within the context of asset monitoring and tracking system. Two objectives were identified to help answer the above question: (1) to create a generic middleware architecture that interconnects at least 4 diverse IoT components and (2) to use a laptop monitoring and tracking system (LMTS) to assess the integrity and responsiveness of the middleware.

The rest of this article is organised as follows: Sect. 2 encompasses associated literature, while Sect. 3 elucidates, the methodology used and Sect. 4 details the discussion and conclusion.

2 Allied Literature

2.1 Cyber Physical Systems (CPSs)

According to [1], a cyber-physical system (CPS) connects the cyber and physical worlds for the purpose of merging and analysing real and cyber information – the analysed data is fed back to the real world. Such systems are capable of controlling movement of reality autonomously – without intervention of humans. This characteristic draws parallels with Internet of Things. CPSs intermingle with the physical world by interrogating and actuating. The main sub-systems that make up CPSs are: (1) wireless/wired sensor networks (WSNs); (2) a decision support system (DSS); and (3) physical systems/elements [4]. In their simplest form, CPSs consist of a mobile asset affixed with a sensor node, in a mobile asset system and that navigates around a monitored area [14].

Of interest to this paper is the mobile asset tracking application domain of CPSs. Embedded computing and low power sensing components have driven developments in this area. These systems can either be based on static or mobile networks [7]. Examples of static systems are described in [15, 16]. Most of the applications under the mobile networks category are found in the health sector where they are used to track hospitals valuable assets as well as the patients [17, 18]. They also have been used in tracking cultural artefacts [6].

2.2 Asset Management Systems

From an organization point of view, asset monitoring and tracking is not an isolated exercise; it is rather part and parcel of the organization's asset management system. The system should in particular capture the assets' types, asset life, asset life cycle and asset life stages. The system also needs to be integrated with other organizational functions such as financial management and human resources management [11]. Some of the basic components addressed in this paper are user profile management, asset life/life cycle management and asset monitoring and tracking.

2.3   Underling Platforms for Asset Tracking Systems

The purpose for the establishment of Internet of Things (IoT) was to make our daily endeavours more convenient and affluent by acting as a link between digital and physical worlds [19]. IoT can trace its history at MIT [20] – since then, many definitions of the concept have emerged. The most recent addition is found the Cluster of European Research projects on the Internet of Things (CERP-IoT) [21]. Here the ITU's [22] 4As vision has been extended to 6As. The internet will host approximately 50 billion devices by 2020, according to research commissioned by Cisco [23]. This proliferation of miniature computing and connected devices presents some integration challenges; there are no (known to the authors) mutual standards to support interoperability, interconnection and security of these heterogeneous devices. One of the prevailing difficulty is obscuring the inherent complexity of the environment by safeguarding applications from absolute management of uncongenial network standards, battery-powered tiny inhomogeneous devices that sometimes have constricted computational power, parallelism, data reproduction and fault intolerant networks [24]. The results of poor integration architectures are evident in applications that have scalability, security, interoperability, synchronization and data management issues [25].

The implementation, operation and maintenance of IoT based applications thrive on utilization of middleware services that amongst other things provide a unique platform that conceals hardware heterogeneousness, manage and dissipate commands to sensor nodes, perform data collation, sifting, transportation and storage and considerably boosts the expansion of diverse IoT applications [26].

Radio frequency identifiers (RFIDs) is a smart contact-free technology used to remotely extract data from or transcribe data to an electronic memory chip enveloped within the microelectronic circuit of tags [27]. RFID is designed to remotely and spontaneously identify and locate tagged objects using radio microwaves. Developments in this technology opened avenues to incorporate the technology in a plethora of applications such as remote asset tracking, healthcare and library systems. Although RFID technology is generally cheaper and more stable, it does not support bidirectional communication, which is essential for mobile devices. Moreover, it becomes uneconomical when deployed for tracking relatively smaller assets.

Biometrics entails the systematic examination of biological data and in the context of security, biological data uniquely identifies people by analysing and comparing distinguishing bodily profiles or patterns [28]. The most common biometric security systems deployed encompass fingerprint, palm-print, footprint, facial, iris and voice recognition technologies. Biometric technology is the most reliable, dependable, fool proof, and unobtrusive form of physical identification mechanism albeit expensive.

2.4   Characteristics of Middleware for Internet of Things

A lightweight software layer can realize the practicable operation of an interconnected IoT architecture that enables interoperability and communication between dissimilar or identical IoT objects or a set of sub-layers interposed between the technological and the application levels known as middleware [29]. In [30], a middleware is defined as a software that "supports flexible integration of hardware and application and provides services such as distributed computing environments, remote procedure calls, messaging to users, regardless of the hardware, operating system and network used". Atzori et al. [29] highlighted that middleware has been gaining momentum due to its ability to facilitate development of new services and the interconnection of legacy technologies into new ones, while precluding programmers from understanding diverse technologies implemented at lower layers. The implementation, operation and maintenance of IoT based applications thrive on utilization of middleware services that amongst other things provide a unique platform that: (1) conceals hardware heterogeneousness; (2) coordinate and dissipate commands to sensor nodes; (3) perform data collation, sifting, transportation and storage and (4) considerably boosts the development of diverse IoT applications [26].

An ideal self-sufficient middleware is one that is resilient enough to uphold self-configuration, self-secure, self-optimization and self-attenuating [1]. This guarantees maintenance of the common prominent features of IoT, regardless of the application domain. Some of these features, as explained in [31] are: (1) Ubiquity - which is the state of being everywhere, in some cases concurrently (and explained in the 4As vision of IoT). (2) Affordance - that is, not unsettling the equipoise/environments as professed by users; in other words, the interaction with the users should be as natural as possible and instinctive. (3) Reliable - make certain no trivial disruptions, perpetuity and self-attenuating. (4) Secure - make sure privacy of data is maintained, similar to other conventional systems. (5) Ambient Intelligence (AmI) - that empowers the system to be 'cognizant of' and 'comprehend' situations.

3 Methodology

3.1 Overview

Constructive research approach (CRA) is a methodology whose primary goal is production of novel contemporary knowledge that can be utilized in resolving real world problems, using freshly gained insights and discernments of a phenomenon to rediscover under explored links in pre-existing knowledge. [32]. The selection of CRA for this research was motivated by the need to concoct a tangible novel solution to address laptop larceny at the Central University of Technology, Free State (CUT). Moreover, it was paramount to evaluate the monitoring and tracking system during development, so prototyping was chosen as the development model as it provides opportunities to test the integration IoT devices and Wireless Sensors.

To effectively evaluate both the system prototype and the middleware, experimental research design was used. The research used the following data gathering methods: (1) document analysis - a thorough examination of asset audit reports; and (2) interviews - a face-to-face engagement with head of security along with victims who lost mobile assets to theft ensued. These interviews enabled the researcher to glean key information about theft hotspots, severity and how insecure some buildings are and the vulnerabilities in the currently deployed security systems at CUT. To ensure that every member of the CUT populace has an equal opportunity to be selected as a potential user of the security system under development, purposeful sampling was used to disseminate questionnaires [33]. The purpose of this undertaking was to get a thorough comprehension of the extent of mobile asset theft and to collect users' discernments about the prototype under development.

3.2 Middleware Development

During the development of the prototype, the researcher injected the middleware code into the application; this was a quintessential technique for two reasons: (1) deployment of the system was targeting laptops running Microsoft Windows 7/8 Operating System (MWOS); (2) this operating environment employs various services to manage diverse computing resources such as virtual location sensors, and fingerprint scanners.

The laptop tracking and monitoring middleware borrowed some characteristics from Cougar middleware. To support exchange of data between the centralized database server and connected laptops, the middleware implemented a database interface that uses structured query language (SQL) query commands. The database server was calibrated to process multiple simultaneous queries ranging from data storage, retrieval, updates to deletion. The database interface was developed with resilience in mind and the result was a fault tolerant middleware aimed to use an intelligent algorithm to establish a new connection to a backup database server when connection to the main database server fails.

To support quality of service (QoS) as in MiLAN [34], the tracking and monitoring middleware used mobile phones to facilitate two way communication. This bi-directional communication was achieved by having a laptop through the middleware transmit messages to a mobile phone and the mobile phone in turn requests the laptop through the middleware perform some action such as sending locus data via short message service (SMS) commands. Quality of service was attained through delivery of acknowledgements; that is to say, a confirmation SMS was generated by the laptop and sent through the middleware to acknowledge receipt of service request command to the mobile phone that requested some operation to be performed. Instant generation and dissemination of security breaches through the middleware's SMS service also corroborated the embodiment of quality of service.

The intelligence in IoT applications is realised through their capacity to react to phenomena triggered by diverse parameters or sensory readings. The LMTS middleware designed to listen and respond to several (ephemeral, intervallic and persistent) events spawned by the application, hardware and database layers, middleware services (SMS, location and database). To support parallelism, the middleware treated each event's action as an independent task that the operating system can independently and concurrently execute. This parallel execution of tasks (parallelism involves, modularizing programs into individual components that execute independently on separate threads) [35], resulted in a middleware architecture that is highly responsive and effective in performing preconfigured actions depending on the generated event.

As depicted in Fig. 2 (Adopted from [30]), the middleware design is comprised of three layers that is application, middleware and hardware. Each layer manages and utilizes several modules and services.

(a) **Gather Assets Data**

The system does not only facilitate the tracking and monitoring of laptops, it is also equipped with the ability to manage high level functions such as registration and storage of laptop information in a database, allocate, re-allocate, transfer or revoke laptop assignment, to or from a university personnel.

(b) **Monitoring and Detection**

This necessitates autonomous and smart techniques to systematically monitor and detect laptop security breaches. In actuality, this module detects unapproved departure of laptops from the university premises. A blend of RFID readers, RFID tags, cellular phones, Global Positioning System (GPS) devices, Geofencing, alarm bells, wireless sensors, and biometric readers/scanners are used to trigger and broadcast this security violation. To simplify turning on/off the laptop-monitoring task, a fingerprint scanner was used to command the middleware to conditionally start/halt interrogating the tag affixed on the laptop, without setting off a security alarm.

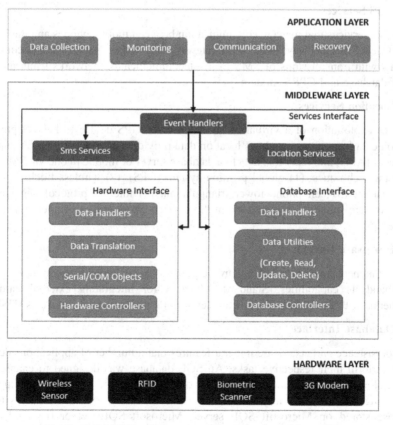

Fig. 2. IoT LMTS middleware architecture adopted from [30]

(c) **Dissemination and Communication**

This component is in charge of transmission of applicable warnings/information concerning to laptop security breaches to all interested parties. It involves triggering alarms; distribution of SMS reports to personnel (security, asset manager in charge of assets at the institution and the person allocated the laptop in question); this prompts the security personnel to take swift action to foil this theft attempt.

(d) **Recovery Capability**

This element entails recovery steps taken in an attempt to track and trace a lost laptop. Despite lacking the much needed intelligence and automation, tracking was achieved through continuous interrogation of the windows virtual GPS sensor to extract the most recent locus data and the same information was delivered via SMS to the victim's mobile phone upon requesting such information using SMS commands. Using locus data periodically saved in the database, Google maps was used to show the physical location of the laptop in question.

3.3 Middleware Services

The following are services and interfaces fulfilled and managed by the middleware:

(a) **SMS Services**

Describes services that manage communication between mobile phones and the LMTS using Ozeki SMS gateway. Ozeki SMS gateway is a software that capacitates computer systems with transmissions of SMS over telecommunication networks using an SQL server database and GPRS modem.

(b) **Location Services**

Involves exploitation of a virtual location sensor or GPS device to harvest physical location data from either windows location data providers or application programming interfaces (APIs) and relay this data to a database server or mobile phone via SMS. The following techniques: (1) global position system (GPS), (2) wireless fidelity (Wi-Fi) triangulation, (3) cell phone tower triangulation, (4) internet protocol (IP address) resolution; are suitable for generation of the physical position of a computer or mobile device [36].

(c) **Hardware Interface**

Entails the mechanism in which electronic peripherals are added to a computer system to expand its capabilities. Standard interfaces for integrating external hardware peripherals with computers systems are serial ports and universal serial bus (USB).

(d) **Database Interface**

Data persistence and access are integral features that a number of applications depend on to perform their respective tasks. An SQL database was designed to enable capturing, storage, retrieval and manipulation of data pertaining to laptop tracking and monitoring. Microsoft's entity framework was used to deliver reliable access to the database stored on Microsoft SQL server. Microsoft SQL Server (is a relational database management system RDBMS).

(e) **Hardware layer**

Individual IoT applications are designed to satisfy different organizational needs, as such, they are inclined to interconnect diverse hardware peripherals. Each hardware peripheral offers distinctive data or service and may employ the capabilities of other hardware to transport data reading, this creates coupled systems that depend on other systems to accomplish their designated mandate.

3.4 System Prototype Application and Evaluation

In line with the four main components of the framework shown in Fig. 2, the implementation was as follows:

(a) **Monitoring**

Laptop monitoring is carried out to detect and foil any attempts to steal the asset. This undertaking utilizes a plethora of hardware peripherals along with middleware services. As indicated in Fig. 3, for the LMTS to monitor a laptop, a user must connect either an RFID scanner or pressure/weight sensor to the laptop using a USB cable. From the system's interface, the user must select the building from which the laptop is sheltered and click button "Start Monitoring" to commence monitoring. In response to this button click action, the system requests fingerprint authentication from the asset owner, the user is expected to scan the finger whose fingerprints were captured during asset assignment and stored on the database. The fingerprint comparison process requires access to the database through the middleware's database services. If the fingerprint on the scanner matches a database stored template, the system conducts asset tag validation to verify if it corresponds to the one assigned to the asset during asset registration. This tag validation step is skipped when monitoring is conducted using a pressure/weight sensor. Once the system has authenticated the asset owner and validated the asset tag, laptop monitoring commences; this is conducted through perpetual interrogation of the asset tag or checking for unreasonable fluctuations in laptop weight

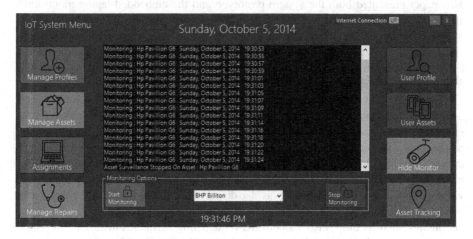

Fig. 3. IoT LMTS monitoring interface

and compare it against the threshold. By clicking "Stop Monitoring" button, the owner requests the system to stop monitoring the asset weight or reading the asset tag without triggering a security breach. In responds to this request, the system requests fingerprint authentication from the laptop owner just to verify if the request is coming from the person who initiated the monitoring process.

(b) Transmission and distribution of alerts

This component operates through utilization of Ozeki SMS gateway (As of June 2017, Ozeki website), GPRS modem, SQL database, middleware services and mobile phones. This module is responsible for the transmission of related warnings or information to relevant personnel (asset owner, security guards and asset manager) via SMS messages upon detection of a laptop security breach.

(c) Laptop Recovery

This module entails recovery steps taken in an attempt to track and trace a lost laptop. Despite lacking the much needed intelligence and automation, tracking was achieved through continuous interrogation of the windows virtual GPS sensor to extract the most recent locus data and the same information was delivered via SMS to the victim's mobile phone upon requesting such information using SMS commands. Using locus data periodically extracted from the virtual sensor and saved in the database, Google maps was used to display the physical location of the laptop in question. Microsoft windows operating system has APIs or dynamic link libraries (DLLs) that make available the location service interface to any application that intends to query locus data from the native code layer. From this code layer, it is possible to calibrate the accuracy level of the virtual sensor to meet the requirements of the host application (As of June 2017, Microsoft MSDN website).

4   Discussion and Conclusion

This paper presented both the system prototype and the embedded laptop monitoring and tracking middleware architecture. The proposed middleware implemented a variety of service components such as: (1) locus data extraction from windows virtual location or GPS sensor; (2) using RFID reader and passive tags to conduct laptop surveillance; (3) two-way transmission of SMS messages; and (4) utilization of database services to facilitate data management through SQL commands.

The adoption of common characteristics found in revered middleware solutions such as MiLAN and Cougar transcended the LMTS middleware architecture into a hybrid middleware that is cost-effective versatile, fault tolerant, reactive, and suitable for the mushrooming Cyber Physical Systems (CPSs). The middleware demonstrated versatility through its support for parallel processing of triggered events and bi-directional communication without compromising the quality of monitoring and other supported services. This quality of being versatile was also displayed by the middleware's ability to use windows operating system services and resources to manage an array of hardware peripherals such as the GPRS modem, RFID and fingerprint scanner. The presented system prototype demonstrated conformance to the objectives set for this case study.

The LMTS middleware in this study was constructed using concepts proposed by Hwang and Yoe [30] and around the IoT paradigm and the outcome thereof was a middleware architecture suitable for use in tracking and monitoring systems within the CPS and IoT paradigms. The middleware provided a proficient and flexible interface to interact with heterogeneous IoT hardware peripherals, trigger events based on generated data, manage, process and consume data generated by diverse interconnected devices. The core purpose of this middleware was to create a standardized environment to manage diverse hardware by concealing their heterogeneity. The evaluation of the middleware and the LMTS was conducted by observing how reactive the system was to diverse events, and measuring the time, it took to detect and broadcast security violations. Other tests comprised of discerning data returned by SQL query commands, the accuracy of locus data generated by the virtual sensor and lastly the ability to correctly interpret SMS commands and trigger the correct action.

Constructive research approach (CRA) was adopted in this research study and a real-life solution was concocted following a seven-step process mooted in [37]. These steps are: (1) identification of real life problem; (2) a thorough investigation of the proposed panacea with respect to long term objectives; (3) an in-depth examination of the problem domain; (4) translation of requirements into system artefacts such as use cases, flow-charts and data-flow diagrams (DFDs); (5) develop a working prototype using designs created in the previous step; (6) prototype deployment, testing and evaluation; and (7) discussion and conclusion.

References

1. Liu, X.F., Shahriar, M.K., Al Sunny, S.M.N., Leu, M.C., Hu, L.: Cyber-physical manufacturing cloud: architecture, virtualization, communication, and testbed. J. Manuf. Syst. **43**, 352–364 (2017)
2. Gubbi, J., Buyya, R., Marusic, S., Palaniswami, M.: Internet of Things (IoT): a vision, architectural elements, and future directions. Future Gener. Comput. Syst. **29**, 1645–1660 (2013)
3. Seo, A., Jeong, J., Kim, Y.: Cyber physical systems for user reliability measurements in a sharing economy environment. Sensors **17**(8), 1868 (2017)
4. Zhou, P., Zuo, D., Hou, K.M., Zhang, Z.: A decentralized compositional framework for dependable decision process in self-managed cyber physical systems. Sensors **17**(11), 2580 (2017)
5. Gunes, V., Peter, S., Givargis, T., Vahid, F.: a survey on concepts, applications, and challenges in cyber-physical systems. KSII Trans. Internet Inf. Syst. (TIIS) **8**, 4242–4268 (2014)
6. Rodriguez-Sanchez, M.C., Borromeo, S., Hernández-Tamames, J.A.: Wireless sensor networks for conservation and monitoring cultural assets. IEEE Sens. J. **11**, 1382–1389 (2011)
7. Kim, K., Jin, J.Y., Jin, S.I.: Classification between failed nodes and left nodes in mobile asset tracking systems. Sensors **16**(2), 240 (2016)
8. Liu, H., Darabi, H., Banerjee, P., Liu, J.: Survey of wireless indoor positioning techniques and systems. IEEE Trans. Syst. Man Cybern. Part C (Appl. Rev.) **37**(6), 1067–1080 (2007)

9. Kim, T.H., Jo, H.G., Lee, J.S., Kang, S.J.: A mobile asset tracking system architecture under mobile-stationary co-existing WSNs. Sensors **12**(12), 17446–17462 (2012)
10. Chen, Z., Xia, F., Huang, T., Fanyu, B., Wang, H.: A localization method for the internet of things. J. Supercomput. **63**(3), 657–674 (2013)
11. ISO: Asset Management – Management Systems Requirements (2014). http://www.iso.org/, http://www.iso.org/iso/iso-55089-colour_pdf.pdf
12. Balakrishnan, D., Nayak, A.: An efficient approach for mobile asset tracking using contexts. IEEE Trans. Parallel Distrib. Syst. **23**, 211–218 (2012)
13. Schadler, T., Yates, S., Wang, N., Sharma, A.: Mobile workforce adoption trends. Forrester Research (2013)
14. Kim, K., Chung, C.W.: In/Out status monitoring in mobile asset tracking with wireless sensor networks. Sensors **10**(4), 2709–2730 (2010)
15. Giannoulis, S., Koulamas, C., Emmanouilidis, C., Pistofidis, P., Karampatzakis, D.: Wireless sensor network technologies for condition monitoring of industrial assets. In: Emmanouilidis, C., Taisch, M., Kiritsis, D. (eds.) APMS 2012. IAICT, vol. 398, pp. 33–40. Springer, Heidelberg (2013). https://doi.org/10.1007/978-3-642-40361-3_5
16. Rajendran, N., Kamal, P., Nayak, D., Rabara, S.A.: WATS-SN: a wireless asset tracking system using sensor networks. In: 2005 IEEE International Conference on Personal Wireless Communications. ICPWC 2005, pp. 237–243. IEEE, January 2005
17. Jeong, S.Y., Jo, H.G., Kang, S.J.: Fully distributed monitoring architecture supporting multiple trackees and trackers in indoor mobile asset management application. Sensors **14** (3), 5702–5724 (2014)
18. Balakrishnan, D., Nayak, A.: An efficient approach for mobile asset tracking using contexts. IEEE Trans. Parallel Distrib. Syst. **23**(2), 211–218 (2012)
19. Gershenfeld, N., Krikorian, R., Cohen, D.: The internet of things. Sci. Am. **291**(4), 76 (2004)
20. Gama, K., Touseaui, L., Donsez, D.: Combining heterogeneous service technologies for building an internet of things middleware. Comput. Commun. **35**(4), 405–417 (2012)
21. Jain, A.K., Hong, L., Pankanti, S.: Internet of Things - strategic research roadmap, Technical report, Cluster of European Research projects on the Internet of Things, September 2009. http://www.internet-of-things-research.eu/pdf/IoTClusterStrategicResearchAgenda2009.pdf
22. International Telecommunication Union: ITU Internet Report 2005: The Internet of Things. International Telecommunication Union, Geneva (2005)
23. Evans, D.: The internet of things: how the next evolution of the internet is changing everything. CISCO white paper, vol. 1, pp. 1–11 (2011)
24. Han, S.W., Yoon, Y.B., Youn, H.Y., Cho, W.-D.: A new middleware architecture for ubiquitous computing environment. In: 2004 Proceedings Second IEEE Workshop on Software Technologies for Future Embedded and Ubiquitous Systems, pp. 117–121. IEEE (2004)
25. Hadim, S., Mohamed, N.: Middleware: middleware challenges and approaches for wireless sensor networks. IEEE Distrib. Syst. Online **7**(3), 1 (2006)
26. Römer, K., Kasten, O., Mattern, F.: Middleware challenges for wireless sensor networks. ACM SIGMOBILE Mob. Comput. Commun. Rev. **6**(4), 59–61 (2002)
27. Finkenzeller, K.: R.F.I.D Handbook. Wiley, Chichester (2003)
28. Jain, A.K., Kumar, A.: Biometrics of next generation: an overview. Second Gener. Biom. **12** (1), 2–3 (2010)
29. Atzori, L., Iera, A., Morabito, G.: The internet of things: a survey. Comput. Netw. **54**(15), 2787–2805 (2010)
30. Hwang, J., Yoe, H.: Study on the context-aware middleware for ubiquitous greenhouses using wireless sensor networks. Sensors **11**(5), 4539–4561 (2011)

31. Rodríguez-Molina, J., Martínez, J.-F., Castillejo, P., López, L.: Combining wireless sensor networks and semantic middleware for an internet of things-based sportsman/woman monitoring application. Sensors 13(2), 1787–1835 (2013)
32. Crnkovic, G.D.: Constructive research and info-computational knowledge generation. In: Magnani, L., Carnielli, W., Pizzi, C. (eds.) Model-Based Reasoning in Science and Technology. SCI, vol. 314, pp. 359–380. Springer, Heidelberg (2010). https://doi.org/10.1007/978-3-642-15223-8_20
33. Teddlie, C., Yu, F.: Mixed methods sampling a typology with examples. J. Mixed Methods Res. 1(1), 77–100 (2007)
34. Heinzelman, W.B., Murphy, A.L., Carvalho, H.S., Perillo, M.A.: Middleware to support sensor network applications. IEEE Netw. 18(1), 6–14 (2004)
35. Silberschatz, A., Galvin, P., Gagne, G.: Applied operating system concepts. Wiley, Hoboken (2001)
36. Doty, N., Mulligan, D.K., Wilde, E.: Privacy issues of the W3C Geolocation API. arXiv preprint arXiv:1003.1775 (2010)
37. Kasanen, E., Lukka, K., Siitonen, A.: The constructive approach in management accounting research. J. Manag. Account. Res. 5, 243 (1993)

Signal Processing, Control and Coordination in an Intelligent Connected Vehicle

Manolo Dulva Hina[1(✉)], Sebastien Dourlens[2], Assia Soukane[1], and Amar Ramdane-Cherif[2]

[1] ECE Paris School of Engineering, 37 quai de Grenelle, 75015 Paris, France
{manolo-dulva.hina, assia.soukane}@ece.fr
[2] LISV Laboratory, Université de Versailles St-Quentin-en-Yvelines, 10-12 avenue de l'Europe, 78140 Vélizy, France
sdourlens@hotmail.com, rca@lisv.uvsq.fr

Abstract. In this paper, we present the functionalities of an intelligent connected vehicle. It is equipped with various sensors and connected objects that enable communication between the driver and its environment. This system provides assistance towards safe and green driving. The driving assistance may be directed towards the driver (semi-autonomous vehicle) or completely towards the vehicle (self-driving, autonomous vehicle). The assistance is based on the driving context which is the fusion of parameters representing the context of the driver, the vehicle and the environment. This cyber-physical vehicle has three main components: the embedded system, the networking and real-time system and the intelligent system. The architecture for data transfer within the connected vehicle is implemented through publish-subscribed infrastructure in which services are transferred and controlled in an orderly manner. These functionalities are tested both in the laboratory and on the road with satisfactory results. This is the fruit of labor of a consortium composed of five industrial and two academic partners.

Keywords: Connected vehicle · ADAS · Internet of things · Intelligent vehicle

1 Introduction

Cyber-physical systems (CPS) are physical and engineered systems whose operations are monitored, coordinated, controlled and integrated by a computing and communication core. CPS is composed of interconnected clusters of processing elements and large-scale wired and wireless networks that connect a variety of smart sensors and actuators [1]. This paper is about a cyber-physical vehicle [2], an intelligent connected vehicle and its smartphone app created to contribute to the reduction of road traffic accident. This connected vehicle proposes safe driving and green driving [3] assistance based on the given driving context. The driving context [4] is the driving situation based on the fusion of various parameters (obtained from sensors, internet of things, etc.) representing the context of the driver, the vehicle, the environment and the infrastructure. An intelligent connected vehicle can be partitioned into three subsystems, each representing a distinct signal processing part. They are given below:

© ICST Institute for Computer Sciences, Social Informatics and Telecommunications Engineering 2019
Published by Springer Nature Switzerland AG 2019. All Rights Reserved
R. Zitouni and M. Agueh (Eds.): AFRICATEK 2018, LNICST 260, pp. 32–43, 2019.
https://doi.org/10.1007/978-3-030-05198-3_3

- *Embedded system*: it is that sub-system responsible for capturing data and signals from the vehicle, and environment. Various sensors, gadgets and actuators of different modalities are associated with embedded system. Altogether, these components form connected objects and Internet of things (IoT) [5].
- *Intelligent System*: it is that sub-system that is responsible for obtaining input data from the embedded system, fusion them in order to deduce the driving situation and determine what action must be undertaken to the specified driving situation. This assistance may be directed towards the vehicle (in which case, the vehicle becomes an *autonomous, self-directing machine*) or the driver (in which case the driver is in complete control of the vehicle, a case of *semi-autonomous vehicle*).
- *Network and Real-time System*: it is that sub-system concerned with communication protocols between components of the system. The communication between embedded system and intelligent system is handled by this component. The repository of vehicle data may be the vehicle itself or the Cloud computing infrastructure.

This paper is a continuation of our previous work [6, 7] only that here the focus is on the detailed treatment of the fusion of signals, the processing for the detection of driving context and the fission process to offer driving assistance.

2 Related Work

As early as 1920's, various efforts have been made to automate vehicle driving [8]. Some promising trials happened in 1950's and research on this has never ceased since then. The first autonomous vehicle was developed in 1980's in Carnegie Mellon University Navlab [9] and AVL in 1984 [10]. It is followed by Mercedes-Benz and Bundeswehr University Munich's Eureka Prometheus Project in 1987. In July 2013, Vislab demonstrated BRAiVE, a vehicle that moved autonomously on a mixed traffic route open to public traffic [11]. Connected and autonomous vehicles (CAV) are a technological revolution, combining radical changes in the design of the road vehicles and understanding of their interactions with the networked infrastructure.

Connected vehicles [12, 13] and autonomous vehicles [14, 15] face different obstacles for further development because their respective technologies are at different stages of development and implementation. Consumers express concern about cybersecurity and privacy issues while safety and consumer readiness to adopt are the perceived barriers for autonomous vehicles [16]. The core science and technology required to support CPS and cyber-physical vehicles (both for connected and autonomous vehicles) are essential for future economic competitiveness. Creating the scientific and technological basis for CPS can pay dividends across wide domains.

According to the survey conducted by Foley & Lardner LLP [16], the technologies for which the connected and/or autonomous vehicles are worth investing are as follows: cybersecurity protection, precision mapping and location technology, vehicle-to-vehicle (V2V) communication technology, advanced driver assistance system (ADAS), machine learning and driving data analysis, infotainment features, and self-driving vehicles for car-sharing. Indeed, this work on ADAS is on the right track. The machine learning [17–19] component of our system is integrated in the intelligent system. The V2V features are a priority by our networking and real-time system component. This paper contributes to the advancement of intelligent connected vehicles.

3 Driving Assistance for a Connected Vehicle

3.1 Objective and Offering a Technological Solution

There is a very wide range of mobility-related applications available in the market these days but most are not directly related to vehicle data. This is in contrast to the norm given that the use of vehicle data and its environment is at the heart of the Advanced Driver Assistance Systems (ADAS) [20, 21]. In order to test and validate the on-board driver assistance systems, it is necessary to equip the test vehicle with the correct sensors that will capture the perceived context of the driver, vehicle and the environment. Furthermore, these sensors should be of quality. The costs incurred in such configuration means that in most cases, ADAS functionalities are generally made available mostly on high-end vehicles and it will take (several) years before they can be made available to family car models. Given such situation, this project aims to address such constraints. Indeed, this project aims to: (i) Create an open environment for the design of innovative applications for smartphone, promoting the emergence of informative driving assistance functions; (ii) Offer an affordable solution by offsetting the processing capacity on the smartphone, optimized by exploiting data of the vehicle and its environment; (iii) Specify a safe and effective interaction between the driver, the mobile software and the synthesis of lives on board the vehicle; and (iv) Reinforce road safety by familiarizing users with ADAS-type functions and optimizing future on-board functions through feedback.

The driving assistance system for connected vehicle is a technological solution centred on the development of a smartphone driving assistance applications based on: (i) The sensors and resources of the smartphone to ensure the perception of the driving environment and the state of health of the driver as well as the treatment of the driving assistance functions; (ii) A communication channel between the smartphone and the vehicle to use vehicle data and activate vehicle functions (Car Easy Apps solution) [22]; and (iii) Establishment of a test platform to simulate the vehicle and its environment in order to develop, validate and demonstrate the applications developed.

To achieve the link with the vehicle data, this project has chosen to use the SDK (software development kit) of the project CEA (Car Easy Apps) [23]; CEA is a project from the Franco-Spanish consortium collaboration led by PSA Peugeot-Citroen[1], in which Continental[2] also participated. This consortium offers a framework under Android that allows wireless (Bluetooth or WiFi) or wired (USB) connection to interface with the multimedia system of the vehicle and thus access a wide variety of signals present on the various CAN (controller area network) bus of the vehicle. The CEA being scalable, one can easily add new signals as needed. See Fig. 1(a).

---

[1] PSA Peugeot-Citroën: https://www.groupe-psa.com/en/.

[2] Continental France: https://www.continental-corporation.com/fr-fr.

3.2   Connected Vehicle Architecture

The architecture of our intelligent vehicle project is shown in Fig. 1(b). The architecture is layered and layers are as follows: (i) the material layer (i.e. this contains pertinent sensors), (ii) the input services layer or pilots that apply the appropriate algorithms related to vision, identification of objects (e.g. road, road sign, weather, vehicles) and the transformation of the data into a low-level event, (iii) the server layer for storing and broadcasting events, (iv) the multimodal fusion layer of events that generate higher-level events, (v) the human-vehicle interface (an exit service) which provides the necessary information to the user in the form of web pages and dashboard utilities of the vehicle, and (vi) Multiple layers of communication to the cloud [24, 25] and road infrastructure.

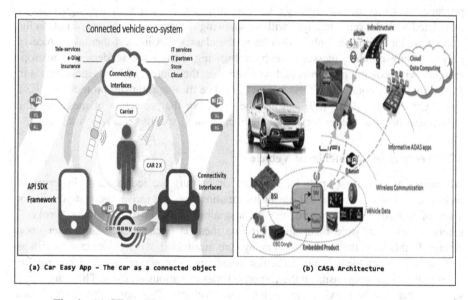

Fig. 1. (a) CEA – The car as a connected object, (b) the CASA architecture

Likewise, as shown in the diagram, the system components are as follows: (i) A vehicle – A PSA vehicle (Peugeot or Citroen) cockpit used as vehicle in the laboratory and the actual road tests; (ii) Various tools inside the vehicle – Given that we are interested in obtaining the driving context, we make use of various tools to realize such objective: (a) BSI – is a back-illuminated, digital-image sensor that uses a novel arrangement of imaging elements to increase the amount of light captured and thereby improve low-light performance; (b) OBD – is an onboard diagnostic gadget; it is a vehicle's self-diagnostic and reporting capability, providing end users with access to the status of various vehicle subsystems; (c) OVIP – is an infotainment platform developed for PSA vehicles; (d) Camera – for driver monitoring, and (e) Bluetooth and LiFi – for wireless communication; (iii) Smartphone – used as HMI (human-machine interaction) tool and to access from IoT and connected objects; and (iv) The CASA App – an Android application developed for this project, installed on the smartphone for driver assistance for safe and green driving.

4 Vehicular Data Communication, Processing and Control

4.1 Publish-Subscribe Architecture

Figure 2(a) shows the data communication structure in an intelligent connected vehicle. Such communication architecture is based on the "publish-subscribe" [26] mechanism: the publication and subscription of messages. In this structure, a publisher publishes messages without knowing a priori who the subscribers to these messages are. The subscriber is the recipient of the message or data. It too does not know who the producer/publisher of the message is. The structure is simple: a message class is associated with the sent messages without knowing if there are recipients or not. In the same way, the recipients only subscribe to the classes that interest them, and receive only the corresponding messages without knowing if there are senders. For interoperability with existing platforms and web services, the content of XML messages is in Javascript object notation (JSON) format [27]. The message transfer protocol is REST over TCP-IP [28]. SOAP [29] can also be used. For the protection of messages, the publication or subscription services authenticate using specific encryption keys.

4.2 Services in an Intelligent Vehicle

All vehicular services (input, intermediate or output) are independent in terms of architecture. For example, if the sensor information does not arrive, the system will not warn of hazard. In this system, the orchestration server (also called the "broker") receives messages, store them and distribute them at once to each subscriber upon receipt. In this way, the transmission delays are minimized. All services can publish as well as subscribe; there is no particular constraint. The server can also control the quality of service by measuring the response times of various services. There are many services that can be provided in an intelligent vehicle. This paper, however, is not going to deal with an exhaustive list of services; it is sufficient that some representative samples of services in an intelligent vehicle are presented. All others would follow the same pattern and principle. As shown in Fig. 2(b), our intelligent vehicle has the following services:

- *Vision Sensor Publisher*: this service collects data related to obstacle (e.g. pedestrian, vehicle, bicycle, etc.) detection and publishes such info whenever it finds one.
- *GPS Location Publisher*: this service obtains the position of the vehicle and publishes it whenever the position coordinates of the vehicle change.
- *Car Sensor Publisher*: this pertains to a group of sensor that monitors the driver status (i.e. fatigued, stressed, etc.) and that of the vehicle (i.e. its distance from vehicle/obstacle in front, presence of stop sign, etc.) and publishes such information.

- *Weather Service Publisher*: this service monitors if there is a fog, rain or snow; if the visibility is poor, and if the road is hazardous due to the weather condition.
- *Event Multimodal Fusion Publisher and Subscriber (EMFPS)*: this is the brain of the system. It subscribes to many signals to be able to fusion such information and deduce the driving situation. It determines if there is a driving assistance to be done for the given driving situation. If so, then it publishes the corresponding signals.
- *Tablet HMI Publisher and Subscriber*: This service is both a publisher and a subscriber. As a publisher, it sends signal the setting configuration for driving assistance preferred by the driver (example: the language of the driving assistance = English | French, etc.). As a subscriber, it receives driving assistance messages published by the EMFPS and it broadcasts a message directed towards the driver, the vehicle or both to assist in the driving situation.
- *Car Dashboard Subscriber*: this service obtains message from the broker to determine if it is going to put the air-conditioner on/off, the music on/off, the heater on/off, activate/deactivate the dashboard wiper, etc.
- *Car Broker*: this is like the maestro of an orchestra. It receives data or messages from the publishers and sends same to its subscribers.

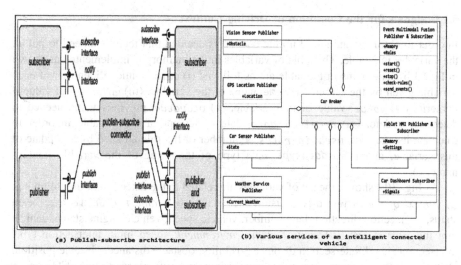

Fig. 2. (a) The publish-subscribe architecture, (b) the various services of an intelligent connected vehicle.

5 The Multimodal Event Fusion Service

The task of Event Multimodal Fusion Publisher and Subscriber (EMFPS) service is to perform the multimodal fusion of various events coming from other services, and to provide them messages and information in higher-level of abstraction in order to inform the user (the driver) on how to react on the new case of interaction. Briefly, it means informing the driver of the situation or of driving assistance message suited for the situation. The EMFPS service is both publisher and subscriber. The detection of context and the adaptation of exit events to the context are realized using a set of rules that are integrated in the service. These rules make use of all input information.

Following receipt of new data or message, the multimodal fusion involves applying a set of rules each time the values of subscribed variables gets updated. Figure 3(a) shows the EMFPS service. As shown, the solid arrows represent data flows between the functions (light blue rectangles) and the memory (cylinder), while the dotted-line arrows correspond to activations of broker server for publication and subscription purposes.

At start-up, the service initializes the array of variables "Memory" to their default values and then subscribes to the various events that it needs to receive. Subscribing means that the program gives the broker server the address of a service function. The call by the server of the call-back function (myCB) which manages the reception of events will be made by the broker server. Upon receiving data or messages related to one or more events, the service retrieves the values of the JSON and updates the variable data in memory and then performs an evaluation of all the rules that are affected by the updated variables. If one or more rules have been triggered, the output events are immediately published to the server.

5.1   Signals for the Cognition of Driving Context

In order to optimize and speed up the code, it is decided that there is a need to put all the variables in a table. The table of variables in the memory is implemented as shown in Fig. 3(b). The items in the table are as follows: (i) *uuid*: a unique identifier of each variable given by the server, (ii) *name*: name of the variable, (iii) *unit*: unit of value if numeric, (iv) *value*: value of the variable, (v) *oldvalue*: previous value needed to detect an update, (vi) *received date*: date of receipt of the variable in order to calculate its age, (vii) *used in rules #*: number of the rule affected by an update of this variable, and (viii) *datatype*: data type of the value of the variable (text or numeric).

As Fig. 3(b) shows, the set of variables are related to the detection of the following: (i) *context of the driver*: driver disturbance status; (ii) *context of the vehicle*: beam status, intersection direction, lane number, vehicle speed, vehicle engine status, vehicle turn indicator status; (iii) *context of the environment*: speed limit, intersection type, intersection signal, intersection distance, visibility, obstacle distance, obstacle position, obstacle speed, obstacle type, time to collision; and (iv) *green driving*: CO_2 driver advise, CO_2 explicit speed limit.

The service also provides driving assistance by sending messages to the server. Such messages are picked up by the Tablet HMI Subscriber and broadcasted to the driver, the vehicle or both. The driving assistance is of three types: (i) *assistance directed to the driver*: speeding status, turn indicator status, stop violation status, obstacle detection status, pedestrian detection status, driver disturbance status; (ii) *assistance directed to the vehicle*: activation of fog light (implemented by the Car Dashboard Subscriber service); and (iii) *assistance for green driving*: CO_2 assist status.

5.2   Human-Vehicle Interaction Interface

The human-vehicle interaction interface [30, 31] adopted for this work is shown in Fig. 4. The images shown in the diagram are mere depiction of the real ones which cannot be shown in this paper due to proprietary restrictions. In this work, there are two types of messages intended for the driver: (i) *Notification* – a message to inform the driver, and (ii) *Alert* – a type of message that attempts to get the driver's attention.

A notification or alert is sent according to the category of driving situation: (i) *Behaviour* – this refers to the driver's conduct of driving. For example, the driver's failure to stop in the Stop light merits an Alert message concerning the driver's behaviour; (ii) *Danger* – a potential risk to the driver or people on the road exists. Entering a foggy zone merits a notification message on danger; and (iii) *Ability* – this concerns about the person's ability to drive a vehicle. For example, if the system detects that a driver is going to fall asleep, a danger message concerning his ability to drive is sent.

When two or more messages need to be sent to the driver then system adopts a priority scheme. Only one message will be sent to the driver at any given time. Here is the priority scheme of this work: (i) *Alert* has a higher priority than *Notification*, and (ii) *Ability* has the highest priority in the message category. Next priority belongs to *Danger* and the last priority belongs to *Behaviour*.

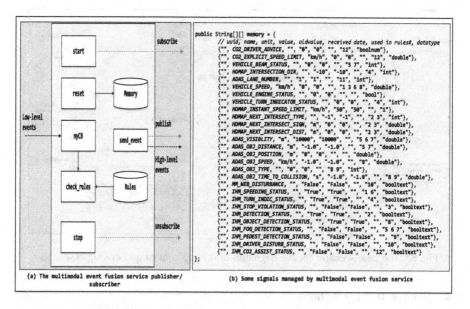

(a) The multimodal event fusion service publisher/subscriber

(b) Some signals managed by multimodal event fusion service

Fig. 3. (a) The multimodal event fusion service structure, (b) Some signals managed by the multimodal event fusion service provider. (Color figure online)

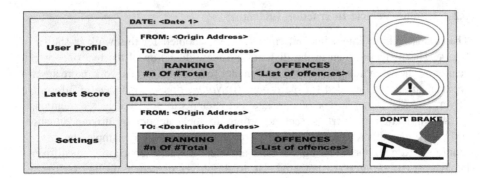

Fig. 4. Human-vehicle interaction interface of project CASA

5.3 Case Study: Scenarios Simulation

There is a need to simulate the multimodal fusion, fission and cognition of driving context that were presented in the earlier sections of this paper. To do this, a sample case scenario is developed and is shown in Fig. 5. Laboratory and road tests reveal that the CASA system is found to be operational and fit for purpose.

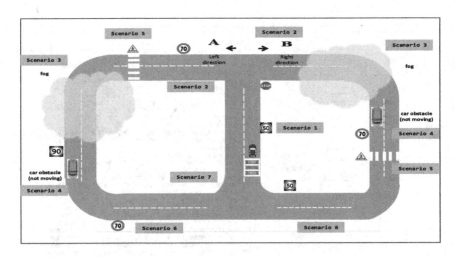

Fig. 5. The case scenario for the cognition of driving context and driving assistance

5.4 Sample Driving Actions

Consider for example the implementation of action "ChangeLane". There are two cases by which this action is invoked, as given below:

Case 1: Obstacle Moving Very Slow. (i) Let X be an instance of class "Vehicle" == Vehicle (?X). (ii) Let there be road R == Road(?R). (iii) Let there be lane

L1 in road R == hasLane(?R, ?L1). (iv) Let there be lane L2 in road R == hasLane(?R,?L2). (v) Let lane L1 be different from lane L2 == differentFrom(?L1, ?L2). (vi) Let there be obstacle W (from previous subsection) == Obstacle(?W). (vii) Let the speed of obstacle W be extra slow == . (viii) Let there be action Z for this driving situation == Action(?Z). If we do fusion of these parameters, we will end up with the following: *Vehicle(?X) ∧ Road (?R) ∧ hasLane(?R,?L1) ∧ hasLane(?R, ?L2) ∧ differentFrom(?L1, ?L2) ∧ Obstacle(?W) ∧ hasSpeed(?W,ExtraSlowSpeed) ∧ Action(?Z) → ChangeLane (?Z)*.

Case 2: Obstacle Has No Speed. (i) Let the description in subsection Case 1 holds true. (ii) Let the obstacle W have no speed (if might be a tree, a rock, etc.) == . If we fusion these parameters, we will end up with: *Vehicle(?X) ∧ Road (?R) ∧ hasLane(?R, ?L1) ∧ hasLane(?R, ?L2) ∧ differentFrom(?L1, ?L2) ∧Obstacle(?W) ∧ hasSpeed(?W, NoSpeed) ∧ Action(?Z) → ChangeLane (?Z)*.

5.5 Contributions

In this paper, the functionalities of an intelligent connected vehicle is presented. The contributions of this work are as follows:

- *A generic, low-cost ADAS*: ADAS in general are reserved for expensive vehicles and closed to proprietary constraints. This work addresses those constraints.
- *A system adaptable for both autonomous and semi-autonomous vehicle*: The driving assistance can be set-up to be directed towards the driver, in which case the system is for a semi-autonomous vehicle. The assistance may be directed directly to the vehicle, in which case we will come up with an autonomous, self-driving vehicle.
- *An efficient publish-subscribe data communication architecture*: In this paper, the publish/subscribe architecture was presented. Publishers send their data or messages to the repository (the broker) without having idea who will consume it. Subscribers obtain the data and messages they need from the broker without having idea of who produced it. The subscribers are only informed that they need to pick-up their data/messages only when they are new. Hence, the data communication is efficient.
- *Assistance towards safe and green driving*: This work also contributes towards the reduction of traffic accident and on lesser fuel consumption while doing the same work. This means lower CO_2 emission, and also reduced cost of voyage.

The first phase of Project CASA was presented to the public during the 2015 ITS European Congress[3], 5–9 October 2015, Bordeaux, France. For five days, the project was presented to the public to get its opinion about the features CASA is offering. We collected data based on the public perception using questionnaires given to some 150 random participants. The results are as follows: (i) Consumers are willing to share their personal data with some applications. Consumers are most willing to grant access to applications that are directly related to navigation and mobility; and (ii) Consumers find that CASA is helpful for road navigation and mobility.

---

[3] http://itsworldcongress.com/.

6 Conclusion and Future Work

Project CASA is conceived with the vision that today's ADAS systems are closed to proprietary constraints and are usually accorded to expensive vehicles. CASA is a generic ADAS and can be used by any vehicle. This is an Android app and is based on smartphone. This project is a collaboration of five industrial and two academic partners, namely PSA-Peugeot-Citroen, Continental, Nexyad, Oktal, DPS and UVSQ. UVSQ, for its part, collaborates with ECE Paris on other intelligent system tasks.

The driving context is the fusion of all parameters related to the context of the driver, the vehicle and the environment. The driving context yields a situation that may or may not need assistance. In the case of it needs an assistance, the system determines the types of assistance using the rules that are stored in the system's knowledge base. The assistance may be directed towards the driver, the vehicle or both (although in this paper, the assistance is almost all directed towards the driver, a case of semi-autonomous vehicle). Taken into account that only one message can be sent to the driver at any given time, priorities are taken into consideration when two or more driving events occur at the same time. Tests and validations are done in the laboratory and on the road. Here, it showed that the use of CASA reduces traffic rules infractions and road accidents. Project CASA was also presented to the public during ITS European Congress in Bordeaux, France in 2015. It was well-received by the public. Future works include further improvement via machine learning component, in particular, the cognitive user interface design [32] and the cognitive component [33] that learns new driving situation, reason with purpose and interact with humans naturally. The component learns from its interaction with system users and from its experiences with the environment.

References

1. Rajkumar, R., Lee, I., Sha, L., Stankovic, J.: Cyber-physical systems: the next computing revolution. In: Design Automation Conference, Anaheim, CA, USA (2010)
2. Wang, S.: Develop Vehicle Control Systems as CPS for Next-Generation Automobiles, March 2015
3. Estl, H.: Paving the way to self-driving cars with advanced driver assistance systems, August 2015
4. Hina, M.D., Thierry, C., Soukane, A., Ramdane-Cherif, A.: Cognition of driving context for driving assistance. In: Presented at the ICAIA 2018: 20th International Conference on Artificial Intelligence and Applications, Kuala Lumpur, Malaysia (2018)
5. Gubbi, J., Buyya, R., Marusic, S., Palaniswami, M.: Internet of Things (IoT): a vision, architectural elements and future directions. Future Gener. Comput. Syst. **29**, 1645–1660 (2013)
6. Hina, M.D., Guan, H., Deng, N., Ramdane-Cherif, A.: CASA: safe and green driving assistance system for real-time driving events. In: Bi, Y., Kapoor, S., Bhatia, R. (eds.) IntelliSys 2016. LNNS, vol. 15, pp. 987–1002. Springer, Cham (2018). https://doi.org/10.1007/978-3-319-56994-9_67
7. Hina, M.D., Guan, H., Ramdane-Cherif, A., Deng, N.: Secured data processing, notification and transmission in a human-vehicle interaction system. In: 19th IEEE International Conference on Intelligent Transportation Systems, ITSC 2016, Rio de Janeiro, Brazil (2016)

8. Sentinel, T.M.: Phantom Auto' will tour city. In: Google News Archive, ed. (1926)
9. Carnegine Mellon University - The Robotics Institute, NavLab: The Carnegie Mellon University Navigation Laboratory. www.cs.cmu.edu/afs/cs/project/alv/www. Accessed Feb 2018
10. Kanade, T.: Autonomous land vehicle project at CMU. In: Presented at the 14th ACM Annual Conference on Computer Science (1986)
11. University of Parma: VisLab, Italy - Public Road Urban Driverless-Car Test 2013 - World premiere of BRAiVE, ed. (2013)
12. Parkinson, S., Ward, P., Wilson, K., Miller, J.: Cyber threats facing autonomous and connected vehicles: future challenges. IEEE Trans. Intell. Transp. Syst. **18**, 2898–2915 (2017)
13. Geng, H.: Connected vehicle. In: Internet of Things and Data Analytics Handbook, ed. Wiley Telecom (2017)
14. RAC Australia: Autonomous vehicle survey (2016). https://rac.com.au/-/media/files/rac-website/pdfs/about-rac/publications/reports/2016/autonomous-vehicles-survey.pdf
15. Ho, J.Y., Koh, W.Y., Veeravalli, B., Wong, J.W., Guo, H.: Secure sensing inputs for autonomous vehicles. In: Presented at the TENCON 2017, Penang, Malaysia (2017)
16. Foley & Lardner LLP: 2017 Connected Cars & Autonomous Vehicles Survey (2017)
17. Louridas, P., Ebert, C.: Machine learning. IEEE Softw. **33**, 110–115 (2016)
18. Tchankue, P., Wesson, J., Vogts, D.: Using machine learning to predict driving context whilst driving. In: Presented at the SAICSIT 2013, South African Institute for Computer Scientists and Information Technologists, East London, South Africa (2013)
19. Witten, I., Frank, E., Hall, M.: Data Mining: Practical Machine Learning Tools and Techniques. Morgan Kaufmann, Burlington (2011)
20. Li, L., Wen, D., Zheng, N.-N., Shen, L.-C.: Cognitive cars: a new frontier for ADAS research. IEEE Trans. Intell. Transp. Syst. **13**, 395–407 (2012)
21. Ithape, A.A.: Artificial intelligence and machine learning in ADAS. In: Presented at the Vector India Conference, Pune, India (2017)
22. PSA Group: Car Easy Apps: Co-designing the connected car of the future (2016). https://www.groupe-psa.com/en/newsroom/automotive-innovation/car-easy-apps/
23. PSA Group: Car Easy Apps: PSA Peugeot Citroën's Application programming interface (2014). https://www.youtube.com/watch?v=3cTsNeKZDTU
24. Oracle: Architectural Strategies for Cloud Computing. Oracle White Paper in Enterprise Architecture, August 2009
25. Yousif, M.: The state of the cloud. IEEE Cloud Comput. **4**, 4–5 (2017)
26. Microsoft: Publish/Subscribe (2018). https://msdn.microsoft.com/en-us/library/ff649664.aspx
27. w3schools.com: JSON – Introduction (2018). https://www.w3schools.com/js/js_json_intro.asp
28. Flanders, J.: Service station - more on REST. MSDN Mag. **27**(7) (2009). http://msdn.microsoft.com/en-us/magazine/dd942839.aspx
29. W3C: Latest SOAP versions (2018). https://www.w3.org/TR/soap/
30. Dumas, B., Lalanne, D., Oviatt, S.: Multimodal interfaces: a survey of principles, models and frameworks. In: Lalanne, D., Kohlas, J. (eds.) Human Machine Interaction. LNCS, vol. 5440, pp. 3–26. Springer, Heidelberg (2009). https://doi.org/10.1007/978-3-642-00437-7_1
31. Oviatt, S.L.: Multimodal interfaces. In: Jacko, A.S.J. (ed.) The Human-Computer Interaction Handbook: Fundamentals, Evolving Technologies and Emerging Applications, pp. 286–304, 2nd edn. CRC Press (2008)
32. Peschl, M.F., Stary, C.: The role of cognitive modeling for user interface design representations. Mind Mach. **8**, 203–236 (1998)
33. Kelly III., J.E.: Computing, cognition and the future of knowing: how humans and machines are forging a new age of understanding (2015)

Applications and IT Services

Embedding a Digital Wallet to Pay-with-a-Selfie, from Functional Requirements to Prototype

Perpetus Jacques Houngbo[1]([⊠]), Joel T. Hounsou[1],
Ernesto Damiani[2,3], Rasool Asal[2], Stelvio Cimato[3], Fulvio Frati[3],
and Chan Yeob Yeun[2]

[1] Institut de Mathematiques et de Sciences Physiques, Avakpa, BP 613,
Porto-Novo, Benin
jacques.houngbo@auriane-etudes.com,
joelhoun@gmail.com
[2] EBTIC-Khalifa University,
Abu Dhabi Campus, PO Box 127788, Abu Dhabi, UAE
{ernesto.damiani,rasool.asal,cyeun}@kustar.ac.ae
[3] Università degli Studi di Milano, Via Bramante, 65 26013 Crema, CR, Italy
{stelvio.cimato,fulvio.frati}@unimi.it

Abstract. The Pay-with-a-Group-Selfie (PGS) project, funded by the Melinda & Bill Gates Foundation, has developed a micro-payment system that supports everyday small transactions by extending the reach of, rather than substituting, existing payment frameworks. In an effort to embed a digital wallet to the PGS, we analysed the system architecture that will be needed and the requirements drive us to opting for blockchain based architecture. We have presented the applicability of a blockchain as platform in a previous paper. The current paper is presenting the functional requirements, the platforms needed for the development as well as the prototypes of the major interfaces.

Keywords: Digital wallet · Mobile payment systems · Trust · Blockchain Distributed ledger

1 Introduction

The Pay-with-a-Group-Selfie (PGS) project, funded by the Melinda & Bill Gates Foundation, has developed a micro-payment system that supports everyday small transactions by extending the reach of, rather than substituting, existing payment frameworks. It is worth to stress on the fact PGS is not intended to replace the current schemes that banks and mainly telecom operators have in place. PGS aims at completing them by going further and reaching those who were unreachable because of lack of network coverage.

Previous works have demonstrated its usage and the current version is evolving towards an accomplished product that will serve people living in remote areas where network coverage is patchy. In the meantime, efforts are being made to improve the way the PGS is expected to perform, that is the reason why it has been decide to equip

R. Zitouni and M. Agueh (Eds.): AFRICATEK 2018, LNICST 260, pp. 47–56, 2019.
https://doi.org/10.1007/978-3-030-05198-3_4

it with a digital wallet. Analyses conducted to that extend lead to the option of basing the architecture of the digital on a blockchain construction. In the wake of our works of improvement, we have presented the applicability of the blockchain based solution. This paper aims at elaborating on the functional requirements and the prototyping of the major interfaces.

The paper is organized as follows: starting by the summary of the requirements for the system architecture, Sect. 2 gives an extensive presentation of the functional requirements. Then, Sect. 3 goes further with the platforms and Sect. 4 is devoted to the prototyping the main interfaces. Finally, Sect. 5 gives our conclusions.

2   Functional Specification

2.1   Summary of Requirements

Regarding the system architecture we have defined the requirements of the PGS digital wallet as follows:

- basic operations: balance on account, payment of purchase, transfer, top up, and withdraw
- purchase of goods and services is the main functionality, but the wallet must also serve for:
  - remittances;
  - social and cultural functions: rewards for artists, dowry, collection during the mass, during any religious ceremony, assistance during grief;
- pivotal role of the "village chief", street corner shops, point of sales (POS) or broker is stressed on;
- performances measured in term of:
  - ease of use and simplicity: the system must be designed for people who are not able to juggle with complicated keyboards;
  - immediate confirmation of transactions, in matters of seconds, in less than ten seconds;
- security aspects:
  - fully-authenticated network;
  - prevent double spending;
  - *Anti-Money Laundering* and *Know Your Customer* issues are to be integrated from design.

All the requirements and properties lead to the choice of implementing the system on a private permissioned blockchain.

Figure 1 presents three groups of use cases for the PGS users, the POS and the institutions.

2.2   Numbers

PGS per se is devoted to serve large group of populations, all the population in rural and remote area with no network coverage. Its digital wallet will then serve that

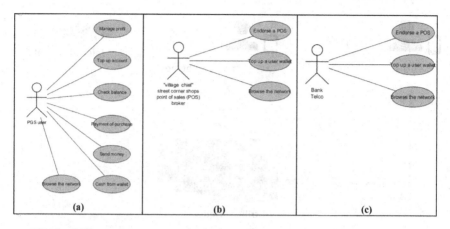

Fig. 1. PGS user use cases (a), POS use cases (b), and institutions use cases (c).

population. It has to be noted that actually every single smartphone user is targeted as they can transfer money to PGS users and vice versa.

The vision is also to plan for big players like banks and telecom operators to join the PGS network. The regulatory authorities may also come in, but they will only be granted read privileges on the ledger. The final number of user is then very large, with groups of specific needs, as shown in the illustration in Fig. 2. That illustration is showing a unit of "System administration and back end". Such unit can be surprising in a decentralized environment.

We estimate that is compulsory at least during the inception phase where there is a need for intense housekeeping at blockchain nodes in term of installing, supporting, and maintaining servers or other computer systems, and planning for and responding to service outages and other problems that may occur. Software maintenance will also be part of their responsibilities.

2.3 Existing System

Currently, in the targeted areas, the payment system is traditionally cash-based. PGS is introducing a new system, still anchored on customs that are already spreading in those areas: the use of smartphone to do selfies. Furthermore, one pivotal actor is the broker, the ambulant banker who is already trusted in the area collector of savings. The broker was introduced [1] to act as a store-and-forward transport layer (where trust in the broker plays the role of security controls [2]), pushing selfies between PGS users on one side and multiple Banks on the other side. The broker will maintain his role with PGS, and this role may eventually be strengthened by the new layer of blockchain that will guarantee the log of all savings collected and their final destinations.

2.4 Uses Case: Direct Purchase

Only one use case (depicted in Fig. 3) is presented here due to its importance in terms of need for immediate result in a peer-to-peer operation. Indeed, when buying an item

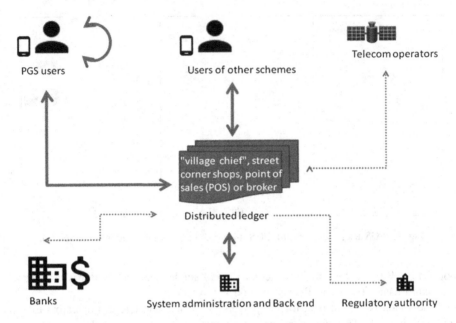

Fig. 2. Overview of the users

in a local market for instance, buyer and seller are facing each other. When the deal is concluded, the merchandise and money are synchronously exchanged. This is where the peer-to-peer payment enters the scene:

- buyer and seller agree on the price;
- buyer launches her PGS on her device and logs in;
- seller launches her PGS on her device and logs in;
- buyer enters amount to pay;
- PGS on the buyer's device checks the balance and alert buyer in case of insufficient credit note;
- PGS offers a list of sellers;
- buyer selects the seller who will receive the money;
- PGS on the buyer's side sends a checking message to seller;
- seller confirms the checking message;
- buyer sends the money;
- seller confirms reception of the money;
- PGS on the seller's side prepares a transaction record to be sent later to the blockchain when a broker will pass by;
- PGS notifies buyer that seller has acknowledged receipt of money;
- PGS on the buyer's side prepares a transaction record to be sent later to the blockchain when a broker will pass by.

All these actions have been done between the two actors using only their own devices. The transaction will be saved later to the blockchain after the broker has passed by and collected the appropriate records to be transferred to the network nodes.

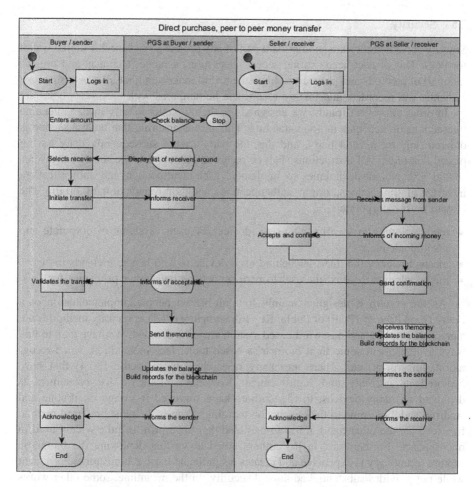

Fig. 3. Activity of direct purchase, peer-to-peer money transfer

2.5   Administration Functions - Support and Maintenance

As mentioned earlier, the system includes the role of system administration. This role is purely devoted to handling technical issues: assistance to network nodes and to final users in setting up their application. The role is totally separated from any interference in the money flowing from one actor to another. The control of all access must clearly prevent any kind of manipulation.

The business model to cover all financial issues of the system is deliberated ignored at this point and sent out of the scope of this paper. It has to be pointed out that the broker and the street corner shops are the most natural point of transfer from cash to the digital wallet. Such services to PGS users are activities that infer risks and costs. When it will be analysed, the business model will also estimate all costs related to the management of the financial transactions and to the service cost.

2.6 Security

Security considerations are an important part of any project so it is for this digital wallet for PGS. This project needs strong security measures, a range (technical and organisational) of methods and procedures implemented to make sure that all transactions are authentic and recorded, and that no record can be tampered with.

In order to prevent frauds, we designed the digital wallet to only manage genuine transactions on accounts in good standing. This means ensuring that the transaction is ordered only by a valid party, and that the party cannot subsequently deny having placed that order. All instructions shall be recorded immutably. The security measures should also include techniques to implement user identification and authentication, integrity of transactions, origin authentication, and non-repudiation of origin. The system must incorporate:

- methodologies to identify all users (devices of users, systems of corporate and institutions, etc.);
- means to verify that the user behind each device is who he/she pretends to be;
- methodologies to allow the user to perform actions he/she has privileges for.

As the system is designed mainly for non-literate people, implementation of a Pretty Good Privacy (PGP) or Public Key Infrastructure (PKI) as security method is not a practical solution and password based system are to be avoided. We have then to find ways to implement some light biometrics based tools: face recognition, voice recognition, fingerprint, etc. There are many researches on biometric [3, 4] that have explored its usability and improvement. Nowadays biometric for consumers is deployed on many devices; in [5], authors have surveyed its usage on iPhone and Android and they came to the conclusion that fingerprint is the most preferred method by users. On the other hand, it has to be noted that fingerprint is quite widely used in microfinance. Furthermore, in [6] authors noted down that deploying the biometric capture technology is expensive and creates a significant barrier to customer enrolment while not provides substantial additional security. In the meantime, some other works [7–9] salute the usage of fingerprint as best practice.

It has then been decided that the security analysis in PGS digital wallet will explore both the "Trusted face" feature of Android and fingerprint at the level of actors interacting with their mobile devices, while all other actors like corporate and institutions, as well as street corner shops and/or brokers, will have "stronger" and more appropriate security management built on a Public Key Infrastructure (PKI). PKI [10] is a system that is comprised of Certification Authority and a Registration Authority; it is managed by the mean of a set of roles, policies, and procedures needed to create, manage, distribute, use, store, and revoke digital certificates and manage public-key encryption.

3   Platforms

The concept of blockchain itself is still in rapid pace development and so is it for entire landscape for developing, testing, and deploying blockchain applications: it is evolving rapidly. Many architectures are available and we opted for Hyperledger. Hyperledger, one of the biggest blockchain standardization efforts, is an open-source initiative overseen by the Linux Foundation. Hyperledger's members are tech companies (Cisco, IBM, Intel, Red Hat, Samsung, VMware, etc.), banks and financial institutions (JPMorgan, Wells Fargo, etc.), blockchain start-ups, global manufacturers and device makers, etc. Hyperledger Fabric is a blockchain framework that offer implementation of permissioned private on a modular and extendable architecture [11–13].

In PGS, We plan to exploit a Hyperledger Composer Business Network Archive (BNA) file for the assets trade and deploying it on a Hyperledger Fabric. Modelling that network, we will define:

- Participants, as the actors who are the PGS users, the users of other schemes, the corporate, the institutions; they will all go through a process of registration and they will then acquire an identity (an enrolment certificate);
- Assets, as the money that move from one participant to another;
- Transactions, as the state change mechanism of the Network.

The platforms to develop this digital wallet for PGS will be comprised of at least three layers: the server, the abstraction layer composed of the applications, the user interfaces. The elements of the platforms are represented in Fig. 4.

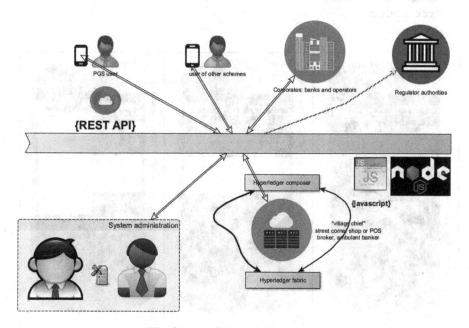

Fig. 4. Hyperledger platform actors

The server

The server must manage network and hence the communications between the client applications and the blockchain itself. The communications relate to the assets, their status, their ownership, and their movements from one participant to another. The server will be implemented in Node.js, an asynchronous event driven JavaScript runtime, designed to build scalable network applications. That server will be part of the Hyperledger Fabric components to be set up.

The abstraction layer

The abstraction layer is the framework where the interactions will take place among the participants, i.e. the network nodes, the assets, based on the transaction logic that drive state changes on the distributed ledger. This is where Hyperledger Composer comes in. It models the business network, containing the assets and the transactions related to them.

The user interfaces

The user interfaces are for all participants to the business network to interact with the distributed ledger. The user interfaces are typically developed using Javascript. As we have the large part of participants using their android device, we will develop the needed part of interfaces using REST API for Android.

4   Interfaces

The PGS user interfaces will provide means for all users to:

- manage their identities;
- check balance;

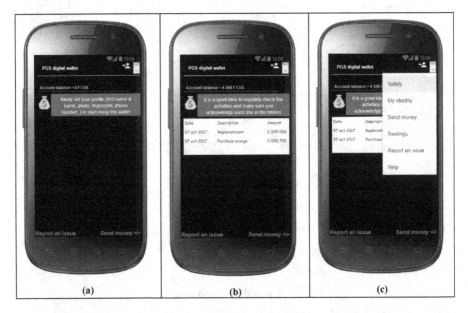

Fig. 5. Initial or empty wallet (a), wallet with some activities (b), and wallet with open menu (c)

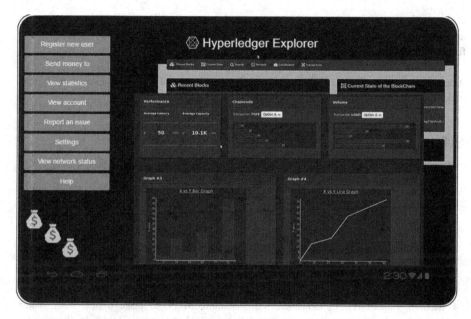

Fig. 6. Tablet at point of service

- send money;
- notify events;
- manage history of transactions.

In the backend, the user interfaces will record all transactions and send them to the blockchain whenever online or in reach of brokers' devices. As showed by the statistics Gartner presented in May 2017, the most popular OS in smartphones[1] is still Android with 86.1%, followed by iOS with 13.7%. As it has been done for the PGS itself, the digital wallet will be developed on Android. Figure 5 shows the three main presentation of the user interface: with an empty wallet, one with some activities recorded, and an interface where the menu is played.

Subsequent interfaces will be needed for every action and for the notifications of events. The elaboration of these detailed interfaces is deferred to the design specification stage. Nevertheless, one more important interface is designed above, the one that is used by actors operating in their capacities of "village chief", street corner shop or POS, or broker/ambulant banker (Fig. 6).

5 Conclusions and Future Work

With the intention to pursue the accomplishment of the Pay-with-a-Group-Selfie (PGS), the digital wallet to embed to it is now evolving a blockchain project. We are currently at an advanced phase of the research and development. The next steps will

---

[1] http://www.gartner.com/newsroom/id/3725117.

then mostly devoted to the coding, testing and improving. This will call on setting up an appropriate network to host the private permissioned blockchain that we have opted for.

Acknowledgement. This work has been partly funded by the Bill & Melinda Gates Foundations under the grant no. OPP1139403.

References

1. Damiani, E., et al.: Porting the pay with a (group) selfie (pgs) payment system to crypto currency. In: Belqasmi, F., Harroud, H., Agueh, M., Dssouli, R., Kamoun, F. (eds.) AFRICATEK 2017. LNICST, vol. 206, pp. 159–168. Springer, Cham (2018). https://doi.org/10.1007/978-3-319-67837-5_15
2. Zarki, M.E., Mehrotra, S., Tsudik, G., Venkatasubramanian, N.: Security issues in a future vehicular network. In: Proceedings of European Wireless (EW02) (2002). https://www.ics.uci.edu/~dsm/papers/2002/sec001.pdf
3. Devi, O.R., Reddy, L., Prasad, E.: Face recognition using fused spatial patterns. Int. J. Adv. Trends Comput. Sci. Eng. **4**(2), 15–21 (2015)
4. Medran, J., Musa1, A., Gonzalez, V., Shadaram, M.: Dual stage optical label switch architecture to create an all optical network based WDM and optical CDMA. In: Proceedings of 2006 IEEE Region 5 Conference, pp. 190–195 (2006). https://doi.org/10.1109/tpsd.2006.5507431
5. Bhagavatula, C., Ur, B., Iacovino, K., Kywe, S.M., Cranor, L.F., Savvides, M.: Biometric authentication on iphone and android: usability, perceptions, and influences on adoption. In: Proceedings of Workshop on Usable Security and Privacy USEC 2015, pp. 1–10 (2015)
6. Muhammad, Z., Rahman, H.U., Makki, B.I., Jehangir, M., Rehman, S.: Branchless banking in pakistan: opportunities and challenges. NFC-IEFR J. Eng. Sci. Res (2017). https://doi.org/10.24081/nijesr.2017.1.0014
7. Buang, A., Suryandari, R.Y., Ahmad, H., Bakar, K.A., Jusoh, H.: Women and liveability – best practices of empowerment from Mozambique. Malays. J. Soc. Space **10**(7), 70–80 (2014). http://ejournal.ukm.my/gmjss/article/view/18992/6091
8. Boateng, F.G., Nortey, S., Asamanin Barnie, J., Dwumah, P., Acheampong, M., Ackom-Sampene, E.: Collapsing microfinance institutions in Ghana: an account of how four expanded and imploded in the Ashanti region. Int. J. Afr. Dev. **3**(2), 37–62 (2016)
9. Maharjan, M., Shakya, S.: Technology acceptance model: understanding local government employees intention in social cash transfer through branchless banking in Nepal. Int. J. Comput. Sci. Mob. Comput. **4**(12), 203–210 (2015)
10. Internet X.509 Public Key Infrastructure Certificate Management Protocols. RFC410 (2005). https://tools.ietf.org/html/rfc4210
11. Li, W., Sforzin, A., Fedorov, S., Karame,. G.O.: Towards scalable and private industrial blockchains. In: Proceedings of the ACM Workshop on Blockchain, Cryptocurrencies and Contracts BCC17, pp. 9–14 (2017). https://doi.org/10.1145/3055518.3055531
12. Cachin, C.: Architecture of the Hyperledger Blockchain Fabric. IBM Research (2016). https://www.zurich.ibm.com/dccl/papers/cachin_dccl.pdf
13. Valenta, M., Sandner, P.: Comparison of Ethereum, Hyperledger Fabric and Corda. Medium (2017). https://medium.com/@philippsandner/comparison-of-ethereum-hyperledger-fabric-and-corda-21c1bb9442f6

A Predictive Model for Automatic Generation Control in Smart Grids Using Artificial Neural Networks

Chika Yinka-Banjo$^{(\boxtimes)}$ and Ogban-Asuquo Ugot

Department of Computer Science, University of Lagos, Lagos, Nigeria
cyinkabanjo@unilag.edu.ng

Abstract. This paper presents a predictive model that estimates the load for an Automatic Generation Control (AGC) system. We start by laying the foundation for our system by discussing the AGC, and the benefits of embedding it in a smart power grid. The AGC as a system is discussed with a keen focus on the mathematical relationship between the load on the system and the frequency deviation. Our predictive model is a deep neural network trained on a multi-variate time series dataset for energy consumption collected over 47 months. The results show that it is possible to predict to a high accuracy, the total load on the power system within the next minute. The goal of the predictive model is predicated upon the notion that the ability to forecast the future load on the system results in the ability to estimate the frequency deviation as well, and thus giving the AGC the ability to forecast risks such as a system overload.

Keywords: Smart grid · Artificial intelligence · Artificial neural networks
Deep learning

1 Introduction

The smart grid power system relies on information technology for the implementation of a system architecture where the major electrical components communicate over an IP network. A typical smart grid architecture consists of generation, transmission, distribution and end user nodes [1]. Each of these components may communicate with each other with a goal of optimizing system performance and reducing risk. In a smart grid power system, one can envision a system design where the end user node through electronic components such as smart meters and smart appliances relays data about energy consumption and load patterns back to the dispatch center. The data is used for instance, to initiate load distribution, just in time to avoid blackouts caused by overloading the system and will therefore save cost due to damage of equipment.

The operational performance of conventional subsystems found in current power grids, such as the Automatic Generation Control (AGC) already benefit from having some form of feedback about the system load [3, 4]. When there is a change in system frequency with respect to an increase or decrease in load, the AGC, based on the corresponding frequency deviation sends control signals to the generator unit to either increase generation or reduce generation to achieve a balance between the system load and system generation. This balance is not always easy to achieve, with sudden peaks

© ICST Institute for Computer Sciences, Social Informatics and Telecommunications Engineering 2019
Published by Springer Nature Switzerland AG 2019. All Rights Reserved
R. Zitouni and M. Agueh (Eds.): AFRICATEK 2018, LNICST 260, pp. 57–69, 2019.
https://doi.org/10.1007/978-3-030-05198-3_5

in system load, the AGC gives up control to an emergency control unit relying on end user load balancing. Over the past decade, researchers have approached the problem of automatic generation through control theory. The literature survey reveals that in general, the AGC problem has been modelled around controller structure and optimization techniques. We review some of these techniques later in Sect. 2.0.

We approach the problem from a relatively different perspective, we observe the direct relationship between the load on the system and the frequency deviation, a key parameter for the AGC. Therefore, the ability for AGC system to forecast the load in the nearest future might serve a huge advantage and solve the problem of handling surprise spikes in load. We propose a neural network based predictive model for the AGC, trained on real energy consumption data that serves the purpose of forecasting the load on the power grid in the next few seconds. Our proposed system design, couples this predictive model to the AGC and the output from the model serves as a parameter for calculating and thus forecasting frequency deviation as well. However, this paper does not present any simulations that determine if truly this proposition improves performance of the AGC or not. We leave such simulations for future work and instead focus on building the ANN model, this paper lays the foundation for the future work. Section 2 lays the theoretical foundations for the proposed system design, in Sect. 3 we present the architecture of the predictive model, the dataset and we report the model performance.

2   Related Work

2.1   Automatic Generation Control

The electric power system, throughout its life cycle, will exists in any of the following four states; normal, preventive, emergency and restorative [4]. These states describe the operational performance of the system with respect to the frequency deviation and the voltage deviation. The normal state is the desirable state where there is a balance between the load and generation [4].

The goal of the control unit in the power system is to keep the system in a normal state. In any case, it is more than likely that contingencies will arise causing frequency deviation and voltage deviations. One of the most common problems is an overload on the power system, resulting in a mismatch between load and generation. Automatic generation control provides an effective mechanism through which the power system can actively balance power by controlling generation to match the load. In a smart grid power system, the AGC is implemented as a software component [3] and is responsible for adjusting the power system generation to minimize frequency deviation.

The AGC achieves generation control by sending signals to control units for the generator. The performance of the AGC system is dependent on how quickly generating units respond to these signals. In general, we can outline the function of the AGC into;

1. Matching an area's generation to it's a load and to control the system frequency
2. Distribute changing loads among available generators so as to minimize costs.

The first function is achieved by secondary control of the generators to minimize frequency deviation. The frequency of the system is the nominal frequency (usually

50 Hz) of oscillations of the alternating current (AC) being generated by the power system. The system frequency rises when the load decreases and may drop if the load increases. However, it is desirable to keep the frequency constant such that $\Delta f = 0$. We can describe the power-frequency relation for any power system, regardless of the primary source of energy. In Eq. 1, we describe this relation for the turbine-governor control. The power-frequency relation for turbine-governor control [3] is;

$$\Delta p_m = \Delta p_{ref} - \frac{1}{R} \times \Delta f \qquad (1)$$

Where Δp_m is the change in turbine mechanical power output, Δp_{ref} is the change in a reference power setting, R is the regulation constant which quantifies the sensitivity of the generator to a change in frequency and Δf is the change in frequency. The first function is also achieved in mutli-area power grid, where each area is connected through a tie-line, by means of load-frequency control (LFC) in which the tie-line power is used. The Area Control Error (ACE) provides each area with an approximate knowledge of the load change and is defined as;

$$ACE = \Delta p_{TL} - \beta \Delta f \qquad (2)$$

Where Δp_{TL} is the tie-line power deviation, β is the frequency bias constant and Δf is the frequency deviation, the ACE serves as feedback for the secondary control [4].

The second function is achieved by distributing the load among different unit generators so as to minimize cost of operation and is based on economic dispatch calculation [3].

Frequency Deviations and Associated Controls
The nominal frequency for a typical power system utility is about 50 Hz, with some countries running utility at about 60 Hz. The frequency deviation Δf is a direct indication of the current changes in utility frequency and says something important about the change in the total load on the utility. The frequency deviation in Eqs. (1) and (2) is a crucial variable required for the AGC as shown in Fig. 2 and determines the control signals required to control the generators. The frequency deviation is given by;

$$\Delta f = -\frac{\Delta p_m}{\beta} \qquad (3)$$

The symbol Δp_m is known as the change in turbine mechanical power but is actually a ratio of the per unit change in load, β remains the frequency bias constant. For example, if the load on a utility drops by 250 MW, and previously, the generators where running on a base load of 500 MW per unit generator. Then, the unit change in load Δp_m is $\frac{-250}{500} = -0.5$. Take note that the numerator is -250 because there was a drop in the load. From this, using Eq. (3), and a frequency bias constant β of 63.2 per unit, the frequency deviation is given as $-\frac{(-0.5)}{63.2} = 0.0079$ per unit. We can then multiply this by 50 Hz (the nominal frequency) to get the frequency deviation in Hertz $\Delta f(\text{Hz}) = 0.0079 \times 50 = 0.3956$ Hz. The purpose of this rather incompletely defined

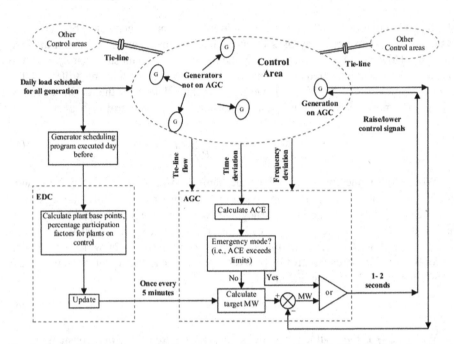

Fig. 1. Typical block diagram for the Automatic Generation Control. The AGC receives input signals including the *frequency deviation*. The input signals are used to calculate the *area control error ACE*, and thus determine the control signals needed to return the utility back to the normal state (image source: Hasan et al.: [4]).

example is to demonstrate symbolically the relationship between the change in load and the frequency deviation, the reader may refer to [15] for a complete example on frequency deviation. The value of Δf along with other parameters, is fed to the AGC and directly influences the type of control signal sent to the utility controllers. The frequency deviation and the corresponding control signal is shown in Table 1.

Table 1. Frequency deviation and associated operating controls.

Range of frequency (f)	Range of frequency at 50 Hz	Types of operation	Types of control
$f^0 - \frac{\Delta f_1}{2}$ to $f^0 + \frac{\Delta f_1}{2}$	50.05 to 49.95	Normal	No controller is required
$f^0 - \frac{\Delta f_2}{2}$ to $f^0 + \frac{\Delta f_2}{2}$	50.20 to 50.05 and 49.8 to 49.95	Normal operation	Primary control
$f^0 - \frac{\Delta f_3}{2}$ to $f^0 + \frac{\Delta f_3}{2}$	50.20 to 51.00 and 49.80 to 49.00	Off-normal operation	Secondary control (AGC)
$f^0 - \frac{\Delta f_4}{2}$ to $f^0 + \frac{\Delta f_4}{2}$	Above 51.00 and Below 49.00	Emergency operation	Emergency control

2.2 Predictive Models for the AGC

Research into various optimization techniques for power systems dates back to the mid 70's and these techniques relied heavily on classical control theory centered around the proportional integral derivative (PID) controller. The nonlinearity of the power system control encouraged researchers to augment the classical controller with optimization strategies and algorithms. Optimization increases the robustness of the PID controller to nonlinearities in parameters such as the load and frequency, however optimization doesn't always lead to successful predictive models. In the literature review, we found that most of the work is centered around optimization techniques, and very little work has been done in predictive modeling for the power system or more specifically the AGC. We classified the work done so far into 2 categories;

1. Optimization

Although reliable to some extent, classical PID controllers and its variants, cannot handle nonlinearities found in power system load and frequency patterns. Thus, classical control theory alone is not sufficient [18]. Modern control theory relies on optimization strategies such as genetic algorithms (GA), particle swam optimization (PSO) and bacteria forging optimization algorithm (BFOA). In [17], the gravitational search algorithm is shown to outperform PID controllers and BFOA. The results show that the optimized control system is quite robust to wide changes in system load conditions and system parameters. The firefly algorithm has been proven to perform well in load frequency control and was demonstrated to outperform PSO, with better response time [16]. Other relevant studies based on optimization strategies such as teaching-learning based optimization [15, 19], have been applied to large scale problems such as the multiarea power system. The Optimization techniques reviewed perform very well and are responsible for the success of modern control applications in power systems. These techniques however have no predictive capabilities.

2. Predictive models

Predicative models for the AGC should be able to estimate with an acceptable accuracy, at least one parameter needed in some aspect of power system control. Predicting parameters for the AGC for instance is not as straight forward as one might assume, again these parameters tend to be highly nonlinear. One technique which has been proven to be quite successful is the model predictive control (MPC). The predict unit of the MPC estimates the AGC system's future output based on its current state, over a finite prediction horizon [22]. The estimated prediction is fed to the control unit to minimize an objective function. The MPC is able to reduce the area control error in multiarea automatic generation control and also provide robustness and faster response [23, 24].

So far, we have reviewed optimization and predictive models that attempt to optimize the whole system response or estimate a set of system parameters. Some interesting studies have focused only on estimating the load of a power system, of the AGC. In [27], a systematic approach for feature selection for predictive modelling of the power system is presented, this is relevant because the features have a direct effect on the predictive potential of a machine learning model. An indirect approach to the load forecasting problem is demonstrated in [25], here the authors predict the state parameters of the system then derive a prediction of the load from the previous estimates, using the support vector regression algorithm. Recurrent neural networks (RNN) have been used for load estimation from a timeseries dataset, RNNs are powerful tools for timeseries forecasting and is quite rightly applied to the load estimation problem, although the accuracies were not too impressive [26]. RNN regression estimates the future load based on previous or past load readings.

From the review, one can infer that there is potential in studying the effects of predictive models for the power system. The issue of nonlinearity is not too big a problem for a robust multilayer deep neural network, these neural networks can be trained on multidimensional datasets to accurately estimate key parameters for power systems. Finally, one can also study the effect of combining deep learning with the optimization techniques reviewed, comparative studies with the MPC strategies are definitely worth looking into.

2.3   Smart Grid Architecture

In this section, we briefly introduce the smart grid in an attempt to consolidate the reason why predictive models in AGC systems are better suited for smart power grids. The main components of a Smart Grid (Fig. 1) are electric power controllers, smart meters, collector nodes, distribution and transmission control generators, electric power substations, transmission and distribution lines, and control centers [6]. Power generators and electric power substations use electronic controllers to control the generation and the flow of electric power.

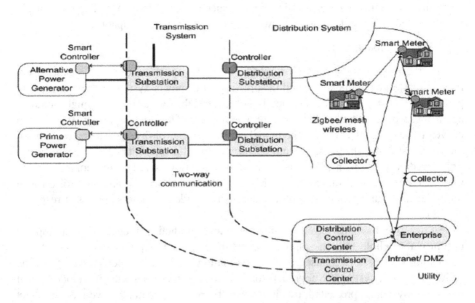

Fig. 2. Typical smart grid architecture (image source: Mavridou et al. [1])

End consumers and collector nodes may communicate through a Zigbee or similar mesh wireless two-way communication network [1]. Two-way communication paths are also used between collectors and the utility. Collector nodes communicate with the utility mostly using the Advanced Metering Infrastructure (AMI) [1, 7] possibly via the Internet. Communication between the transmission and distribution substations and the control center guide the operational process. Like existing power grids, a Smart Grid includes a control system that accommodates intelligent monitoring mechanisms and keeps track of all electric power flowing in a more detailed and flexible way [1]. The fact that as a system, the smart grid relies heavily on information technology makes it more suitable to implement modern innovative solutions that can benefit from online data streams and can exist as a software component embedded within any smart grid electronic component.

Although still theoretical for the most part, many can agree that current and proposed smart grid systems are highly reliable and efficient and secure, [2, 5, 8]. Other features of the smart grid include;

- Flexible network topology: the smart grid architecture has been shown to allow bidirectional energy flow, where the grid can generate energy sources as well receive energy from other sources [11].
- Load balancing/adjustment: the total load on a grid varies highly and is dependent on variables with high uncertainty. When the load on the grid indicates a spike in demand it is essential to redistribute the load or to call on standby generators to support the increase in demand. Smart grid can solve this problem with real-time communication with appliances to efficiently redistribute the load [12].
- Demand response support: Demand response support allows generators and loads to interact in an automated fashion in real time, coordinating demand to flatten spikes. Eliminating the fraction of demand that occurs in these spikes eliminates the cost of adding reserve generators, cuts wear and tear and extends the life of equipment, and allows users to cut their energy bills by telling low priority devices to use energy only when it is cheapest [13].
- Sustainability: the improved flexibility of the smart grid allows for the implementation of more renewable sources of energy. This is due to fact that the smart grid architecture allows for a more distributed feed-in networks.
- Security: The exposure of Supervisory Control and Data Acquisition systems (SCADA) in such an open network introduces security risks. Therefore, the security of smart grids is paramount when designing the architecture. The security of smart grids is a thriving research area, several institutions have proposed cybersecurity protocols for smart grids [9, 10, 12, 14].

3 Proposed System Design

The success of the AGC is guaranteed only when the frequency deviation is still within the range of $49\,Hz \leq f \leq 51\,Hz$ as shown in the Table 1. When the frequency and thus the frequency deviation is suddenly increased or decreased beyond that range, the utility is at the risk of a blackout and a resulting damage in equipment costing millions.

The problem with current models of the power system and the AGC is that the control systems cannot deal effectively with the non-linearity of the load patterns on a utility. This is why there is an emergency control to take over from the AGC in worse case scenarios. The load on a utility at any given point in time is subject to fluctuations that are difficult to predict. Based on this problem, we present a predictive model for the automatic generation control. At the heart of our design is the regression model, in the form of an artificial neural network (ANN) trained on electric consumption data (i.e. the load) collected over 47 months. The goal is to be able to predict the total base load in the next minute. The predicted load should then be used to estimate the frequency deviation, which is then fed to the AGC for processing the output control signals.

3.1 Data Analysis and Feature Engineering

The dataset used for the training is a multivariate time-series dataset collected from a single household over 47 months [20]. The data attributes include the date, time (in minutes), global active power (kW), global reactive power (kW), voltage and sub meter readings 1, 2 and 3. Each of the electrical readings are collected per minute, the result of this a large dataset of 2075259 instances. The date attribute is split into day and month attributes, all attributes except the sub meter readings are used as input attributes. The desired output label for the supervised learning required is the total energy consumption, the total load. Since the total load was missing, we had to derive the output label using the formula (Fig. 3);

$$Total\,load = \frac{Global\,active\,power \times 1000}{60} \tag{4}$$

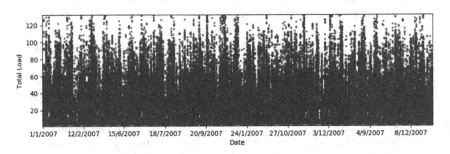

Fig. 3. Scatter plot of the *total load* for just one year. *Total load* is in Kilowatt.

Due to the fact that the data was collected per minute, the data points are highly dense, we show a scatter plot for the total load for just' one week and a day in Figs. 4 and 5 respectively.

The scatter plots in Fig. 4 illustrate the times at which there is a peak load in the system, which is at about 9.30pm, this is the time at which electricity consumption is highest. Some studies have shown that peak loads usually occur in the evening. Some primary reasons for this are the need for more electric bulbs because of the darkness, evening Tv shows and higher number of people are indoors during the evening. Finally, we show a histogram of frequency of total load in kilowatt.

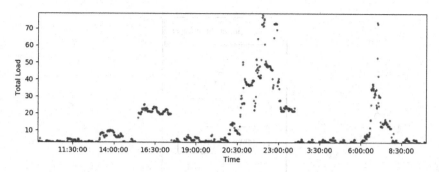

Fig. 4. Scatter plot of the *total load* for one day. *Total load* is in Kilowatt.

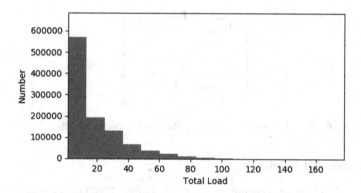

Fig. 5. Total load and their frequency.

3.2 ANN Architecture

The regression model is a simple model that has two fully connected hidden layers with 7 input attributes. The model is built using the Keras deep learning framework [21]. The network weights are uniformly initialized (Fig. 6).

The rectified linear unit activation function is used for the hidden layer. No activation function is used for the output layer because it is a regression model and we are interested in predicting the numerical values directly without an affine transform. The efficient ADAM optimization algorithm is used and a mean squared error (MSE) loss function shown in Eq. (5) is optimized. This will be the same metric used to evaluate the performance of the model. The MSE gives us an error value we can directly understand in the context of the problem. We also include dropout in the hidden layers to reduce overfitting.

$$MSE = \frac{1}{n}\sum_{i=1}^{n}\left(Y_i - \widehat{Y_i}\right)^2 \tag{5}$$

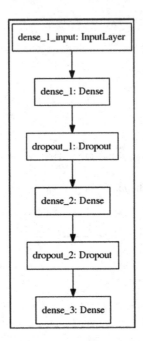

Fig. 6. Model architecture showing the input, hidden and output layers

3.3   Training and Validation

The training data contains a sample of 21,992 instances spread over the period of 2006 to 2007 (Fig. 7).

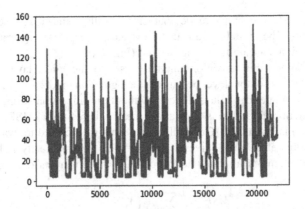

Fig. 7. Scatter plot showing output label y in training set.

The kfold cross validation technique is used for training and validating the model. A batch size of 10 and epochs of 100 was used for cross validation scoring. The mean square cross validated score is shown below (Table 2).

Table 2. Mean square error for cross validated scoring.

Mean square error (MSE)	Mean absolute error (MAE)
0.0014	0.0121

4   Results

The model is tested on an isolated test data from the period between 2008 and 2009, a sample size of 18,100 is used for testing (Fig. 8), (Table 3).

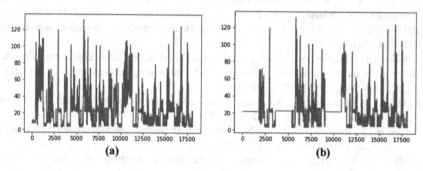

(a)   (b)

Fig. 8. (a) Scatter plot for test data output label (b) Scatter plot showing predicted output results on the test set.

Table 3. Mean square error for cross validated prediction on test data.

Mean square error (MSE)	Mean absolute error (MAE)
0.0076	0.0111

Although we observe some bias in the first 5000 instances, it can be observed that the variance is in general, relatively low on the test data. The results show that the predictive model performs quite well on the test data and is able to correctly predict the total load given an instance of the input parameters for the date, time, global active power and reactive power, and the voltage.

5   Future Work and Conclusion

The work presented here lays the foundation for a more intensive design for a predictive automatic generation control system. Future work presents the opportunity of training the model on larger training and test samples. The dataset for energy consumption from an area (a state for instance) should be used and the input attributes may be increased to accommodate for some social events such as "festive season or not", which may directly influence total base load. From here, simulations should be run using the predictive model in conjunction with the AGC software so as to consider the effect of other parameters.

In conclusion, a predictive model for the AGC model was developed and trained on a dataset for energy consumption from a single household. The mean square error from the test set shows that there is a tolerable balance between the bias-variance tradeoff. The model provides evidence that it is possible to train a deep neural network to predict the total load on a power grid at any given time and day with a very high accuracy.

References

1. Mavridou, A., Papa, M.: A situational awareness architecture for the smart grid. In: Georgiadis, C.K., Jahankhani, H., Pimenidis, E., Bashroush, R., Al-Nemrat, A. (eds.) ICGS3 2011. LNICST, vol. 99, pp. 229–236. Springer, Heidelberg (2012). https://doi.org/10.1007/978-3-642-33448-1_31
2. Yih-Fang, H., Werner, S., Jing, H., Kashyap, N., Gupta, V.: State estimation in electric power grids: meeting new challenges presented by the requirements of the future grid. IEEE Sig. Process. Mag. **29**(5), 33–43 (2012)
3. Keyhani, A., Chatterjee, A.: Automatic generation control structure for smart power grids. IEEE Trans. Smart Grid **3**(3), 1310–1316 (2012)
4. Hasan, N., Khatoon, S., Ibraheem, N., Singh, Y.: Automatic generation control problem in interconnected power systems 1310–1316 (2012)
5. Global Security Index 2017. https://www.itu.int/dms_pub/itu-d/opb/str/D-STR-GCI.01-2017-PDF-E.pdf
6. U.S. Department of Energy Office of Electricity Delivery and Energy Reliability: Study of Security Attributes of Smart Grid Systems – Current Cyber Security Issues (2009)
7. National Energy Technology Laboratory for the U.S. Department of Energy Office of Electricity Delivery and Energy Reliability: Advanced Metering Infrastructure (2008)
8. Electric Power Research Institute: Report to NIST on Smart Grid Interoperability Standards Roadmap, Contract No. SB1341-09-CN-0031-Deliverable 7 (2009)
9. Federal Energy Regulatory Commission. http://www.ferc.gov/about/ferc-does.asp. Accessed 21 Feb 2018
10. North American Electric Reliability Corporation. http://www.nerc.com. Accessed 21 Feb 2018
11. Tomoiagă, B., Chindriş, M., Sumper, A., Sudria-Andreu, A., Villafafila-Robles, R.: Pareto optimal reconfiguration of power distribution systems using a genetic algorithm based on NSGA-II. Energies **6**, 1439–1455 (2013)
12. Sinitsyn, N.A., Kundu, S., Backhaus, S.: Safe protocols for generating power pulses with heterogeneous populations of thermostatically controlled loads. Energy Convers. Manag. **67**, 297–308 (2013)
13. Energy Future Coalition, Challenge and Opportunity: Charting a New Energy Future, Appendix A: Working Group Reports, Report of the Smart Grid Working Group. https://web.archive.org/web/20080910051559/http://www.energyfuturecoalition.org/pubs/app_smart_grid.pdf. Accessed 21 Feb 2018, Accessed 21 Apr 2018

14. Power systems chapter 5. http://nptel.ac.in/courses/Webcourse-contents/IIT-KANPUR/power-system/chapter_5/examp_5.5.html. Accessed 21 Feb 2018
15. Rao, R.V., Savsani, V.J., Vakharia, D.P.: Teaching–learning-based optimization: an optimization method for continuous non-linear large-scale problems. Inf. Sci. (Ny) **183**(1), 1–15 (2012)
16. Padhan, S., Sahu, R.K., Panda, S.: Application of firefly algorithm for load frequency control of multi-area interconnected power system. Electr. Power Compon. Syst. **42**(13), 1419–1430 (2014)
17. Sahu, R.K., Panda, S., Padhan, S.: Optimal gravitational search algorithm for automatic generation control of interconnected power systems. Ain Shams Eng. J. **5**, 721–733 (2014)
18. Shabani, H., Vahidi, B., Ebrahimpour, M.: A robust PID controller based on imperialist competitive algorithm for load-frequency control of power systems. ISA Trans. **52**(1), 88–95 (2013)
19. Rao, R.V., Kalyankar, V.D.: Parameter optimization of modern machining processes using teaching–learning based optimization algorithm. Eng. Appl. Artif. Intell. **26**(1), 524–531 (2013)
20. UCI Machine Learning Repository. http://archive.ics.uci.edu/ml. Accessed 21 Mar 2018
21. Keras deep learning framework. http://keras.io. Accessed 21 Mar 2018
22. Kumar, K., Tyagi, B., Kumar, V.: Multiarea automatic generation control structure using model predictive based control in deregulated environment (2015). 978-1-4673-7492-7/15
23. Qin, S.J., Badgwell, T.A.: A survey of industrial model predictive control technology. Control Eng. Practice II **11**, 733–764 (2003)
24. Venkat, A.N., Hiskens, I.A., Rawlings J.B., Wright, S.J.: Distributed MPC strategies with application to power system automatic generation control. In: Texas Wisconsin Modelling and Control Consortium, No. 2006-05 (2006)
25. Tajer, A.: Load forecasting via diversified state predication in multi-area power networks. IEEE Trans. Smart Grid **8**, 2675–2684 (2017)
26. Kong, W., Dong, Z.Y., Hill, D.J., Luo, F., Xu, Y.: Short-term residential load forecasting based on resident behaviour learning. IEEE Trans. Power Syst. (2017). https://doi.org/10.1109/tpwrs.2017.2688178
27. Abedinia, O., Nina, A., Hamidreza, Z.: A new feature selection technique for load and price forecast of electrical power systems (2016). http://www.ucalgary.ca

Exploring Users' Continuance Intention Towards Mobile SNS: A Mobile Value Perspective

Aseda Mensah[1], Kwame Simpe Ofori[2(✉)] [iD],
George Oppong Appiagye Ampong[3], John Agyekum Addae[3],
Affoue Nadia Kouakou[3], and John Tumaku[4,5]

[1] Department of Marketing and Entrepreneurship,
University of Ghana Business School, Accra LG78 Ghana
aseda_mensah@outlook.com
[2] Department of Computer Science, Ho Technical University, Ho, Ghana
kwamesimpe@gmail.com
[3] Ghana Technology University College, Accra, Ghana
{gampong, jagyekum}@gtuc.edu.gh,
nadiakouakou10@gmail.com
[4] Zhongnan University of Economics and Law, Wuhan, China
johntumaku@gmail.com
[5] Ho Technical University, Ho, Ghana

Abstract. The functionalities of most Social Networking Sites allow users to enjoy practical benefits like maintaining important social and business relationships, communicating with others, and getting feedback on important shared information. However, the place of SNSs as a source of entertainment and enjoyment is also well-documented. The purpose of the paper is to identify the factors that predict continuance use of social networking sites from the perspective of mobile value. Data was collected from 452 students in three leading universities in Ghana and analyzed with Partial Least Square-Structural Equation Modeling. Results from the study revealed that both hedonic value and utilitarian value were significant predictors of continuance intention. Satisfaction was also found to be a significant predictor of continuance intention. In all, the model accounted for 55.6% of the variance in continuance intention. The study also provides important contributions to the literature, by demonstrating the significance of both utilitarian and hedonic value in leading to satisfaction with the usage of mobile SNS services. The implications and limitations of the current study are discussed and directions for future research proposed.

Keywords: Social networking sites · Hedonic value · Utilitarian value
Satisfaction · Continuance intention

1 Introduction

The motivations for consumption have been evolving in recent years. Whereas consumers previously made consumption decisions based on utilitarian considerations [1], customers now contemplate less functional and straightforward solutions to their needs

© ICST Institute for Computer Sciences, Social Informatics and Telecommunications Engineering 2019
Published by Springer Nature Switzerland AG 2019. All Rights Reserved
R. Zitouni and M. Agueh (Eds.): AFRICATEK 2018, LNICST 260, pp. 70–78, 2019.
https://doi.org/10.1007/978-3-030-05198-3_6

[2], favoring instead those value offerings which attend to their needs in a manner that entertains and addresses their emotional concerns also [3]. Such shifting values have spurred a flurry of research on what has been termed 'hedonic' values of consumers [4], with academics studying the effects of such motivations on traditional outcomes like loyalty [2], purchase intention [5], and quality perceptions [6], among others. This dichotomy of desired value has also been considered in the online context, with some researchers examining how utilitarian and hedonic motivations affect the usage of online services [7].

Moreover, the advent of social networking sites (SNS) has provided a unique context in which such perceptions of value can be assessed. López and Ruiz [8] and van der Heijden [9] propose that users on social media are motivated by both utilitarian and hedonic factors. For instance, the functionalities of most SNSs allow users to enjoy practical benefits like maintaining important social and business relationships [10], communicating with others [11], and getting feedback on important shared information [12]. However, the place of SNSs as a source of entertainment and enjoyment is also well-documented in the literature [13]. More relevantly, an increasing number of consumers access SNSs on mobile devices [14], and academics like Zhou et al. [15] opine that such mobile SNS is distinct from traditionally-accessed SNSs. This provides an important gap in the literature for researchers who seek to comprehend how such mobile application of an existing phenomenon may result in different consumer responses.

2 Literature Review

2.1 Continuance

One of the more important results of brands' marketing efforts is continued patronage from their customers. Sufficient evidence from existing literature indicates that it is much more expensive for organizations to serve and satisfy existing customers than for them to find new ones [16]. As such, it has been important for organizations to retain their consumers and encourage them to continue their purchase and/or engagement behavior. Antecedents of such continuance behavior have been studied in the literature, and include a number of constructs like, most pertinently, perceived value and cus-tomer satisfaction. For instance, Patterson and Spreng [17] and Pura [18] found a direct relationship between consumers' perceived value and their intention to continue the usage of services. Again, the role of satisfaction in leading to continuance intention has been observed by researchers in electronic contexts like self-service technology [19], mobile payment services [20], and the usage of Web 2.0 services [21], among others. Studies specific to mobile applications of social networking sites are still nascent, though, and there therefore remains significant gaps to be filled in the literature.

2.2 Mobile Value

Mobile technology has become a focal issue in both research and practice as it has gained a foothold among consumers of various brands. Kim [22] observed that a large proportion of users now access internet services using mobile devices. This has been made possible by the increasing quality of mobile devices which provide immersive experiences that even larger screens and devices may not offer [15]. Indeed, prior literature has established that users' satisfaction with mobile internet usage and intention to continue use is largely dependent on their perceptions of its quality [6]. It is little wonder then that research from the consumer perspective has sought to identify and understand the perceived value gained from the usage of mobile internet services [23]. This has been referred to as mobile value, and Kim and Hwang [6] observe that in the consumer behavior literature, users typically enjoy two forms of mobile value: hedonic value, and utilitarian value [1]. These value perceptions have been found to be important predictors of consumer behavior, such as mobile internet adoption [24] and customer satisfaction [25].

3 Hypotheses Development

3.1 Hedonic Value (HV)

One form of mobile value, as has been previously mentioned, is hedonic value, which the literature identifies as "consumers' enjoyment of the shopping experience itself" [2]. Such value is motivated by the desire to be immersed in the world of the brand or activity, such that pleasure is derived from the entire process of interacting with the brand. Within the information systems literature, such perceived hedonic value is a strong motivator for the usage of entertaining information systems [9]. Interestingly, Pöyry et al. [7] identify that users with hedonic motivations may participate more on a brand's Facebook page, but have much less intention to purchase than utilitarian users who are silent browsers. Thus, it is evident that hedonic value can and does affect consumer behavior, but there remains the need for how the relationships work in various contexts. Hence, though Eroglu et al. [26] found that hedonic value is a stronger pre-dictor of satisfaction than utilitarian value, and Chiu et al. [27] found that hedonic value is a significant indicator of consumer continuance intention, these results have not been substantiated in the mobile SNS context. Thus, the current study puts forth that:
H1:   Hedonic value significantly predicts satisfaction
H2:   Hedonic value significantly predicts user continuance intention.

3.2 Utilitarian Value

On the other hand, utilitarian value has been described in the literature as merely functional, attained from consumer attitude and behavior which may even "be thought of as work" [28]. It stems from the pursuit of a specific outcome in participating in an interaction with the brand or activity in question. Utilitarian perspectives have been used to explain user behavior for several years, and while the literature has pointed out its inability to comprehensively explain consumption patterns [1], its importance in predicting user variables remains uncontested. Anderson et al. [2], for instance, found that utilitarian motivations are an important part of users' participation in retail pages on Facebook, citing specific motivations like time savings and information access.

Interestingly, Babin et al. [4] and Ryu et al. [28] both found utilitarian value to be stronger than the hedonic in resulting in satisfaction. In leading to continuance intention, also, and Ryu et al. [28] found utilitarian value to be greater than hedonic in the restaurant sector. As there is little evidence within the mobile SNS context, however, the current study proposes that:

H3:   Utilitarian value significantly predicts satisfaction
H4:   Utilitarian value significantly predicts user continuance intention.

3.3   Satisfaction (SAT)

Satisfaction is a crucial element of marketing because of its prediction of several other desirable metrics for marketers [29]. Basically understood as the consumer's evaluation of the actual product or service as compared to their expectations of it [30], satisfaction begins and ends with the consumer, and is necessarily based on their perceptions of the value they have benefitted from. Satisfaction is often linked to continuance intention in the literature e.g. [29, 31], as a user is most likely to return to a product or service only when they are confident that it provides the value they seek for the sacrifices they made for it [17]. Researchers like Ryu et al. [28] and Namkung and Jang [32] concur on the importance of such a relationship. In the mobile SNS literature, however, the link has not often been confirmed. Moreover, the place of satisfaction as a possible mediator in the perceived value-continuance intention relationship remains murky.

The current study therefore hypothesizes that:
H5:   Satisfaction significantly predicts continuance intention.

4   Methodology

The items for the latent variables used in this study were drawn from previous studies and the questions were reworded to fit the social networking context. Items for hedonic value and utilitarian value were derived from Lin and Lu [33]. Satisfaction and continuance intention on the other hand were derived from Bhattacherjee [34]. The measurement instrument had 18 items in all. Items were presented in English and measured using a 5-point Likert scale anchored between 1 (Strongly Disagree) and 5 (Strongly Agree). Survey data was collected over a period of 5 days from students in three universities in Ghana using paper-based questionnaires. Data from 452 responses were used for the analysis. Of this number 209 were male and 243 were females.

5   Results and Analysis

Data were analyzed using the Partial Least Square-Structural Equation Modeling. Using the two-step process recommended by Chin [35], we first analyzed the measurement model and then went on to test the measurement model.

5.1   Measurement Model Assessment

The measurement model was assessed with reliability, convergent validity and discriminant validity. As recommended by Henseler et al. [36] it can be seen from Table 1 that all the latent variables are reliable since the values of both Cronbach's alpha and composite validity are compellingly higher than 0.7. Convergent validity was assessed with the Average Variance Extracted. Hair et al. [37] recommend that for convergent validity to be assured, AVE values must be greater than 0.5. Support for this is also provided in Table 1.

Table 1. Loadings-cross loadings and reliability statistics

	INT	HV	SAT	UV	α	CR	AVE
INT1	**0.902**	0.582	0.506	0.616	**0.922**	**0.944**	**0.810**
INT2	**0.927**	0.515	0.533	0.610			
INT3	**0.904**	0.425	0.501	0.553			
INT4	**0.864**	0.425	0.460	0.510			
HV1	0.459	**0.871**	0.241	0.494	**0.913**	**0.939**	**0.793**
HV2	0.471	**0.886**	0.283	0.477			
HV3	0.531	**0.913**	0.283	0.501			
HV4	0.477	**0.891**	0.294	0.465			
SAT1	0.412	0.229	**0.820**	0.287	**0.892**	**0.918**	**0.650**
SAT2	0.453	0.325	**0.820**	0.369			
SAT3	0.488	0.241	**0.848**	0.333			
SAT4	0.444	0.263	**0.779**	0.271			
SAT5	0.430	0.207	**0.785**	0.315			
SAT6	0.461	0.225	**0.783**	0.343			
UV1	0.563	0.454	0.355	**0.893**	**0.929**	**0.950**	**0.825**
UV2	0.569	0.488	0.357	**0.916**			
UV3	0.585	0.505	0.349	**0.918**			
UV4	0.602	0.526	0.386	**0.906**			

Note: α - Cronbach's Alpha, CR - Composite reliability, AVE - Average Variance Extracted, INT - Continuance intention, HV - Hedonic value, SAT - Satisfaction, UV - Utilitarian value

Discriminant validity was assessed using the Fornell –Larcker criterion, which states the square root of the AVE for each construct must be greater than the correlation between that construct and any other construct [38]. The results in Table 2 provide support for this criterion. In all, the results showed that the psychometric properties of the measures used in the study were adequate.

Table 2. Fornell-Larcker criterion

	INT	HV	SAT	UV
INT	**0.900**			
HV	0.545	**0.891**		
SAT	0.557	0.310	**0.806**	
UV	0.639	0.544	0.399	**0.908**

Note: Square root of AVEs are shown on the diagonal in bold

5.2 Structural Model Assessment

In assessing the structural model we examined the magnitude significance and sign of the path coefficients. We also examined the overall fitness of our model. Results for the structural model assessment are provided in Table 3.

Table 3. Hypotheses testing of paths

Hypotheses	Path	Path coefficient	P values	Results
H1	HV → SAT	0.132	0.031	Supported
H2	HV → INT	0.238	0.000	Supported
H3	UV → SAT	0.327	0.000	Supported
H4	UV → INT	0.377	0.000	Supported
H5	SAT → INT	0.333	0.000	Supported
	Model fit			
	SRMR	0.047		

Hedonic value was found to have a significant positive effect on satisfaction ($\beta = 0.132$ p = 0.031) thereby providing support for H1. Hedonic values was again seen to have a positive effect on Continuance intention ($\beta = 0.238$ p = 0.000). Utilitarian value was also found to be significant predictor of satisfaction ($\beta = 0.327$ p = 0.000) and continuance intention ($\beta = 0.377$ p = 0.000) providing support for H3 and H4 respectively. Of the three predictors of continuance intention Utilitarian value is the most significant. Lastly satisfaction was found to be a significant predictor of continuance intention ($\beta = 0.333$ p = 0.000).

6 Discussions and Implications

The current study aimed to identify how consumers' perceptions of hedonic and utilitarian values affect their satisfaction with mobile social networking sites, as well as their continuance intention. The results of the study indicate that all proposed hypotheses were supported by the data. Firstly, it was found that the perception of both utilitarian and hedonic value from the mobile SNS are predictors of continuance intention. The results of the study also indicate that utilitarian value is a stronger predictor of both customer satisfaction and continuance intention when it comes to mobile SNS applications. Though in a different context, these results are similar to those found by the likes of Babin et al. [4] and Ryu et al. [28]. It is therefore most important for brands and organizations to ensure that their mobile SNS pages meet the rational expectations of their users, providing useful and practical information, as this is what will keep consumers satisfied and draw them to keep coming back. It is also necessary for marketers to provide some hedonic value for users to enjoy pleasurable experiences on SNS pages, as our results show that such experiences are also useful in creating satisfaction and return visits.

The study has also provided important contributions to the literature, by demonstrating the significance of both utilitarian and hedonic value in leading to both satisfaction and continuance intention in the usage of mobile SNS services.

6.1 Limitations

The current study found some exciting result that endorses previous studies, however a few limitations must be taken into consideration when interpreting and generalizing results. First, data were collected from students in three universities in Ghana. Even though this sample represents a fairly typical band of SNS users it is still not representative of all SNS users. Secondly, our study employed a cross-sectional design, however, since user behavior changes over time it would be interesting to consider a longitudinal design in future studies.

References

1. Hirschman, E.C., Holbrook, M.B.: Hedonic consumption: emerging concepts, methods and propositions. J. Mark. **46**, 92 (1982)
2. Anderson, K.C., Knight, D.K., Pookulangara, S., Josiam, B.: Influence of hedonic and utilitarian motivations on retailer loyalty and purchase intention: a Facebook perspective. J. Retail. Consum. Serv. **21**, 773–779 (2014)
3. Batra, R., Ahtola, O.T.: Measuring the hedonic and utilitarian sources of consumer attitudes. Mark. Lett. **2**, 159–170 (1991)
4. Babin, B.J., Darden, W.R., Griffin, M.: Work and/or fun: measuring hedonic and utilitarian shopping value. J. Consum. Res. **20**, 644 (1994)
5. Jones, M.A., Reynolds, K.E., Arnold, M.J.: Hedonic and utilitarian shopping value: investigating differential effects on retail outcomes. J. Bus. Res. **59**, 974–981 (2006)
6. Kim, D.J., Hwang, Y.: A study of mobile internet user's service quality perceptions from a user's utilitarian and hedonic value tendency perspectives. Inf. Syst. Front. **14**, 409–421 (2012)
7. Pöyry, E., Parvinen, P., Malmivaara, T.: Can we get from liking to buying? Behavioral differences in hedonic and utilitarian Facebook usage. Electron. Commer. Res. Appl. **12**, 224–235 (2013)
8. López, I., Ruiz, S.: Explaining website effectiveness: the hedonic–utilitarian dual mediation hypothesis. Electron. Commer. Res. Appl. **10**, 49–58 (2011)

9. van der Heijden, H.: User acceptance of hedonic information systems. MIS Q. **28**, 695 (2004)
10. Aharony, N.: Relationships among attachment theory, social capital perspective, personality characteristics, and Facebook self-disclosure. Aslib J. Inf. Manag. **68**, 362–386 (2016)
11. Lipford, H.R., Wisniewski, P.J., Lampe, C., Kisselburgh, L., Caine, K.: Reconciling privacy with social media. In: Proceedings of the ACM 2012 Conference on Computer Supported Cooperative Work Companion - CSCW 2012, pp. 19–20 (2012)
12. Liu, D., Brown, B.B.: Self-disclosure on social networking sites, positive feedback, and social capital among Chinese college students. Comput. Hum. Behav. **38**, 213–219 (2014)
13. Lin, K., Lu, H.: Why people use social networking sites: an empirical study integrating network externalities and motivation theory. Comput. Hum. Behav. **27**, 1152–1161 (2011)
14. Xie, W.: Social network site use, mobile personal talk and social capital among teenagers. Comput. Hum. Behav. **41**, 228–235 (2014)
15. Zhou, T., Li, H., Liu, Y.: The effect of flow experience on mobile SNS users' loyalty. Ind. Manag. Data Syst. **110**, 930–946 (2010)
16. Berry, L.L.: Relationship marketing of services perspectives from 1983 and 2000. J. Relatsh. Mark. **1**, 59–77 (2002)
17. Patterson, P.G., Spreng, R.A.: Modelling the relationship between perceived value, satisfaction and repurchase intentions in a business-to-business, services context: an empirical examination. Int. J. Serv. Ind. Manag. **8**, 414–434 (1997)
18. Pura, M.: Linking perceived value and loyalty in location-based mobile services. Manag. Serv. Qual. Int. J. **15**, 509–538 (2005)
19. Chen, S.-C., Chen, H.-H.: The empirical study of customer satisfaction and continued behavioural intention towards self-service banking: technology readiness as an antecedent. Int. J. Electron. Financ. **3**, 64–76 (2009)
20. Zhou, T.: An empirical examination of continuance intention of mobile payment services. Decis. Support Syst. **54**, 1085–1091 (2013)
21. Chen, S.C., Yen, D.C., Hwang, M.I.: Factors influencing the continuance intention to the usage of Web 2.0: an empirical study. Comput. Hum. Behav. **28**, 933–941 (2012)
22. Kim, B.: Understanding antecedents of continuance intention in social-networking services. Cyberpsychol., Behav. Soc. Netw. **14**, 199–205 (2011)
23. Chun, H., Lee, H., Kim, D.: The integrated model of smartphone adoption: hedonic and utilitarian value perceptions of smartphones among Korean college students. Cyberpsychol., Behav. Soc. Netw. **15**, 473–479 (2012)
24. Kim, H.-W., Chan, H.C., Gupta, S.: Value-based adoption of mobile internet: an empirical investigation. Decis. Support Syst. **43**, 111–126 (2007)
25. McDougall, G.H.G., Levesque, T.: Customer satisfaction with services: putting perceived value into the equation. J. Serv. Mark. **14**, 392–410 (2000)
26. Eroglu, S.A., Machleit, K., Barr, T.F.: Perceived retail crowding and shopping satisfaction: the role of shopping values. J. Bus. Res. **58**, 1146–1153 (2005)
27. Chiu, C.-M., Wang, E.T.G., Fang, Y.-H., Huang, H.-Y.: Understanding customers' repeat purchase intentions in B2C e-commerce: the roles of utilitarian value, hedonic value and perceived risk. Inf. Syst. J. **24**, 85–114 (2014)
28. Ryu, K., Han, H., Jang, S. (Shawn): Relationships among hedonic and utilitarian values, satisfaction and behavioral intentions in the fast-casual restaurant industry. Int. J. Contemp. Hosp. Manag. **22**, 416–432 (2010)
29. Cronin, J., Brady, M., Hult, G., Tomas, M.: Assessing the effects of quality, value, and customer satisfaction on consumer behavioral intentions in service environments. J. Retail. **76**, 193–218 (2000)

30. Anderson, E.W., Sullivan, M.W.: The antecedents and consequences of customer satisfaction for firms. Mark. Sci. **12**, 125–143 (1993)
31. Zhao, L., Lu, Y., Zhang, L., Chau, P.Y.K.: Assessing the effects of service quality and justice on customer satisfaction and the continuance intention of mobile value-added services: an empirical test of a multidimensional model. Decis. Support Syst. **52**, 645–656 (2012)
32. Namkung, Y., Jang, S.: Does food quality really matter in restaurants? Its impact on customer satisfaction and behavioral intentions. J. Hosp. Tour. Res. **31**, 387–409 (2007)
33. Lin, K.-Y., Lu, H.-P.: Predicting mobile social network acceptance based on mobile value and social influence. Internet Res. **25**, 107–130 (2015)
34. Bhattacherjee, A.: Understanding information system continuance: an expectation confirmation model. MIS Q. **25**, 351–370 (2001)
35. Chin, W.W.: The partial least squares approach to structural equation modeling. In: Modern Methods for Business Research, pp. 295–336 (1998)
36. Henseler, J., Hubona, G., Ray, P.A.: Using PLS path modeling in new technology research: updated guidelines. Ind. Manag. Data Syst. **116**, 2–20 (2016)
37. Sarstedt, M., Ringle, C.M., Smith, D., Reams, R., Hair, J.F.: Partial least squares structural equation modeling (PLS-SEM): a useful tool for family business researchers. J. Fam. Bus. Strateg. **5**, 105–115 (2014)
38. Fornell, C., Larcker, D.F.: Evaluating structural equation models with unobservable variables and measurements error. J. Mark. Res. **18**, 39–50 (1981)

Smartphone Cyber Security Awareness in Developing Countries: A Case of Thailand

Feren Calderwood[✉] and Iskra Popova

Department of Computer and System Sciences, Stockholm University,
NOD-Huset, Borgarfjordsgatan 12, 164 55 Kista, Sweden
feca4014@student.su.se, ipopo@su.se

Abstract. Cyber security awareness among smartphone users is becoming one of the main challenges of cyber security in both developed and developing countries. This paper focuses on Thailand, a developing country that is ranked among the riskiest countries in the world with regards to cybercrime. Through a survey exploring the knowledge and practices of Thai student smartphone owners, as the young population is the largest user group, we seek to estimate the level of their cyber security awareness about the most common risks. The findings reveal that they are most susceptible to identity theft or data compromise, while they were on the whole found to have a higher level of security awareness than students in other countries. We argue for Thailand's digital economy to be sustainable, ICT4D projects need to extend their focus to this population of smartphone users to increase security awareness.

Keywords: ICT4D · Cyber security awareness · Smartphone users
Developing country · Thailand · Risk

1 Introduction

With the increase of cyber-attacks and their diversification, so is the threat to the growth of the digital economy in both developed and developing countries. Cyber-attacks are specifically challenging for developing countries. At the same time that they try to build or further develop their information and communication technology (ICT) infrastructure, they also have to build resilience to ward off these threats [1]. It is critical that they do so and align with Goal 9 of the UN Sustainable Development Goals[1], to ensure that their digital infrastructure will become sustainable.

In the recent years the number of smartphones in many developing country shows a trend of constant growth. While smartphone operating systems have been increasingly designed with inbuilt security to be enabled after acquiring a smartphone device, the accountability of caring about and practicing cyber security is placed upon the individuals. For people in developing countries, many will get their first Internet access through smartphones. Besides being exposed to attacks common to computers they are threatened by other events that come from the specifics of these small devices. The

---

[1] Goal 9 concerns "build a resilient infrastructure, promote sustainable industrialization and foster innovation" and includes targeting upgrade of infrastructure by 2030 to make them sustainable.

© ICST Institute for Computer Sciences, Social Informatics and Telecommunications Engineering 2019
Published by Springer Nature Switzerland AG 2019. All Rights Reserved
R. Zitouni and M. Agueh (Eds.): AFRICATEK 2018, LNICST 260, pp. 79–86, 2019.
https://doi.org/10.1007/978-3-030-05198-3_7

human element in cyber security should be addressed through estimating the cyber security knowledge and practices of the end users, and through providing the relevant education and training. This is in particular important for developing countries with significant penetration of smartphones used for Internet access and the expansion of mobile services offered by various actors in the society.

There is plenty of research dedicated to estimating cyber security knowledge and practices of smartphone users. Most of it has been carried out in developed countries [2–5] with very few in the developing world [6]. The studies show that the smartphone security practices are weak and that their cyber security knowledge poor. However, no published articles in English dealing with cyber security awareness of smartphone users in Thailand have been found.

Thailand is a middle-income developing country in South East Asia. Its government has digital development high on its agenda and has established its Digital Economy and Society Development Plan [7] that sets out to extend Internet access and enable e-commerce as well as e-payments. It received support under the auspices of the International Telecommunication Union (ITU) through the ICT for development (ICT4D) project No. 9THA150306 to build human capacity in cyber security and critical infrastructure protection [8]. While this project focused on strengthening the capacity of the government agencies, not visible on the cyber security roadmap in Thailand is the role of end users, and specifically, smartphone end users as 82% of them use the phones for accessing the Internet [9]. Out of the whole population in Thailand accessing the Internet through smartphones, 83% are 18–34 years old, and only 27% are 35 + years old with the smartphone owner group more likely having secondary or higher education (82%) [10].

This paper presents the research about cyber security awareness of Thai students performed as a part of the thesis work at the ICT4D master programme at Stockholm University [11]. The next section provides an overview of the smartphone cyber security risks followed by the section describing the methodology and the limitations. The findings and the conclusions are presented in the last two parts of the paper.

2   Smartphones Cyber Security Risks

The European Union Agency for Network and Information Security (ENISA), acting also as regional advisory body for Asia [13] identified the top six risks for the smartphone users [14].

Data leakage Resulting from Device Loss or Theft: Data leakage can have a severe impact as 97% of smartphone users according to the Kaspersky global survey [15] store a combination of self-created photos/videos/music, personal email, SMS, passwords/PIN codes, phone contacts, banking details. Users are particularly vulnerable if they don't use any form of authentication on their device.

Unintentional Disclosure of Data: This is related to mobile applications gaining excessive permission to the phone content by which it may disclose this data online or to the developer. Using unprotected transmission of data via public Wi-Fi spots can also cause data disclosure.

Attacks on Decommissioned Phones: Digital forensic software has advanced so that data can be retrieved from phones even if they have been factory reset before being re-sold, thrown away or given to a mobile phone decommissioning centre. It is usually recommended that after the factory reset, the user uploads fake data and performs the factory reset again. If the procedure is repeated several times, the probability of discovering the original data is drastically reduced.

Phishing Attacks: An attacker collects user credentials, such as passwords or credit card numbers, using fake applications, SMS or email messages that seem genuine. Smartphone users can be susceptible if they are unaware of how to detect malicious e-mails, SMS messages or forged web links asking for passwords or other sensitive information.

Spyware Attacks: Malicious applications (malware) that can record, steal and transfer data to its creators, the attacker, can end up on the smartphone through downloading and installing applications from untrusted sources. Threats usually come from third-party app stores. However, even apps on Google Play or Apple Store can occasionally mask malware.

Network Spoofing Attacks: This commonly happens in free Wi-Fi hotspot environments, whereby an attacker gives a Wi-Fi a name that may seem legitimate to observe the data being sent and received by those who connect to it. Even legitimate open Wi-Fi networks can be used for such activities. Often when these networks are password protected, the access to the password can be easily obtained or guessed.

3   Methodology and Limitations

The research sets out to explore cyber security practices of student smartphone users in Thailand, to discover the aspects where there is a lack of knowledge and to recommend directions for development of future programmes in raising cyber security awareness. The objectives are broken down as follows.

- Identify the top cyber security risks for Thai smartphone student end users
- Estimate the level of protection that their practices provide against cyber-attacks;
- Depict the cyber security aspects requiring increased cyber security awareness.

A questionnaire gathered the information on security practices of Thai students who own smartphones. The same data collection method was already used in the majority of the research on the same topic, [4–6]. This is a productive method for data collection when the information required is relatively brief and uncontroversial and can be obtained directly from the informants [15]. Simple and short questions on how smartphones are used or what actions users take when there is a danger from cyber-attacks provide information about cyber security knowledge, attitudes and behaviours without any sensitive issues being tackled.

A web platform easily accessible with a smartphone was used to administer the questionnaire. Answers from the Thai students were collected in the autumn of 2016 through HaiSurvey, an incentive-based online system operated by the public opinion expert agency W&S Asia who provided the translation of the questions in Thai language and made them available to a panel of 10,000 potential respondents.

The ethical issues were addressed by presenting to the participants an introductory text that described the purpose of the research, the rights to voluntarily participate in the survey with the possibility to exit at any time and by emphasizing their anonymity was guaranteed. The HaiSurvey system protects the anonymity of the participants and does not capture nor share any personally identifiable information with the researcher. Because of the limited budget of the student researcher, the following limitations are present.

1. The questionnaire consists of 24 questions. 17 of them dedicated to exploring the Internet usage and the security practices, two screening questions filter respondents who are student smartphone owners, and five questions collect demographic data.
2. All the questions are closed with five of them having an open field.
3. The number of valid responses is 115.

4   Results

The questions included in the online questionnaire are based on the work previously done by [4] and [5]. Table 1 lists the questions in the questionnaire and the responses obtained with the two screening questions not included.

The analysis of the demographics data obtained with Q1 to Q5 shows that that the sample can be considered as approximately representative of the population of Thai students although the sampling strategy used was not a strictly representative one. According to [16] the majority of Thai students start with tertiary education at age 18 or take some professional education. This is in support to having the majority or 74% of our respondents at the age 19 to 25. This number is aligned with the responses about the level of education where 76% are at the undergraduate level or take the professional education. The statistics from 2015[2] shows that 58. 3% of the students in the tertiary education in Thailand are females. This is very close to the gender distribution in our sample with 60% females. The distribution of the students according to the regions is similar to that of the population in Thailand[3] not taking into account Bangkok that houses the majority of the tertiary institutions. Regarding the operating systems (OS), our distribution with 60% Android and 40% iOS is not far from the statistics[4] showing personal use of Android is 59% and of iOS 31%.

The responses to Q6 to Q10 picture Thai students having large range of devices, a variety of applications installed on the smartphone with significant amount of sensitive data stored. The majority spend on the Internet more than two hours per day.

---

[2] Source: http://data.uis.unesco.org/#, Percentage of students in tertiary education who are female.
[3] Source: http://www.citypopulation.de/Thailand-Cities.html, Thailand regions.
[4] Source: https://www.statista.com/statistics/563664/thailand-types-of-smartphone-operating-systems-used-for-personal-purposes/, Smartphone OSes used for personal purpose.

Table 1. The questions in the questionnaire and the responses obtained

Q#	Questions	Responses
Q1	What is your age?	19 to 25 (74%); 26 to 34 (26%)
Q2	What is your gender?	Male (39%); Female (60%); Other (1%)
Q3	What part of Thailand do you live in?	Central including Bangkok (56%); North, Northeast (30%); East, West, South (14%)
Q4	What level of education are you enrolled in?	Undergraduate (60%); Master level (24%); Other professional degree (16%)
Q5	What OS does your smartphone have?	Android (60%); iOS (40%)
Q6	Please tell us which electronic devices you own?	Smartphones (100%); Computers (78%); Microwave (73%); Dishwasher (0%)
Q7	How many hours per day on average are you connected to the Internet using your smartphone?	More than 2 h (92%); Between 1 and 2 h (6%); Less than one hour (2%)
Q8	How do you access the Internet using your smartphone? Please rate 1-5 in order of most often to never.	Mobile data plan: (47% most often, 30% often, 16% not very often, 3% rarely, 4% never); Home password protected network (40% most often, 36% often, 13% not very often, 6% rarely, 5% never)
Q9	What type of data do you store on your smartphone?	Photos (96%); Emails (86%); Passwords: social networks, email accounts (69%), bank accounts, credit card numbers (63%)
Q10	What types of applications do you use on your smartphone?	Shopping (72%); Transportation (63%); News (57%); Social (89%); Communication (77%); Games (80%); Finance and banking (79%); Entertainment (79%); Productivity (38%); Tools (48%); Security (42%)
Q11	Where from do you install your mobile applications?	Physical mobile store (6%); Authorized online shop, iTunes or Google Play (74%); Any site where the needed application can be found (20%); Other (0%)
Q12	What type of access protection do you use on your smartphone?	Password with capital and small letters (32%); Password with mixed letters and numbers (33%); Password pattern (10%); Biometrics (19%); None (6%)
Q13	Have you set up access protection to any of your smartphone applications?	Yes, to all of them (17%); Yes, to some of them (56%); No I have not (27%)
Q14	Have you got rid of an old smartphone? If so, what did you do with it?	Gave it or sold to a family member or a friend (54%); Gave it or sold it to an unknown third party (28%); Threw it in the garbage (2%); I have never got rid of my smartphone (16%)
Q15	If you answered yes to the previous question, did you do this beforehand?	Factory reset my smartphone (65%); Factory reset the smartphone, then loaded fake data on to the phone and factory reset the smartphone again (12%); Repeat the previous option several times (6%); I never got rid of it (17%)
Q16	Do you click on links in e-mails or SMS from unknown senders?	Always (49%); Sometimes (43%); Never (8%)
Q17	Do you check what permissions applications require when installing them?	Always (75%); Sometimes (22%); Never (3%)
Q18	Do you read news about smartphone security?	Always (62%); Sometimes (36%); Never (2%)
Q19	Have you ever misplaced your smartphone?	Always (20%); Sometimes (56%); Never (24%)
Q20	Have you ever decided against the using of an application because the app wanted to access your personal data?	Yes (84%); No (11%); I do not know (5%)
Q21	Do you have some security software installed on your smartphone?	Yes (74%); No (21%); I do not know (5%)
Q22	What kind of security software do you have installed on your smartphone?	Anti-virus (73%); Anti-theft (42%); Ant-spam (39%); Data encryption (34%); Firewall protection (26%); Other (0%)

Two specific findings about the cyber security awareness standout 1) students show a high likelihood of being victims of social engineering and phishing; 2) they highly appreciate their privacy and protect themselves from spyware. These results are due to Q16 and Q20. Figure 1 shows the distribution of the answers with the dark areas presenting the negative habits or bad security practices leading to high risks. The fact that the majority of the downloaded applications are from an authorized app store, as per the answers to question 11, indicates a rather low risk from spyware attacks. The answers to question 17 shows that three-quarters of the respondents always pay attention to the permissions asked by the applications, additionally show their concern about privacy.

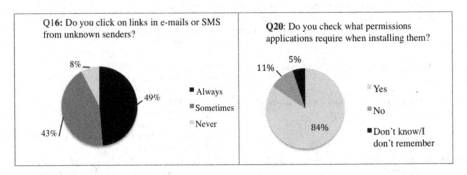

Fig. 1. Distribution of the responses to Q16 and Q20, the dark areas showing negative habits

Regarding other aspects of smartphone cyber security, the findings point to a moderate level of security awareness. According to the answers to question 8, students most often or often connect to the Internet via a protected home Wi-Fi network and rarely to public ones, thus avoiding the risk of network spoofing attacks. The risk from leakage of data due to displacement or loss of the device is not that high because a large portion of respondents use appropriate passwords for locking the screen and for accessing the applications (questions 12 and 13). Also, the responses to question 19 show that not too many respondents are prone to always displacing their phone (only 20%). The risk from attacks on a decommissioned phone is moderate as per the answers to questions 14 and 15 about the respondents getting rid of the old phones either in the most proper or in a proper manner. Questions 18, 21 and 22 asked about the interest in cyber security. The answers showed that the informants having moderate interest in following the news on cyber security, however many of them have some security software installed on their device.

5   Conclusion

According to the reported security practices and behaviours, these Thai students exhibit a moderate level of awareness about cyber security risks except for the risk from phishing attacks about which they have low awareness, and the risk from spyware, where they have high knowledge on how to protect themselves. The respondents show a higher concern and knowledge about the threats from downloading and giving permissions to applications than most students in developed countries [2–5]. When it comes to the threats from phishing attacks, their unawareness is higher than that of students in developed countries. 82% of Thai students who either always or sometimes click on links in phishing emails is much higher when compared with 58% of respondents in the UK not being familiar with phishing [2], and 49% of students in Australia not considering that phishing emails could have negative consequences [5].

Humans are always the weakest link in the cyber security chain in any country. The vulnerability of developing countries is higher due to the limited resources they have to address all the aspects of cyber security, as is the case with Thailand. Therefore we suggest that ICT4D programmes involve training and education of end users. The programmes should be based on the findings of the knowledge gaps and bad practices. They should be led as a joint initiative by the government, mobile industry and education sector. Government has the power to give the mandate for the industry and education system to play an active role in building the e-society. The mobile industry promotes their brand value through providing education in the form of smartphone risk simulations games that consumers play. This is supported by the findings by Fung et al.'s [17] pilot study which showed that e-learning, through a game, significantly increased the students more in depth knowledge and understanding of information security.

Through being capable of protecting themselves against cyber-attacks, the smartphone users contribute towards better cyber security at a national level. This in turn has a positive impact on building confidence and trust in the mobile services offered and contributes to the sustainability of the online economy.

References

1. Tagert, A.C.: Cybersecurity challenges in developing nations. Doctoral dissertation. Carnegie Mellon University (2010)
2. Lazou, A., Weir, G.: Perceived risk and sensitive data on mobile devices. In: Weir, G.R.S. (ed.) Cyber forensics, issues and perspectives, pp. 183–196. University of Strathclyde, Glasgow (2011)
3. Chin, E., Felt, A.P., Sekar, V., Wagner, D.: Measure user confidence in smartphone security and privacy. In: Symposium on Usable Privacy and Security (SOUPS) (2012)
4. Mylonas, A., Kastania, A., Grizalis, D.: Delegate the smartphone user? Security awareness in smartphone platforms. Comput. Secur. **34**, 47–66 (2013)
5. Imgraben, J., Engelbrecht, A., Choo, K.R.: Always connected, but are smart mobile users getting more security savvy? A survey of smart mobile device users. Behav. Inf. Technol. **33** (12), 1347–1360 (2014)
6. Ophoff, J., Robinson, M.: Exploring End-User Smartphone Security Awareness within a South African Context. Information Security for South Africa (ISSA) (2014)
7. Thailand Digital Economy and Society Development Plan. http://www.digitalthailand.in.th/drive/Digital_Thailand_pocket_book_EN.pdf. July 2016
8. ITU project 9THA150306 website. http://www.itu.int/net4/ITU-D/CDS/projects/display.asp?ProjectNo=9THA15030. July 2016
9. Thailand Internet User Profile 2015. EDTA (2016)

10. Internet Seen as Positive Influence on Education but Negative on Morality in Emerging and Developing Nations – Internet Usage More Common among the Young, Well-Educated and English Speakers. http://www.pewglobal.org/files/2015/03/Pew-Research-Center-Technology-Report-FINAL-March-19-20151.pdf. 16 Apr 2016

11. Calderwood, F.: Cyber security risks for smartphone users in Thailand. Master thesis. Stockholm University (2017)

12. Choucri, N., Madnick, S., Ferwerda, J.: Institutions for cyber security: international cyber responses and global imperatives. Inf. Technol. Dev. **20**(2), 96–121 (2014)

13. ENISA: Critical Applications – Smartphone Security Top Ten Risks. https://www.enisa.europa.eu/activities/Resilience-and-CIIP/critical-applications/smartphone-security-1/top-ten-risks. May 2016

14. Kaspersky Lab: One in every six users suffers loss or theft of mobile devices, 21 October 2013. http://www.kaspersky.com/about/news/press/2013/one-in-every-six-users-suffer-loss-or-theft-of-mobile-devices. July 2016

15. Denscombe, M.: The Good Guide Research Guide for Small-Scale Social Research Projects, 4th edn. Open University Press, Maidenhead (2010)

16. OECD/UNESCO. Education in Thailand: An OECD-UNESCO Perspective, Reviews of National Policies for Education. OECD Publishing, Paris (2016)

17. Fung, C.C., Khera, V., Depickere, A., Tantatsanawong, P., Boonbrahm, P.: Raising information security awareness in digital ecosystems with games – a pilot study in Thailand. In: 2008 2nd IEEE International Conference on Digital Ecosystems and Technologies, pp. 375–380 (2008)

Development of an Artificial Neural Network Model for Predicting Surface Water Level: Case of Modder River Catchment Area

Jandre Janse van Vuuren, Muthoni Masinde[(✉)], and Nicolaas Luwes

Unit for Research in Informatics for Droughts in Africa,
Central University of Technology, Bloemfontein, Free State, South Africa
JandreJansevanVuuren@outlook.com,
muthonimasinde@yahoo.com

Abstract. Water is vital for life; however, water is a scarce natural resource that is under serious threat of depletion. South Africa and indeed the Free State is a water-scarce region, and facing growing challenges of delivering fresh and adequate water to the people. In order to effectively manage surface water, monitoring and predictions tools are required to inform decision makers on a real-time basis. Artificial Neural Networks (ANNs) have proven that they can be used to develop such prediction models and tools. This research makes use of experimentation, prototyping and case study to develop, identify and evaluate the ANN with best surface water level prediction capabilities. What ANN's techniques and algorithms are the most suitable for predicting surface water levels given parameters such as water levels, precipitation, air temperature, wind speed, wind direction? How accurately will the ANNs developed predict surface water levels of the Modder River catchment area?

Keywords: Artificial Neural Networks · Modder River · Free State
Surface water · Predication and monitoring

1 Introduction

Water is vital for life; every living entity needs water in order to prosper. On the other hand, water is a scarce natural resource that is under serious thread of depletion from events such as climate change, population and economic growth and poor management of its use around the world (Schewea and Heinke 2014). South Africa and indeed the Free State is a water-scarce region; the constant droughts, very low annual rainfall, poor infrastructure support (rusty water pipes and leaks) and unpredictable water usage patterns by large-scale farmers and other irrigation activities in the province only makes things worse (Ishmael and Msiza 2007). There is evidence that the current challenges of delivering fresh and adequate water to people of the Free State will only get worse as the effects of climate change, population and economic growth become a reality (Blerk 2012).

The government, relevant stakeholders and parties have put measures and strategies in place; they include water restrictions to inform the masses on the sustainable water usage patterns. There is however, an urgent need to develop accurate models for predicting future water levels (Hedden and Cilliers 2014). One way to effectively

© ICST Institute for Computer Sciences, Social Informatics and Telecommunications Engineering 2019
Published by Springer Nature Switzerland AG 2019. All Rights Reserved
R. Zitouni and M. Agueh (Eds.): AFRICATEK 2018, LNICST 260, pp. 87–92, 2019.
https://doi.org/10.1007/978-3-030-05198-3_8

manage surface water is a monitoring and prediction tool that is able to accurately inform decision makers on real-time basis, of the amount of water available for a period of time: short-term, medium-term and long-term. Surface water is found in lakes, rivers, dams and streams, which is drawn into the public water supply. Despite their various shortcomings, Artificial Neural Network's (ANN) have proven that they can be used to develop such prediction models (Govindaraju and Rao 2013). ANN has evolved as a branch of artificial intelligence and has been regarded as an efficient tool for the learning of any nonlinear input-output systems (Chiang et al. 2010).

2 Related Literature

2.1 Water Management in Free State

Water management is the control and movement of water resources to minimize damage to life and property while maximizing the benefits of water (Agriculture n.d.).

The Free State is the third largest province in South Africa covering approximately 129 825 km^2 and is located in the centre of the country. Bloemfontein is the capital of the province which comprises five district municipalities and nineteen local municipalities (Reform 2013).

The Orange River and the Vaal River together with their tributaries, are the main sources of surface water in the Free State province. The Orange River Basin stretches over six other provinces of the country's nine provinces. The Orange River System drains approximately 47% of South Africa's total surface area and approximately 22% of the country's mean annual rainfall run-off (Reform 2013).

2.1.1 Study Area: Modder River

The whole Modder River is a large basin with a total of 1.73 million hectares. It is divided into three sub-basins, named as the Upper Modder, Middle Modder and the Lower Modder. It is located within the Orange water management area (WMA) to the east of the city of Bloemfontein (central South Africa) (Woyessa and Pretorius 2005).

The Upper Orange WMA lies to the centre of South Africa and extends over the southern Free State and parts of the Eastern and Northern Cape provinces. The WMA also borders on Lesotho to the east, where the Orange River originates as the Senqu River. Draining in the Highlands of Lesotho, the Senqu River contributes close to 60% of the surface water associated with the Upper Orange WMA, at the point where it enters South Africa to become the Orange River (Tetsoane and Woyessa 2008).

2.2 Current Surface Water Level Prediction Processes

Water availability of surface water resources is determined by a combination of measurement and modelling. The long-term availability of the surface water resources is determined using rainfall-runoff models. The models that have been used in South Africa include WRSM2000, ACRU, SWAT, VTI and HSPF. The monthly time step WRSM2000 model is widely used in DWAF water resource studies for large catchments. ACRU and SWAT are essentially daily time-step models, while VTI and HSPF are short-time-step models. The latter four models have as yet only found niche or "special question" applications in the determination of water availability for water resource studies. WSM2000 and HSPF are conceptual models of the hydrological cycle while ACRU, VTI and SWAT have a more physical basis (Coleman and van Rooyen 2007).

2.3   Artificial Intelligence

Artificial Intelligence (AI) refers to the computing paradigm that aims to develop solutions that mimic human perception, learning and reasoning to solve complex problems (Masinde et al. 2012). Although AI is usually thought of as part of computer science, AI overlaps with disciplines as diverse as philosophy, linguistics, psychology, electrical engineering, mechanical engineering and neuroscience (Shoham 2014).

2.3.1   Neural Networks

Neural Network (or Artificial Neural Network) are computational networks which attempt to simulate the decision process in networks of nerve cells (neurons) of the biological central nervous system. The neural network, by its simulating of a biological neural network, is in fact a novel computer architecture and a novel algorithm architecture relative to conventional computers. It allows the use of very simple computational operations (addition, multiplications, and fundamental logic elements) to solve complex, mathematically ill-defined problems, nonlinear problems or stochastic problems (Graupe 2013).

2.4   Artificial Neural Networks

ANN's are widely applied in a broad range of fields such as image processing, signal processing, medical studies, financial predictions, power systems, pattern recognition and more. Their success has also inspired applications to water resources and environmental systems, because ANN models have the ability to recursively learn from the data, they can result in significant savings in the time required for model development and are particularly useful for applications involving complicated, nonlinear processes that are not easily modelled by traditional means (Govindaraju and Rao 2013). The ANN model can be broadly divided into the following three types (Chhachhiya and Sharma 2013):

Feed-forward network – In this network output from one layer of neurons feeds forward into the next layer of neurons. There are never any backward connections and connections never skip a layer (Chhachhiya and Sharma 2013). Can make use of supervised or unsupervised learning (Karayiannis 2013).

Recurrent network – This type of network has at least one feedback loop and is mainly used for associative memory and optimization calculation (Chhachhiya and Sharma 2013).

Self-organization network – This network is based on unsupervised learning. In this network, the target output is not known to the network. Mainly used for cluster analysis (Chhachhiya and Sharma 2013).

3 Research Questions

- What ANN's techniques and algorithms are the most suitable for predicting surface water levels given parameters such as water levels, precipitation, air temperature, wind speed, wind direction, atmospheric pressure and evaporation?
- How accurately will the ANNs developed using the algorithms in question 1 above, predict surface water levels of the Modder River catchment area?

4 Research Objectives

The main objective of this research project is to investigate and develop an effective ANN model that is able to predict surface water levels for short-term medium-term and long-term lead-times. The model will be based on data from the Modder River catchment area of Free State.

This main objective will be achieved through the following sub-objectives:

- To develop a custom ANN model that is capable of predicting surface water levels given a set of pre-defined, pre-processed parameters such as water level, precipitation, air temperature and humidity.
- To evaluate and implement interfaces that will use the ANN model above to provide a real-time surface water level prediction system prototype.
- Evaluate the working of the system prototype for a specific period of time.

5 Methodology

Quantitative data that included temperatures, humidity, wind speed, wind direction, rainfall must be requested and received from the South African Weather Services (SAWS) that is in relationship around Case study of the Modder River catchment area. Water level data has been received from the Department of Water Affairs online website. All of this data is pre-processed using a custom developed application to ensure the data is in a generalized form and stored in a database for use. The feed forward back-propagation ANN framework is developed using Visual Studio C#. Using the pre-processed data from the database, experimenting with different data sets in the ANN is in order. Using the weather data as inputs and the water level data as output for the ANN during training, the data set that produces the least amount of error measurements, will be used as the main data set to train the ANN and develop a real-time prototype, where the entities that produced the training data, can connect through some interface to the ANN to provide real-time data.

6 Preliminary Results and Discussion

The graph below is an example of the raw data before being processed. The rain fall is in mm, the temperature in Celsius degrees, the wind speed in km/h and wind direction is between 0 and 360°.

B	C	D	E	F	G	H	I	J
StasName	Latitude	Longitude	DateT	Rain	Temperature	WindSpeed	WindDir	Humidity
QUEENSTOWN	−31.92	26.88	17-Nov-1998 18:00	3.4	11.1	5.6	110	91
QUEENSTOWN	−31.92	26.88	17-Nov-1998 19:00	0.2	11.3	4.8	120	91

This raw data is then pre-processed into a better format for data management and stored in the database, for example: the rain might be 3.4 mm in the raw data, but the pre-processed value might be 4 mm. The pre-processed data is then formatted again to have generalized values and have a smaller number of nodes to work with, for example: Identifying the minimum and maximum value of each input parameter, the level of nodes is developed for the value, for example: using the value of 30 mm rainfall, 0–20 mm rainfall might have minimum impact, there for the range of 0–20 mm rainfall is assigned only 1 input node, but 21 mm–25 mm might have a bigger impact, and therefore every 5 mm after the 0–20 mm range is given 1 input node each. Another generalization example is the temperature, where it can be −5 or −10 °C, which can be placed in the generalization range of cold, therefore giving it 1 input node for the range of any value beneath 0 to range 10.

The generalized data is then retrieved from the database, and put through the developed ANN in C#. The output of the ANN will consist of range 0 to 110, there for having 110 output nodes, this can also be generalized at a later stage to reduce the number of nodes. Each output node represents 1% of the water level, so if the final output is 70 nodes as true, then the surface water level is predicted to be 70%.

References

U.S. Agriculture: Natural Resources Conservation Service—Water Management (n.d.). http://www.nrcs.usda.gov/wps/portal/nrcs/main/national/water/manage/. Accessed 8 Aug 2016

Blerk, J.V.: Water for equitable growth and development, Chap. 2. In: Natural Water Resource Strategy (2012)

Chhachhiya, D., Sharma, A.: Recapitulation on transformations in neural network back propagation algorithm. Int. J. Inf. Comput. Technol. 3, 323–328 (2013)

Graupe, D.: Principles of Artificial Neural Networks. World Scientific, Singapore (2013)

Ishmael, S., Msiza, F.V.: Artificial neural networks and support vector machines for water (2007)

Schewea, J., Heinke, J.: Multimodel assessment of water scarcity under climate change. PNAS 111, 3245–3250 (2014)

Masinde, E.M.: Bridge between African Indigenous knowledge and modern science on drought prediction. ITIKI (2012)

Karayiannis, N., Venetsanopoulos, A.N.: Artificial Neural Networks: Learning Algorithms, Performance Evaluation, and Applications. Springer, New York (2013)

Govindaraju, R.S., Rao, A.R.: Artificial Neural Networks in Hydrology. Springer, Heidelberg (2013)

Reform, N.D.: Free State Province Provincial Spatial Development Framework (PSDF), 2 (2013)

Tetsoane, S.T., Woyessa, Y.: Impact of rainwater harvesting on the hydrology of Modder River Basin. Water Institute of SA (2008)

Shoham, Y.: Artificial Intelligence Techniques in Prolog. Morgan Kaufmann, Burlington (2014)

Hedden, S., Cilliers, J.: The emerging water crisis in South Africa. African Futures Paper (2014)

Coleman, T.J., van Rooyen, P.: Framework for future water resource analysis in South Africa (2007)

Woyessa, Y.E., Pretorius, E.: Implications of rainwater harvesting in a river basin management: evidence from the Modder River basin, South Africa. Prog. Water Resour. 12 (2005)

Chiang, Y.-M., Chang, L.-C., Chang, F.-J.: Dynamic neural networks for real-time water level predictions of sewerage systems-covering gauged and ungauged sites. Hydrol. Earth Syst. Sci. 14, 1309–1319 (2010)

UmobiTalk: Ubiquitous Mobile Speech Based Translator for Sesotho Language

John Nyetanyane and Muthoni Masinde[(✉)] [iD]

Unit for Research on Informatics for Drought, Central University of Technology,
Free State, Bloemfontein, South Africa
jnyetanyane@cut.ac.za, muthonimasinde@yahoo.com

Abstract. The need to conserve the under-resourced languages is becoming more urgent as some of them are becoming extinct; natural language processing can be used to redress this. Currently, most initiatives around language processing technologies are focusing on western languages such as English and French, yet resources for such languages are already available. Sesotho language is one of the under-resourced Bantu languages; it is mostly spoken in Free State province of South Africa and in Lesotho. Like other parts of South Africa, Free State has experienced a high number of non-Sesotho speaking migrants from neighboring provinces and countries. Such people are faced with serious language barrier problems especially in the informal settlements where everyone tends to speak only Sesotho. As a solution to this, we developed a parallel corpus that has English as a source and Sesotho as a target language and packaged it in UmobiTalk - Ubiquitous mobile speech based learning translator. UmobiTalk is a mobile-based tool for learning Sesotho for English speakers. The development of this tool was based on the combination of automatic speech recognition, machine translation and speech synthesis. This application will be used as an analysis tool for testing accuracy and speed of the corpus. We present the development, testing and evaluation of UmobiTalk in this paper.

Keywords: UmobiTalk · Automatic speech recognition (ASR)
Machine translation (MT) · Text to speech (TTS) and parallel corpora

1 Introduction

Under-resourced languages are languages that lack unique writing systems or stable orthography, limited presence on the web and lack of electronic resources [6]. These languages are difficult to computerize through the use of natural language processing because large amount of data is required to train the current recognizers [21]. These kinds of languages are becoming unpopular; less economically viable and doomed to lose currency since the attention placed on them is of limited acknowledgement [3].

The choice of Sesotho language was reached based on the fact that it is one of the under resourced languages mostly spoken in the Free State province of South Africa; it is spoken by approximately 4 million South Africans as a home language [31]. In 2011, the province experienced approximately 35 000 migrants coming from outside South Africa with in-migration of approximately 128 000 of population from different

R. Zitouni and M. Agueh (Eds.): AFRICATEK 2018, LNICST 260, pp. 93–106, 2019.
https://doi.org/10.1007/978-3-030-05198-3_9

provinces [31]. One of the reasons South Africa experiences higher migration rates is because it is one of Africa's economic giants, thus acting as a catalyst to motivate immigrants from the neighbouring countries, especially those that are facing socio-economic challenges [30].

The tool described in this paper was motivated by the problems brought by the language barrier that exists between Sesotho speakers and non-Sesotho speakers in Free State. Despite the advancement and proliferation of speech-to-speech technologies and tools, there exist no mobile phone based tool (known to the authors) that can effectively aid learning of the Southern Sotho language. Such a tool is very useful to foreigners, non-Sesotho speakers, migrants as well as people with special needs who are usually faced with a unique challenge on how to integrate themselves to Southern Sotho language speaking society in the province. Although English is seen as an intermediary language that bridges language barriers between different races, people especially in the rural areas of Free State do not know (speak, read and write) English, hence the Sesotho translating tool is seen as an asset. The technological aspects included in UmobiTalk and discussed in this paper are: speech based technology (this caters for both the source and target language), natural language understanding (NLU) modules (such as morphological, syntactic and semantic analyzers), language corpus and machine translation (MT).

We present the details of the design, implementation, testing and evaluation of UmobiTalk. The rest of the paper is structured as follows: Sect. 2 details the underlying theory on which the UmobiTalk is based, Sect. 3 is implementation while the methodology used is in Sect. 4. The details of the tool's evaluation, conclusion and results are in Sect. 5.

2   Literature Review

A speech-to-speech application must have the following components: Automatic Speech Recognition (ASR), Machine Translation (MT) and Text-to-Speech (TTS) [11, 20]. As shown in Fig. 1 below, ASR receives an input (source language), MT converts (processing) a source language to target language and TTS speak (output) the target language.

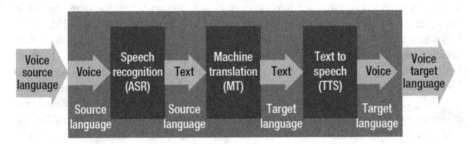

Fig. 1. A speech-to-speech application's events sequence [11, 20].

ASR technology makes life easier because spoken words can be used to communicate with the machine. According to [24], speech is the easiest way to communicate and is faster than typing and more expressive than clicking. Still on the same topic, recent research of [29] reveals that speech to text applications can also improve system accessibility by providing data entry options for blind, dyslexic, deaf or physically challenged users. The most recent example here is 'Be My Eyes'; iPhone app that lets blind people contact a network of sighted volunteers for help with live video chat (http://www.bemyeyes.org/). Research into speech processing and communication for the most part, was motivated by people's desire to build a mechanical model to emulate human verbal communication capabilities [4]. Speech is the most natural form of human communication; ASR has made it possible for computer to follow human voice commands and also understand the human languages.

Evidence from literature demonstrates the fact that, unlike entering input on a fully-sized keyboard, entering text on a mobile device is often sluggish and error prone [1]. Additionally, using a touch screen on small mobile device to input data is time consuming and frustrating. The use of ASR in mobile devices is more effective and flexible than in desktops because they can be used while a person is "on the move" [24]. Researchers have suggested that ASR is very important especially for users with low literacy or little script knowledge such as those in the developing regions.

2.1 Machine Translation

Machine translation (MT) technology is a process of substituting a source text with a target text, but because of language implications, a well-constructed parallel corpus is essential to handle text and phrase translation processes [24]. The viability of machine translator has been experimented by several researchers. According to [27], MT has been seen as an asset that can be used by learners to learn foreign languages. MT translator has been used by most applications such as UmobiTalk, Google translate, dictionary applications, and many more. Earliest research of [19] expounds the idea of using machines to translate started at 1940s and it was seen as an indispensable technology on the basis that it is economically viable compare to human translators, but on the other hand it was posing a threat to professional human translator as it was taking all over. Although the machine translators are quick, inexpensive, always available, and language independent that correlates highly with human translators they will always have flaws compared to professional human translators [15].

To obtain an outmost performance and quality of machine translation, collaboration of machines and human performing post editing of language translation is fundamental [15]. The measuring of the machine translator is determined by its closeness to a professional human translator. According to [10], as they were using the MT to translate from Arabic to English they concluded an MT as an analysis tool to evaluate the parallel corpus' correctness, robustness, reliability, accuracy, flexibility and many more.

2.2 Language Corpus

In order to build any speech engine, whether speech recognition or speech synthesis engine, one needs a corpus. Language corpus is a collection of pieces of language text in electronic form selected according to external criteria to represent as far as possible a language as a source of data for linguistic research [22, 23]. Corpus build raised rapidly from 1960 to 1980 and corpus usage is not only becoming an important foundation of modern linguistic studies, but as other specialized academic research in the field of medicine, architecture, technology, law, English and other premises [35]. Earliest research of [2] explain that corpus usage has extended to areas such as translation studies, stylistics, and grammar and dictionary developments. In addition, [14] expounded a corpus as a tool that can be used for many diverse language technology applications such as word sense disambiguation, anaphora resolution, information extraction, statistical machine translation, grammar projection, unsupervised part of speech tagging or learning multilingual semantic translation. There are different types of corpora (collection of corpus) which are general, specialized, parallel, historical, multimodal, and learner corpus [13, 36].

General corpus can be spoken (speech corpora) or written corpora aim to provide knowledge for the whole language and is considered as a very large monolingual corpus with millions of words that will be used to match the input [13]. General corpora also known as sample corpora or reference corpora can be used to capture the language variety such as Britain English and American English or Lesotho's Sesotho and South African Sesotho [36]. It is reference corpora in such a way it can be used as a snapshot of a language collected at a particular point in time [36].

Specialized corpus is restricted to a certain domain and is compiled for a specific purpose and represents a particular context, genre, text or discourse and subject matter or topic [13]. [35] define specialized corpora as collecting a particular field of corpora to build ideal library collection. On the other side, [36] explain a specialized corpora as a tool that captures the specific type of a language use and dwell on it by using highly contextualized terminologies. Learner corpus is another type of a specialized corpus focusing on some basic aspects of a language and is used specifically by non-native speakers of a language represented to facilitate the teaching and learning processes and material.

Parallel corpus is a widely used multilingual translation containing two or more language text samples aligned at sentence level in which one language represents the source and another one represents the target [28, 36]. This technology is one of the indispensable resources that emerges wide range of multilingual applications such as machine translation and cross lingual information extraction [28]. Additionally, parallel corpus can be explained as a valuable resource for cross-language information retrieval and data-driven natural language processing systems especially for statistical machine translation (SMT) [26, 34]. The translation flow can either be unidirectional (one way direction from source to target) or bidirectional (from source to target and vice-versa) [32].

Historical corpus known as diachronic corpus is a corpus that can unhide or track the language and language writing used from centuries (ancient orthogonal) that can be compared with the currently used language with the aim to obtain rational finale on how language evolves [36]. Example on Sesotho orthography which can be explained as a way of writing or text spelling. The convention of South African Sesotho orthography used in ancient times such as old testimonial bibles (20th centuries ago) is quite different from the one used lately [9]. Lesotho still retains an ancient original orthography while the one used in South Africa has evolved [9].

According to [18], the development of historical corpus in Arabia assists linguistic and Arabic language learners to effectively explore, understand and discover interesting knowledge hidden in millions of instances of language use. A historical corpus of electronic art music has been successfully developed and is now available online from UbuWeb art resource site [8]. Despite its flaws in terms of bias whereby male com-posers are dominant, it provides an interesting test ground for automated electronic music analysis in terms of historical and cultural coverage [8].

Multimodal corpus is a corpus that is done through audio and video recording normally during the discussion meeting [16]. Multimodal corpus includes transcripts that are aligned or synchronized with the original audio or visual recording [13]. Earliest research of [7] said multimodal corpus was developed based on multimodal communicative behavior and can be recorded through visual display which can be writable such as speech or non-writable such as shoulder orientation, gesture, head orientation, and gaze relate to spoken content. Sign language is a good example of why multimodal corpus is necessary where it represents non-verbal language and non-verbal aspects of the language [16].

2.3   The Sesotho Language

Sotho or Southern Sotho language is one of the 11 official South African languages. According to statistics, Sesotho language is primarily spoken by 1 717 881 people in Free State and secondly 1 395 089 in Gauteng province [31]. Southern Sotho, Northern Sotho (Setswana) and Western Sotho (Sepedi) are all derived from Sotho languages and all the speakers are called Basotho [9]. The Sotho languages are closely related to Southern Bantu language such as Nguni languages that comprise of Xhoza, Zulu, Swazi, Hlubi, Phuthi and Ndebele.

Sesotho language is considered as a highly morphological language because a single word is formed by the concatenation of morphemes [9]. A morpheme is an immature or an undeveloped word normally called linguistic unit with a minimal meaning [9], and proper concatenation of them result into normal word. These mor-phemes include a head morpheme called prefix, a stem morpheme called an infix and a tail morpheme called suffix [17]. A stem morpheme can derive on many new words once different affixes are attached to it [9].

2.4   Related Work

[12] presented the rapid development of an Afrikaans-English speech to speech translator which is a prototype that incorporates the use of ASR, MT and TTS and designed to run on laptops or desktops computers using a close talking head-set microphone. Google translate and Google Translate Android App are Google appli-cations that helps with the learning of multi-languages [20]. [5] described Lwazi corpus

for ASR which is a new telephone speech corpus for nine South African Bantu languages; this corpus aims to facilitate the development of the applications that will enhance education, speech enabled software and information dissemination through media. [33] expressed the TTS application for call centre automation; here, TTS engine monitors live call centre calls between live callers and live operators and detects certain key words that are spoken; these keywords are used to facilitate the report about call issues and real-time assistance of the call centre operator. [6] postulates automatic speech recognition for under resourced languages technology which focuses on integrating Bantu languages (considered as under-resourced languages) and technologies that make use of speech recognition such as In Car Messaging application.

3   Research Methodology

Given the nature of the proposed solution, qualitative research was deemed most applicable because it enabled elicitation of ideas and views of the phenomena in order to get descriptive and accurate findings. Prototyping was applied in the development of the mobile application system prototype while experimentation was used to evaluate the usability of this prototype. Given the enormous scope of developing a corpus, case study research design was adopted; for this purpose, only, a selected representation of the Southern Sesotho language was modelled and used to develop and evaluate the system prototype.

In evaluating the usability of the system prototype, sample method (involves taking a representative selection of the population and using data collected as research information [25]) was applied. The results obtained from the sample were generalized to the entire population. This research's sample was based on the population in Free State. Purposive sampling was used because the participants have some defining characteristics that make them the holders of the data needed for the study, e.g. foreigners and non-Sesotho speakers that are faced with the problem of integration to Sesotho speaking population. Once the sample was determined, the tools to obtain the data were selected. Open-ended interview was conducted; there was a conversation between the researcher and the participants, and the aim was to extract the ideas or views about the proposed application. As a qualitative data gathering technique, observations were conducted; users were videotaped while installing and using the application on their mobiles. The aim was to obtain the behavioral patterns of the participants without necessarily questioning or communicating with them. The aspects that were being evaluated using observation were: speed, robustness, compatibility and usability of the application.

4   Implementation

4.1   System Framework

UmobiTalk's development was based on the framework in Fig. 2 below; it focuses on three important aspects of the speech based machine translator: ASR, MT and TTS.

Parallel corpus was first developed and UmobiTalk app was used as a tool to evaluate the functionality of the corpus.

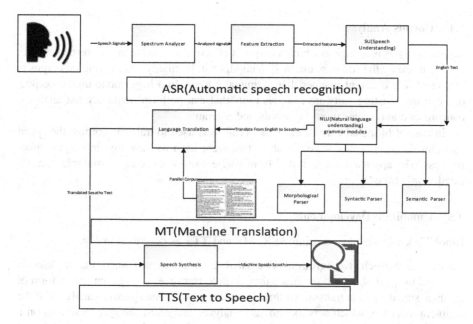

Fig. 2. Summary of processes taking place during the development of UmobiTalk

4.2   Parallel Corpus Collection

We conducted the quantitative research with the aim to obtain basic Sesotho language that migrants need to know; collected data was stored in two different files aligned at a sentence level. The first file known as the source file containing English texts and the second file known as a target file containing Sesotho translated texts. The corpus was then narrowed to only six domain aspects of the language learning: greetings, small talk, tourism (food, culture, places etc.), business, emergency words and etiquette.

4.3   Corpus Annotation

Firstly, each word forming a sentence was assigned its part of speech tag; this made it easy for the machine to understand and categorize their word class. Words that are considered to have grammatical ambiguity or words with more than one grammatical features were assigned more than one part of speech tag e.g. book_NN/VB. The phrase annotation layer was added in which sentences were broken down in to phrases; each phrase was assigned an appropriate phrase tag, forming constituents (syntactically analyzed phrases). The Sesotho texts were tagged using numerical codes that uniquely identify a word or a phrase in a sentence. These numerical codes were used to link the

Sesotho translations with English constituents in a corpus. For each two parallel lines in a corpus, the number of constituents from the source language was equal to the number of Sesotho translations from the target corpus.

4.4   Corpus Analysis

Corpus analysis is a stage in which a corpus's effectiveness, robustness, correctness etc. are evaluated by the software that will manipulate it. Normally, a monolingual corpus is evaluated in a different manner than bilingual corpus. In a huge monolingual corpus, one can use existing software analysis tools that can perform frequency list analysis, concordance and collocation, keywords and n-Grams.

In case of bilingual corpus, the UmobiTalk was used to train the corpus; the speed and translation accuracy were variables that were used to measure the corpus effectiveness. The application was tested from single word translation to multiple complicated words translation.

4.5   Umobitalk Developments

UmobiTalk was developed using ASR, MT and TTS as described in Fig. 1.

Automatic Speech Recognition. The ASR is implemented such that a user is expected to speak the word or phrase they wish to translate. The speech is in a form of acoustic signals, and is transmitted through sound waves. The spectrum analyzer of the recipient machine, which acts like an ear, analyzes and maps the speech signals on a spectrum. Feature extractor then extracts phonemes from analyzed speech signals and finally the speech understanding technology converts the extracted phonemes in to text depending on the language of interest such as English. In UmobiTalk, the recognized English text is displayed on a screen for user verification and edits. This way, the user is certain that the translated word is the correct word he/she is looking for. In Fig. 3 below, the user is prompted to speak to the machine; the spoken words will be displayed on a text box.

Fig. 3. Allow the user to speak to the machine

Machine Translator. Before the machine translates the inputted text, it needs to 'understand' the grammatical features of the text. In order to make this possible, a NLU (natural language understanding) module was developed; it comprises of morphological, syntactic and semantic analyzers. The morphological analyzer uses the tokenizer method to break down the sentence in to words known as elements, each element is then passed to the part of speech tagger which uses the machine dictionary to check the legality of word and assign it a relevant part of speech tag. The tagged words are sent to the syntactic analyzer which uses the phrase structure rules to analyze and group the words based on their grammatical dependency. The phrase structure rules are applied in a form of a parse tree, where by the analytical procedure analyzes the sentence from top to bottom and from left to right. Finally, the semantic analyzer tries to figure out the changes of meaning of words. Semantic analyzer is further explained below.

Semantic Analyzer. The semantic analyzer focuses on identifying and solving word sense ambiguity. A word sense ambiguity is a word having more than one meaning, its correct meaning is determined by its location in a sentence. Those words are labeled with more than one part of speech tag such as book_NN/VB in a machine dictionary. The semantic analyzer is encapsulated with the word sense disambiguation (WSD) module that can detect inputted single words ambiguity (Fig. 4) and in-text word ambiguity (Fig. 5).

The screenshots below demonstrate how UmobiTalk respond to above mentioned ambiguities.

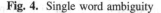

Fig. 4. Single word ambiguity   **Fig. 5.** In-text word ambiguity

As shown in Fig. 4 above, a user will select from the list which book is he/she referring to. From Fig. 5, WSD module is provided with the set of rules that can identify the position of word with ambiguity in a given context, and disambiguate the word based on what precedes and follows it. It should be noted that the machine 'noticed' that "may" is not a "may" of a month because it is followed by the noun instead of a verb; secondly, the first "book" has been recognized as a verb because it is followed by a noun instead of a verb or possessive part of speech. The last book is recognized as a noun because it is followed by the possessive part of speech.

When the language has been analyzed, the machine translator will take over. The machine translator is implemented to run all the lines inside a corpus by comparing each inputted constituent against the list of existing constituents in a source corpus to find the best match; if the match is found, then the specific Sesotho translation is extracted from a target corpus and presented on a screen.

TTS Developments. Sesotho words audio files were compiled and incorporated into UmobiTalk; these files are used when reading the Sesotho translations. The Umobi-Talk's TTS operation compares each translated text with the set of audio files to find the best match. The selected audio files are stored in a media player list that is later manipulated. Time interval between the successive audio files is set to approximately 10 s to allow successive audio files to be executed immediately after the preceding one has complete. Without setting the time interval, the audio files will be executed at once or concurrently making it difficult to hear the words. The shortcoming of Sesotho TTS approach is that it has been designed to predict existing Sesotho words; therefore, new words (words not in corpus such as proper nouns) cannot be read by the application. This is currently addressed by integrating the customized Sesotho TTS with the existing English TTS to read unknown words in English.

5 Evaluation, Conclusion and Further Work

5.1 Evaluation of Umobitalk Speed and Accuracy

The system testing and evaluation was conducted by the researcher through experiments, to meticulously observe and document the language translation accuracy and the response time. The response time was basically based on the time it takes from when button translate is clicked and to when the output is displayed on a screen. To record the response time, we modified the application to have timer that will determine the speed of the language translation. The experiments were conducted to determine the overall translation speed of the application. The experiments were based on translation of word patterns known as n-Gram (number of words in a sentence) inputted by the user. These words were inputted in a form of phrases that were analyzed as constituents. Constituent is word(s) in a sentence that can be grouped and analyzed together based on their grammatical dependencies. Based on the experimentation, we concluded that the translation speed is determined by the response time of the machine, the shorter the response time the higher the translation speed. The response time is dependent on the number of constituents that are inputted by the user. The more the inputted constituents the longer the response time. Translation speed was analyzed in a form of a graph below (Fig. 6).

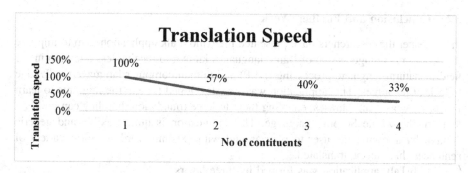

Fig. 6. Modelling of translation speed using the line graph

The overall translation speed of the machine is 57.5%.

We tested the translation accuracy in the same manner with the translation speed, by evaluating it against the number of constituents inputted. We ensured that constituents inputted abides to language grammatical rules. The translation accuracy was calculated by comparing the machine translated text with the correct Sesotho text determined by the Sesotho linguistic, to determine the closeness. Therefore, the higher the closeness the higher the accuracy rate (Fig. 7).

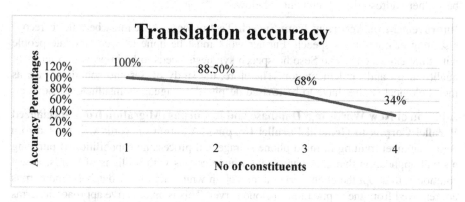

Fig. 7. Modelling of translation accuracy using the line graph

From the graph above, the more the constituents are feed to the system, the less the accuracy. The overall translation accuracy of UmobiTalk is 72.6%, the motive behind achieving such a good score was depending on well-structured parallel corpus. However, main challenge that degrades the accuracy rate was difficulties that were encountered when trying to intertwine two different languages, having two different language structures.

5.2 Conclusion and Further Work

In this paper the researchers have presented the Umobitalk application, aim to improve the Sesotho language as one of Bantu languages known to receive less attention in the field of natural language processing (NLP) and human computer language (HCL) due to lack of resources. This application was also developed to help the migrants to learn few basic words and phrases, enabling them to have foundation that they can build on to learn the whole Sesotho language. This application is quite flexible and generic enough by allowing the user to play around with existing words to form variety of sentences that can be translated.

UmobiTalk application was formed by three layers

1. Automatic speech recognition (ASR), used for input purposes
2. Machine translation (MT), used to process data
3. Speech synthesizer, used to output data.

This prototype is developed as an analysis tool to assess and improve the parallel corpus implemented; since the quality of the corpus cannot be evaluated directly, hence a tool to manipulate the corpus is prerequisite. This prototype was tested and evaluated by the researcher and group of respondents. The software proven to be quite easy to use, can work without having to access the data connection, unless a user need to use Google speech technology. Using the application lights up some aspects that needs to be further addressed as documented below.

Improvement of Accuracy from Speech Technology. ASR must be able to recognise long or continuous speech. Further work must be done to accommodate people with different accents. The Sesotho speech synthesis needs to be improved in terms of quality audio and implementation. Therefore, the study of Sesotho sounds known as morphological studies have to be revised despite the language's insufficient resources.

Addition of New Words in a Database and in Corpus (Migration from Specialized Parallel Corpus to General Parallel Corpus). Addition of words was limited to a certain number, putting in mind phone storage and processing capabilities. If pursuing a small application that can manipulate a huge corpus with millions of words, a best solution is to adopt the client server approach in which dictionary database and corpus are removed from the application to cloud server. This is an effective approach in terms of improving system functionality. However, it cannot be viable due to cost ineffectiveness, since the user must always be online to operate the system.

Integrate Translation to Other Languages. The functionality level will increase; single application can solve more than one problem. The major challenge will be the level of complexity which will increase not only on a technical basis but also on graphical user interface. The user before performing translation must first use combo box tool to select maybe the source and the target language.

Bidirectional Translation Between Two Languages. Vice versa translation between two languages will require dictionary database and parallel corpus to be extensively modified to allow backward translation from Sesotho to English. This idea will help the Sesotho speaking individuals who wants to learn English language.

Sesotho Pronunciation Learning Technology. A translated Sesotho phrase such as "setjhaba sa Qwaqwa" is difficult to be read and properly articulated by a non-Sesotho speaker such as Indians or Chinese speaking people, thus a need to learn pronunciation is vivid. As a further work UmobiTalk will integrate Sesotho pronunciation training, to enforce a proper pronunciation of Sesotho words for an effective communication principle. The only deterioration that will hinder the successful implementation of this tool is language insufficient resources and speech based technology that require thorough learning of Sesotho morphemes. The predicted advantage of Sesotho speech based technology is to help the non-native Sesotho speakers to learn complex phonological aspects of Sesotho consonants such as "kg, tl, tlh, qwa, qha" and many more that are used most of the time.

References

1. Alumäe, T., Kalijurnd, K.: Open and extendable speech recognition application architecture for mobile environments. In: Spoken Language Technologies for Under-Resourced Languages (2012)
2. Anthony, L.: AntConc: design and development of a freeware corpus analysis toolkit for the technical writing classroom. In: Proceedings International Professional Communication Conference. IEEE (2005)
3. Anodo, T.: Open source spelling checker for Kimiiru language. Doctoral dissertation, University of Nairobi (2013)
4. Anusuya, M., Katti, S.: Speech recognition by machine, a review. arXiv preprint arXiv:1001. 2267 (2010)
5. Barnard, E., Davel, M., Van Heerden, C.: ASR corpus design for resource-scarce languages. In: ISCA (2009)
6. Besacier, L., et al.: Automatic speech recognition for under-resourced languages: a survey. Speech Commun. **56**, 85–100 (2014)
7. Chen, L., et al.: VACE multimodal meeting corpus. In: Renals, S., Bengio, S. (eds.) MLMI 2005. LNCS, vol. 3869, pp. 40–51. Springer, Heidelberg (2006). https://doi.org/10.1007/11677482_4
8. Collins, N.: The UbuWeb electronic music corpus: an MIR investigation of a historical database. Organised Sound **20**(1), 122–134 (2015)
9. Demuth, K.: Accessing functional categories in Sesotho: interactions at the morpho-syntax interface. In: Meisel, J.M. (ed.) The Acquisition of Verb Placement. SITP, vol. 16, pp. 83–107. Springer, Dordrecht (1992). https://doi.org/10.1007/978-94-011-2803-2_4
10. Devlin, J., et al.: Fast and robust neural network joint models for statistical machine translation. In: Proceedings of the 52nd Annual Meeting of the Association for Computational Linguistics (Volume 1: Long Papers), vol. 1 (2014)
11. Duarte, T., et al.: Speech recognition for voice-based machine translation. IEEE Softw. **31**(1), 26–31 (2014)
12. Engelbrecht, H., Schultz, T.: Rapid development of an Afrikaans-English speech-to-speech translator. In: International Workshop on Spoken Language Translation (IWSLT) (2005)
13. Arshavskaya, E.: The Routledge Handbook of Language Learning and Technology, pp. 103–106 (2018)
14. Graën, J., Batinic, D., Volk, M.: Cleaning the Europarl corpus for linguistic applications (2014)

15. Green, S., Heer, J., Manning, C.: The efficacy of human post-editing for language translation. In: Proceedings of the SIGCHI Conference on Human Factors in Computing Systems. ACM (2013)
16. Gries, S.T., Berez, A.L.: Linguistic annotation in/for corpus linguistics. In: Ide, N., Pustejovsky, J. (eds.) Handbook of Linguistic Annotation, pp. 379–409. Springer, Dordrecht (2017). https://doi.org/10.1007/978-94-024-0881-2_15
17. Guma, S.: An Outline Structure of Southern Sotho. Shuter and Shooter, South Africa (1971)
18. Hammo, B., et al.: Exploring and exploiting a historical corpus for Arabic. Lang. Resour. Eval. **50**(4), 839–861 (2016)
19. Hutchins, J.: From first conception to first demonstration: the nascent years of machine translation: 1947–1954. A chronology. Mach. Transl. **12**(3), 195–252 (1997)
20. Hyman, P.: Speech-to-speech translations stutter, but researchers see mellifluous future. Commun. ACM **57**(4), 16–19 (2014)
21. Imseng, D., et al.: Impact of deep MLP architecture on different acoustic modeling techniques for under-resourced speech recognition. In: 2013 IEEE Workshop on Automatic Speech Recognition and Understanding (ASRU). IEEE (2013)
22. Jakubíček, M., et al.: The ten ten corpus family. In: 7th International Corpus Linguistics Conference CL (2013)
23. Kennedy, G.: An Introduction to Corpus Linguistics. Routledge, Abingdon (2014)
24. Kumar, A., et al.: Rethinking speech recognition on mobile devices (2011)
25. Latham, B.: Sampling: What is it: Quantitative research methods 5377 (2007)
26. Nakazawa, T., Kurohashi, S., Kobayashi, H., Ishikawa, H., Sassano, M.: 3-step parallel corpus cleaning using monolingual crowd workers. In: Hasida, K., Purwarianti, A. (eds.) Computational Linguistics. CCIS, vol. 593, pp. 79–93. Springer, Singapore (2016). https://doi.org/10.1007/978-981-10-0515-2_6
27. Niño, A.: Machine translation in foreign language learning: language learners' and tutors' perceptions of its advantages and disadvantages. ReCALL **21**(2), 241–258 (2009)
28. Paulussen, H., et al.: Dutch parallel corpus: a balanced parallel corpus for Dutch-English and Dutch-French. In: Spyns, P., Odijk, J. (eds.) Essential Speech and Language Technology for Dutch. NLP, pp. 185–199. Springer, Heidelberg (2013). https://doi.org/10.1007/978-3-642-30910-6_11
29. Reddy, R., Mahender, E.: Speech to text conversion using android platform. Int. J. Eng. Res. Appl. (IJERA) **3**(1), 253–258 (2013)
30. Sibanda, O.: Social ties and the dynamics of integration in the city of Johannesburg among Zimbabwe migrants. J. Sociol. Soc. Anthropol. **1**(1-2), 47–57 (2010)
31. Statistics South Africa. Population Census (2011). [dataset]. http://www.statssa.gov.za/census2011/Products/Census_2011_Census_in_brief.pdf
32. Sundermeyer, M., et al.: Translation modeling with bidirectional recurrent neural networks. In: Proceedings of the 2014 Conference on Empirical Methods in Natural Language Processing (EMNLP) (2014)
33. Thenthiruperai, B., Kates, J., Miller, K.: Use of speech recognition engine to track and manage live call center calls: U.S. Patent No. 8,130,937, 6 March (2012)
34. Tian, L., et al.: UM-corpus: a large English-Chinese parallel corpus for statistical machine translation. In: LREC (2014)
35. Yang, L., Zhang, D., Tang, Y.: The realization of food corpus based on database technology. J. Simul. **2**(6), 327–330 (2014)
36. Vaughan, E., O'Keefe, A.: Corpus analysis. In: The International Encyclopedia of Language and Social Interaction (2015)

Short Paper Session

Embedding a Digital Wallet to Pay-with-a-Selfie, Defining the System Architecture as Blockchain Based

Perpetus Jacques Houngbo[1]([✉]), Joel T. Hounsou[1],
Ernesto Damiani[2,3], Rasool Asal[2], Stelvio Cimato[3], Fulvio Frati[3],
and Chan Yeob Yeun[2]

[1] Institut de Mathematiques et de Sciences Physiques,
Avakpa, BP 613, Porto-Novo, Benin
jacques.houngbo@auriane-etudes.com,
joelhoun@gmail.com
[2] EBTIC-Khalifa University,
Abu Dhabi Campus, PO Box 127788, Abu Dhabi, UAE
{ernesto.damiani,rasool.asal,cyeun}@kustar.ac.ae
[3] Università degli Studi di Milano, via Bramante 65, 26013 Crema, CR, Italy
{stelvio.cimato,fulvio.frati}@unimi.it

Abstract. The Pay-with-a-Group-Selfie (PGS) project, funded by the Melinda & Bill Gates Foundation, has developed a micro-payment system that supports everyday small transactions by extending the reach of, rather than substituting, existing payment frameworks. PGS is designed to work with devices with limited computational power and when connectivity is patchy or not always available. Once the concept of PGS has been accepted as demonstrated by the experimentation, we move to integrating elements and tools intended to ease federation or incorporation of the large spectrum of stakeholders. Embedding a digital wallet is one step in that vision. We analysed the system architecture that will be needed and the requirements drive us to opting for blockchain based architecture. We are then presenting the applicability of a blockchain as platform.

Keywords: Digital wallet · Mobile payment systems · Visual cryptography
Trust · Blockchain · Distributed ledger

1 Introduction

Nowadays, mobile devices are everywhere around the world, and many users have them in their pockets or in their purses instead of a regular wallet, and use their own devices to make payments or transfer money to each other. In the last 15 years, many apps (such as Google Wallet, or Samsung Pay) and technologies (like NFC) have become available supporting smartphone users in their payment needs.

In developing economies, the number of people with access to mobile phones is high and increasing from year to year, but the availability of the overall technological infrastructures and the usage habits are very different from those of the western world.

© ICST Institute for Computer Sciences, Social Informatics and Telecommunications Engineering 2019
Published by Springer Nature Switzerland AG 2019. All Rights Reserved
R. Zitouni and M. Agueh (Eds.): AFRICATEK 2018, LNICST 260, pp. 109–124, 2019.
https://doi.org/10.1007/978-3-030-05198-3_10

The availability of financial, health-care, agricultural, and educational services via mobile terminals is changing traditional relationships inside previously remote local communities, and it is bringing increasing economic opportunities. For example, many people living in rural areas of Africa and Asia have started using SMS services to find out daily prices of agricultural goods, to improve their bargaining position in local markets, and to select markets that offer the maximum income [1].

There are research works that focus on finding appropriate ways for illiterate people in rural areas to benefit from the development and expansion of the digital world [2]. The *Pay with a (Group) Selfie (PGS)* System is designed with the same ambition. In fact, the PGS [3] is an innovative payment system that uses a *group selfie* to collect all information items behind a purchase: the seller, the buyer, the service/product and the agreed price. The need for such system in rural areas where network coverage is patchy clearly moderates the enthusiasm created by the mobile boom earlier in the 2010 [4].

This paper is an attempt to present the research and development steps of the extension of the PGS by embedding a digital wallet in it. Its overall aim is to show the achievability of that extension and the technical viability of the proposed solution to be based on distributed ledger. Blockchain is a hot topic that keeps coming in every talk. Although many seem to just be "buzzword compliant with the latest and greatest", blockchain is unquestionably among the hottest technologies in the enterprise security, data storage and file-sharing arenas. Blockchain is an emerging and strategic trend, Gartner[1] ranks it 6 out of 10 in its *"Top 10 Strategic Technology Trends for 2017"*. The interest of blockchain for this work resides in its properties of trust-free, tamper-proof and resilience. A blockchain system is:

- a peer-to-peer (P2P) distributed system that:
  - is used for storing a single sequence of events;
  - admits only appending new events;
  - enforces a fixed or user-defined protocol (contract) for appending;
  - does not require trusted parties;
- a distributed ledger with no single trusted/privileged guardian.

The paper is organized as follows: Sect. 2 presents a light introduction to block-chain. As blockchain is an important part in the design of the solution, it is worth presenting that introduction before gearing towards to the design of the solution. Section 3 briefly recalls the status of PGS and its experimentation. Upon analysis of the need for digital wallet for PGS, Sect. 4 presents the state of the art in designing digital wallet. Section 5 elaborates on the system architecture, from the requirements analysis up to the system design. That section basically explains the rationale of relying on a blockchain platform to scaffold that system architecture. In that layout, the paper presents the initial steps of research and development: research solutions, requirements analysis, and system design. The further steps from functional specification up to the design of first prototype are out of the scope of this paper. Finally, Sect. 6 draws our conclusions.

---

[1] https://www.gartner.com/doc/3471559/top–strategic-technology-trends.

2 Blockchain

The innovation of blockchain is so breakthrough that currently there are numerous research and publications related to it. After that Nakamoto [5] has opened the path to crypto currencies, many institutions performed adaptation on them. Blockchain operates as a shared ledger recording the history of electronic business transactions that take place among participants in the P2P network. The participants then need a consensus mechanism, a collaborative process that they use to agree that a transaction is valid and to keep the ledger consistently synchronized. Participants agree to the transaction and validate it before it is permanently recorded in the ledger. The great value of the consensus mechanism is that it lowers the risk of fraudulent transactions, because tampering with transactions added to the ledger would have to occur across many places at the same time. Blockchain platforms use a range of consensus models [6]. From the original form of Proof of Work initiated by Bitcoin [5] and the Practical Byzantine Fault Tolerance algorithm (PBFT) implemented as modular consensus protocol to be plugged into Hyperledger [7, 8], other models have been proposed, such as Proof-of-Stake (PoS) and Proof-of-elapsed-Time (PoeT) and Proof-of-Activity (PoA).

One of the key properties of blockchain is information security, King [9] elaborates on how blockchain can help in combating a large spectrum of issues in the cyber threats landscape. The immutability of the blockchain records resides on the common shared ledger whose state is collectively maintained by the network in a decentralized fashion [10–13]. This is a consensus protocol [14] that ensures a common, unambiguous ordering of transactions and blocks and guarantees the integrity and consistency of the blockchain.

The World Economic Forum [14] elaborates on the governance challenges and multi-stakeholders cooperation opportunities that arise from the blockchain development. The same way as other authors did [15], Crosby et al. [16] insisted on the difference between bitcoin and a blockchain. The core technology of blockchain is abundantly explained [17, 18]. As a means to navigate through the multiple platforms and architectures offered, Xu et al. [19] have proposed a taxonomy to classify and compare blockchains and blockchain-based systems while Ellervee, Matulevicius, and Mayer [20] attempted to overcome lacks of standardization and uniform understanding. Because of the ubiquity of the phenomena of bockchain, the temptation is high to serve it almost any way. Xu et al., Ellervee, Matulevicius, and Mayer [19, 20] and most importantly Wüst and Gervais [21] offer frameworks to determine whether a blockchain is the appropriate technical solution.

3 Status of PGS

PGS development was carried out by three teams: one in charge of the client-side back end (that generates shares [22] at the seller's device), one in charge of the point-of-service back-end (reconstruction of the original selfie from the shares, validation of the purchase and interface with external payment systems), and one in charge of the user interface on the mobile devices.

3.1 Development Environment

Android was selected as the execution environment at the client side. According to Gartner[2] report for August 2016, as of Q2 2016, Android represents over 86% of market share and dominates the market together with iOS that counts for 13%. Also, it is by far the preferred choice in Africa and particularly in the Republic of Benin, where PGS has been experimented.

The PGS is currently designed in the form of four modules playing distinct roles. The Seller module triggers the process by taking the photo. Then, it compresses the photo, computes the shares using visual cryptography, and sends appropriate files to the Buyer module. The Buyer module receives the files and can later send them to the Broker one. Finally, the Broker module receives files from both the Seller and the Buyer and transfers them to the Bank module.

3.2 Experimentation

The experimentation phase has defined the following objectives:

- assessment of the viability of PGS design;
- functional testing and experimentation;
- user acceptance;
- checking of unexpected results.

It is a great satisfaction to notice that the concept of PGS has been quite widely accepted. Almost 80% of those who came across the two teams have clearly accepted the idea and many of them have also expressed the will to get more information about it.

Observations at the level of the software are also element of great satisfaction. The numerous challenges that the lab tests have help fix turn to be advantageous for the current version. From the captcha to the taking of the selfie, from transferring files from Seller to Buyer, and exchanging files with the Broker, the software modules performed as expected. The functionalities previously validated during of lab experimentation have been confirmed. The option of relying on Bluetooth as main channel of communication has been proved to be efficient.

One of the objectives of this experimentation was to observe unpredicted or unexpected results. This experimentation went through with almost no unpredicted or unexpected results, apart from the surprise about the type of telephones in use, to be discussed in the next section.

With the continuously increasing offer of Android applications due to the predominance of Android devices in Africa, this experimentation was expecting to confirm the omnipresence of Android devices in the suburb of Porto-Novo. Mainly the common belief was that Samsung (mostly fake Samsung) as a brand is dominating the market. It was really a surprise to see from the figures that the most common mobile phones in use are not the Samsung like as it was previously thought. Nobody from the

---

[2] http://www.gartner.com/newsroom/id/3415117.

team was expecting that it would be, but Nokia and Itel are on the top, ahead of the Samsung only ranked as third.

The current design of the PGS software requires the user to be at a certain level of literacy. The experimentation has been run by people who can be perceived as smartphone savvy as they very easily master the entire process. Nevertheless, that full process requires several steps to complete:

- seven taps on buttons from the Seller:

  1. take the selfie;
  2. take the photo;
  3. confirm the photo;
  4. validate to continue at the end of encryption;
  5. send the share to the buyer;
  6. find the buyer device in the list;
  7. select the buyer's device in the list;

- data entry for item purchased and price from the Buyer
- four taps on buttons from the Buyer;
- four taps on buttons from the Broker;
- identification of the name of the receiver device in a list of available Bluetooth devices.

While some studies confirm importance of "ease of use" in mobile-payment services adoption [23], other studies demonstrate that "*ease of use had no significant effect on perceived usefulness and intention to use*" [24]. Nevertheless, we consider enhancing the current stage of ease of use of PGS. All these steps may need to be simplified for the PGS to come to be usable by people who are less smartphone savvy, as it may be expected in remote rural areas.

The design around the introduction of the Broker has proved to be efficient in terms of assuring the shares reach the bank asynchronously, without disrupting the system. Even though the current design relies on human action to trigger the file exchange, it is conceivable that this data transfer can be performed automatically whenever the broker's device comes close to a seller's or a buyer's device.

3.3 Conclusion of the Experimentation

The experimentation meets expectations: it showed that the PGS concept is accepted, the software performed well and the experimentation gave clues on the level of smartphone literacy level the software currently requires. The experimentation then shows path for improvement of the software in terms of need for more automation for devices to actively operate in machine to machine interface. Finally, the experimentation highlighted the need for a further study of the actual devices in use in the remote rural areas.

4 Digital Wallet for PGS, State of the Art of Digital Wallets

PGS completely integrates the prediction of transforming *"the mobile phone from a pure person-to-person communication device to an electronic wallet"* [25]. While the current version of PGS only simulates the transfer of money from one account to another, the product cannot be complete without a practical way of handling those transactions.

Simply put, a digital wallet is an application running on an electronic device that allows an individual to make electronic transactions. With the user's payment information and credentials stored in it, the digital wallet, also known as an *e-wallet*, can be used with mobile payment systems that allow consumers to pay for purchases with a smartphone equipped with the proper application and a near-field-communication (NFC) microchip or with the capabilities of scanning a QR (Quick Response) at a Point-Of-Sale (POS) terminal. This is also referred as a contactless payment.

In a previous work, we have attempted to clarify the numerous terms and concepts that run around virtual currencies, e-money, digital wallets, crypto currencies [22]. This paper starts from the assumption that a digital wallet is not limited to crypto currencies, but it is supposed to adapt to store any kind of currency. PGS is designed with the clear intention to offer mobile payment for any kind of currency, including cryptocurrencies. But that vision will be implemented later. As for now, PGS offers its services on the base of the currency currently in use. In that framework, the digital wallet facilitates transactions by allowing users and merchants to transfer the currency among themselves, making sure that the right parties are credited and charged. In a research to identify the security challenges that mobile payment faces, [26] have depicted the layers pertaining to traditional card payment process and those added by mobile payment process. They then divide mobile payment systems into five categories: mobile payment at the point of sale, mobile payment as the point of sale, mobile payment platform, independent mobile payment system, and direct carrier billing.

Mobile Payment at the Point of Sale

In the category "mobile payment at the point of sale", the customer uploads his traditional credit card data into the mobile device and then performs transactions by presenting her mobile device to the terminal at the merchant. All big players like Android Pay[3], Apple Pay[4], Microsoft Wallet[5] and Samsung Pay[6] offer this type of specific digital wallet[7]. Their main property is that they allow user to add credit cards to mobile device by taking a photo or entering account information. Users can do the same for loyalty cards, digital coupons and gifts card. When making a purchase at a

---

[3] https://www.android.com/pay/.

[4] http://www.apple.com/apple-pay/.

[5] https://www.microsoft.com/en-us/payments.

[6] http://www.samsung.com/us/samsung-pay/.

[7] MasterCard's new MasterPass program is an attempt to simplify further: it is a partnership with the major big players. That unifying approach may solve the issue of fragmentation in the marketplace. While consumers will operate one single account, merchants will access one single Application Programming Interface (API) to process transactions.

store, the user places the mobile device over the card reader, selects the appropriate card for payment and approves the payment via fingerprint or password.

Mobile Payment as the Point of Sale

In the case of "mobile payment as the point of sale", the merchant transforms his mobile device into a point of sale by installing appropriate applications. This trend comes as a must for merchants as they are stressed to upgrade their POS terminals to better protect the customer's financial information. Unfortunately, there is no single standard solution for the POS terminals. In the meantime, the option of deploying multiple solutions will be complex and expensive, and merchants should opt for installing a digital wallet on their mobile device. This allows them to stay away from a lot of hassle while benefiting from numerous advantages.

Mobile Payment Platform (Can Be "Independent Mobile Payment System")

The mobile payment platform option integrates many features. By the mean of an application, the consumer uses her mobile device to access several payments services like the pure digital wallet, cardless (and contactless) ATM cash withdrawals or mobile airtime top up for instance. When the system is dedicated to a specific company, it is termed as "independent mobile payment system".

Direct Carrier Billing

The category of direct carrier billing defines the cases where the cost of purchase is charged on the mobile subscriber's account at the operator. This system does not require a credit or debit card.

Of special note is the case of the Peer-to-Peer (P2P) Payment systems championed these days by Venmo[8]. This type of payment enables consumers to send, receive, or request a payment to or from another person and are most frequently used for sharing the cost of a restaurant bill, sending a cash gift, or paying a babysitter. Such peer-to-peer payment is the one that suits most the digital wallet PGS will embed but unfortunately, the traditional design backs it on credit cards and bank accounts. For PGS to be able to implement that scheme, it has to find way around bank accounts.

One of the main drawbacks of these digital wallets described above is that it is not obvious how the user adds money (cash) to his wallet. The different cards have their direct link to the issuer bank, but moving cash directly to the wallet is mostly silenced, the operation must be from a credit card or a bank account.

Overall, digital wallet offers some tangible advantages directly appreciated by the consumer: transaction fees are lessened, more flexibility with the possibility to pay in a combination of credit, points and coupons, fast checkout at stores. The reduction of monetary and environmental costs of physical cards and receipts that can be digitized, and the improvement in security are two other significant advantages to be noted. It is therefore wise to predict that the development of digital wallets will only improve in the future and PGS must enter that development by embedding its own version of digital wallet.

---

[8] https://venmo.com/.

5 System Architecture

This section aims at answering the question of what is needed for implementing a digital wallet, through the analysis of several types of requirements. Numerous frameworks are available to conduct such analysis, going from some light and almost linear steps like offered by [27] up to more complex roadmap similar to the Checklist-Oriented Requirements Analysis (CORA) framework presented by [28]. At this stage, we took the option to proceed by using a slightly adapted model of requirements analysis that is comprise of customer requirements, functional requirements, performance requirements, design requirements.

5.1 Customer Requirements

The customer requirements in this paragraph derive from the overall ambition of the PGS itself. Based on the objective of opening digital opportunities for people living in rural areas with no network coverage, PGS must embed a digital wallet that will cover all financial parts of transactions in such areas. One can think of the basic checkout of purchase of goods and services. But many other needs are to be covered as well, and remittances are one of them. Beyond the traditional conditions where the digital wallet uses to serve, there are some social and cultural functions in which it will get involved: rewards for artists, dowry, collection during the mass and any religious ceremony, assistance during grief, etc.

Rewards for Artists

It is quite common that any ceremony, baptism, initiation rites, bridal, wedding, or grief and funeral, turns to be an opportunity for performances of bands, artists, orchestras. Apart from the cachet the artist got for performing, they essentially receive rewards and gratuities during their show. The principle is the more people come and give money, the better. Giving many times a small amount of money, instead of donating a big amount at a time makes much more impact.

Dowry

The dowry of the bride is key element during the African bridal ceremony. It has to comply with numerous characteristics, one of them being the quality of banknotes; they have to be quite new. Whatever the amount being donated, the dowry is giving in bank notes. The digital wallet has to incorporate the function of making the dowry the same way as the rewards for artists, because the most important thing in those cases is the number of brand-new banknotes (big notes) that are displayed to the receiver.

Collection During the Mass, During any Religious Ceremony

Christianity has spread in several remote areas and numerous churches are active. Collection during the mass and other ceremonies holds many significations for all the faithful of the churches and thus is very important.

Assistance During Grief

Money plays an important role in terms of assistance to someone during grief. Even though the assistance is also common for happy events like baptism, in several places, it has reached a very specific extend when it comes to funerals. This is probably due to the fact that people have usually enough time to get prepared to happy events, whereas deaths often arrive unexpectedly. The social organization and the management of death practically occupy a central place in traditions, thus the importance of financial assistance during mourning. Funerals in such places are events where people invest lot of money, but also a lot of energy and a lot of time.

It is not expected that the digital wallet of PGS performs the same for all the social and cultural events evoked above. While some of them perfectly suit the secrecy of transaction, others on the other hand are really rooted in the exposure and hype made around them. As people go around in all those places with their devices, the digital wallet embedded within the PGS can offer its services even though the core concept of taking a selfie for the PGS may not apply in some of the cases.

The digital wallet of PGS will mainly enter the scene when the transaction is coming to the settlement, when the money is supposed to move from one actor to the other. In terms of performance, this operation implies some data entry from the buyer. Voice recognition to enter the amount and/or image analysis from the original selfie can ease the process. The same can apply for the selection of the recipient of the money. Operating systems offer variety of such tools, and many have been ported to mobile [29–31]. Improvements in PGS will benefit from those tools that are available.

5.2 Functional Requirements

As PGS is mainly intended to unbanked customers, the digital wallet that it will embed cannot rely on any form of credit or debit card. A mechanism to replenish users' accounts is then compulsory. From the many mechanisms to top up digital wallet account that can be implemented, PGS will not research in integrating credit or debit cards. However, street corner shops or point of sales are a must, as well as peer to peer money transfers. In [32], we have stressed the role and importance of a specific intermediary in PGS: it is the broker. Being it point-of-service, "village chief", street corner shops, point of sales or broker, this actor operates as a trusted third party whose main mission is to discourage users' malicious behaviour in the long term. It can then perform and adequately record replenishment actions of the digital wallet. The same actor is then one of the most important actors in the chain as we will describe it below in the next sections.

Basic operations on the digital wallet of PGS will include balance on account, payment of purchase, transfer, top up, and withdraw.

5.3 Performance Requirements

The main constraint in all cases is that PGS and its digital wallet should be operating for users who can be not computer savvy, even not-literate at all; it is then compulsory to minimize at the extreme any need of text typing. This brings the importance of ease of use and simplicity in a sense that the entire system is designed for people who are not able to juggle with complicated keyboards. Ease of use and simplicity are of paramount importance for PGS.

Another aspect in terms of performance is that all status information must be displayed at the device immediately at any change so that users are alerted about the final status of their account after the operation has been concluded. It is of paramount importance that that information will arrive in less than ten seconds. This performance requirement is of great importance in an environment where there is no network coverage to perform any online transaction with any central authority.

5.4   Operational Constraints and Security Issues

One of the constraints imposed to a digital wallet for PGS is that it must comply with two of the mains constraints of today's financial world: *Anti-Money Laundering* and *Know Your Customer*. It may not seem accurate to impose those constraints in areas where the expected amount of transactions are known to be very low but we have opted to fully integrate them from the beginning in order to be able to deploy the system with very few roadblocks in the future. These constraints impose then the PGS network to rely on a fully-authenticated network. The system must then incorporate enhanced security.

Beyond the challenge of authentication, the digital wallet that PGS will embed will also have to pay attention to the issue of double spending. *Stricto sensu*, double spending is the case to use the same quantity of money in two different purchases. In the digital wallet of PGS, that scenario has very probability to happen since all spending are requested to immediately reflect on the balance. And the accuracy of the balance is then more valuable. Nevertheless, even if the scenario of insufficient credit note can be programmatically controlled, the case of double spending needs specific solution. When analyzing innovations in payments systems, authors in [33] have presented the security issues as well as some solutions. This issue is of high importance in the case of PGS as the system will operate mainly out of the control of banks. Because the target customers are located in areas with scarcity of modern infrastructures and services like bank or mobile coverage, PGS is built without relying on any bank account or credit card. This implies that appropriate solution must be in place to prevent customer to spend more than they have in their balance. The solution is presented below in Sect. 5.7.

5.5   PGS Network

As described above, in the traditional way, a digital wallet is designed by merchant offering e-services to its customers. PGS is connected to a central authority, a bank where some specific actors plays their respective roles. In our case, the main actors are as follow:

- user/consumer: the one who owns the device and who uses it for transactions as payer or payee;
- street corner shop: this is the first point of replenishment of the digital wallet, the place where money is moved from cash unto the digital wallet.

The system might be able to operate fully working only with those two basic actors, but it is foreseen that banks and telco operators will join when they will appreciate the extend of the PGS and regulators[9] will more than probably also enter in the game. The complete system will then resemble to the illustration in Fig. 1 - Illustration of the actors of PGS.

---

[9] Regulator and supervisor of financial institutions, law enforcement, national security, etc.

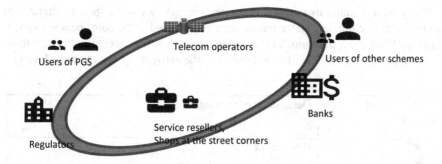

Fig. 1. Illustration of the actors of PGS

This illustration shows a network of participants transferring money among themselves, some of them being restricted to the level of observers: they are not active participants actually transferring money. The users of other schemes have been included in the network as they may also willing to use their current scheme as payers or payees. The appropriate interface must be added in the future for them to be fully integrated, even if this implies solutions, to be analyzed separately, for interoperability. The properties of that network are:

- actors are numerous, but also clearly known and identified when boarding;
- actors are very demanding on security, and they only trust information their own device displays to them;
- actors have diverse read and write needs, regulators can only read, banks may only read, payers and payees will read and write to the specific transaction they are involved in;
- "always online" is not an option, while whenever internet connection is available it must be used;
- status storing is a must, the network will have the responsibility to provide accurate balance of any wallet;
- scalability is of high importance, because most transactions are performed offline, whenever network coverage is available, fast replications will take place;
- throughput should be pushed to "high";
- network latency should be pushed to "fast", ten seconds is a maximum of delay between the order to pay and the confirmation message displayed on the payee's device.
- Linking the actors together is achievable by the mean of:
- common [distributed] ledger with privacy service to determine who can see what;
- consensus, who validate or approve transactions;
- provenance, audit trail or complete record of who own what asset throughout its life cycle;
- immutability, one block linked with the next block, impossible to tamper.

Every actor is doing its business (or is performing) by using a specific interface to manage its transactions and all the transactions are recorded by the core operating system that is the blockchain platform. The complete network is represented in Fig. 2 - Illustration of the full network. In that configuration, the network operates in three layers:

Symbols of the rings (layers)	Description of the rings
O	Business network
⬭	User interface [java-based module or android based module] to manage transactions handled either over message broker
⬭	Core operating system: platform for decentralized applications where smart contracts get executed to process transaction messages

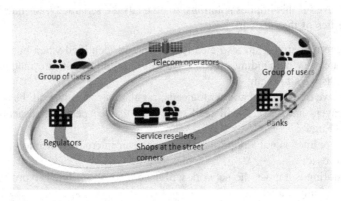

Fig. 2. Illustration of the full network

5.6   PGS Blockchain

The properties beforehand enumerated have paved the way for the blockchain-based digital wallet PGS will embed. Some of those properties are: number of actors, importance of trust-less network where permissions to read and write the data are distributed among all the users connected to the network and no user is given any special privileges, high need for security, storage of state, immutability of records. To be sure, we have also confronted this option with the flow chart designed by [21] to determine whether a blockchain is the appropriate technical solution. As shown in Fig. 3 - Flow chart to determine whether a blockchain is the appropriate technical solution, that framework confirms our option. As indicated by the blue arrows, the process led to the selection of **private permissioned blockchain**:

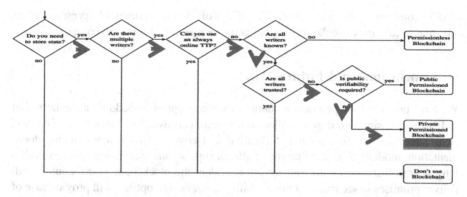

Fig. 3. Flow chart to determine whether a blockchain is the appropriate technical solution

- Do you need to store state? → Yes
- Are there multiple writers? → Yes
- Can you use an always online trusted third party (TTP)? → No
- Are all writers known? → Yes
- Are all writers trusted? → No
- Is public verifiability required? → No

5.7 Solutions to Specific Security Issues

The option of basing the system architecture on blockchain offers also a solution to the specific security issue of preventing double spending. As the system will then be decentralized, copies of the ledger are shared among participants, with appropriate consensus model in order to validate transactions. The next question is then about the implementation of the consensus.

It is obvious that we do not opt for the Proof of Work as pioneered by the Bitcoin blockchain: it requires a massive expenditure of energy. Alternatives include Tendermint[10]. Tendermint consists of two chief technical components: a blockchain consensus engine and a generic application interface. The consensus engine, called Tendermint Core, ensures that the same transactions are recorded on every machine in the same order. The application interface, called the Application BlockChain Interface (ABCI), enables the transactions to be processed in any programming language. For this issue of consensus, we are also considering the approach that Microsoft has taken in developing the Coco Framework[11]. The approach consists in implementing a trusted network of physical nodes without requiring the actors that control those nodes to trust one another. In that configuration, it is then possible to control what code is run and guarantee the correctness of its output — thereby simplifying consensus and reducing duplicative validation. The network nodes operate distributed key value store with

---

[10] https://tendermint.com/.

[11] https://azure.microsoft.com/en-us/blog/announcing-microsoft-s-coco-framework-for-enterprise-blockchain-networks/.

RAFT consensus [6]. Moreover, the Microsoft Coco Framework presents other advantages in term of scalability, confidentiality and consortium governance.

6 Conclusions and Future Work

We have presented the practical potential of the concept of embedding a digital wallet to PGS and basing that digital wallet on a private permissioned blockchain. The next steps start with the functional specification and cover software requirements documentation, modelling, first prototype, platform support and integration. There is still a long way to that integration, and we are confident the blockchain based solution will deliver promises in security and immutability; other design options will provide ease of use and simplicity.

Acknowledgement. This work has been partly funded by the Bill & Melinda Gates Foundations under the grant n. OPP1139403.

References

1. Kochi, E.: How The Future of Mobile Lies in the Developing World. TechCrunch (2012). https://techcrunch.com/2012/05/27/mobile-developing-world/
2. Duncombe, R., Boateng, R.: Mobile phones and financial services in developing countries: a review of concepts, methods, issues, evidence and future research directions. Third World Q. **30**(7), 1237–1258 (2009). https://doi.org/10.1080/01436590903134882
3. Cimato, S., Damiani, E., Frati, F., Hounsou, J.T., Tandjiékpon, J.: Paying with a selfie: a hybrid micro-payment framework based on visual cryptography. In: Glitho, R., Zennaro, M., Belqasmi, F., Agueh, M. (eds.) AFRICOMM 2015. LNICST, vol. 171, pp. 136–141. Springer, Cham (2016). https://doi.org/10.1007/978-3-319-43696-8_15
4. Kizza, J.M.: Mobile money technology and the fast disappearing African digital divide. Afr. J. Sci. Technol. Innov. Dev. **5**(5), 373–378 (2013). https://doi.org/10.1080/20421338.2013.829298
5. Nakamoto, S.: Bitcoin: a peer-to-peer electronic cash system (2008). https://bitcoin.org/bitcoin.pdf
6. Baliga, A.: Understanding blockchain consensus models. Technical report, Persistent Systems Ltd. (2017). https://www.persistent.com/wp-content/uploads/2018/02/wp-understanding-blockchain-consensus-models.pdf
7. Castro, M., Liskov, B.: Practical Byzantine fault tolerance and proactive recovery. ACM Trans. Comput. Syst. TOCS **20**(4), 398–461 (2002). https://doi.org/10.1145/571637.571640
8. Gramoli, V.: From blockchain consensus back to Byzantine consensus. Future Gener. Comput. Syst. (2017). https://doi.org/10.1016/j.future.2017.09.023
9. King, C.: Ensuring secure enterprise blockchain networks: a look at IBM blockchain and LinuxONE. Pund-IT whitepaper (2017). https://www-01.ibm.com/common/ssi/cgi-bin/ssialias?htmlfid=ZSW03359USEN
10. Zheng, Z., Xie, S., Dai, H., Chen, X., Wang, H.: An overview of blockchain technology: architecture, consensus, and future trends. In: Proceedings of 2017 IEEE International Congress on Big Data (BigData Congress), pp. 557–564. (2017). https://doi.org/10.1109/bigdatacongress.2017.85

11. Zheng, Z., Xie, S., Dai, H.-N., Chen, X., Wang, H.: Blockchain challenges and opportunities: a survey. Int. J. Web Grid Serv. **14**(4), 352–375 (2017). https://www. henrylab.net/pubs/ijwgs_blockchain_survey.pdf
12. Poon, J., Buterin, V.: Plasma: scalable autonomous smart contracts. White Paper (2017). https://plasma.io/plasma.pdf
13. Debus, J.: Consensus methods in blockchain systems. Frankfurt School Blockchain Center (2017). https://medium.com/@fsblockchain/consensus-methods-in-blockchain-systems-d2eae18b99b7
14. Ongaro, D., Ousterhout, J.K.: In search of an understandable consensus algorithm. In: Proceedings of the 2014 USENIX Conference, pp. 305–320 (2014). https://web.stanford. edu/~ouster/cgi-bin/papers/raft-atc14
15. Tapscott, D., Tapscott, A.: Realizing the potential of blockchain: a multistakeholder approach to the stewardship of blockchain and cryptocurrencies. World Economic Forum White Paper (2017). https://www.weforum.org/whitepapers/realizing-the-potential-of-blockchain
16. Crosby, M., Pattanayak, P., Verma, S., Kalyanaraman, V.: Blockchain technology: beyond bitcoin. Appl. Innov. Rev. **2**, 6–10 (2016). https://j2-capital.com/wp-content/uploads/2017/11/AIR-2016-Blockchain.pdf
17. Beck, R., Czepluch, J.S., Lollike, N., Malone, S.: Blockchain-the gateway to trust-free cryptographic transactions. In: Proceedings of European Conference in Information Systems ECIS 2016, Research Paper 153 (2016). https://aisel.aisnet.org/ecis2016_rp/153
18. Gupta, M.: Blockchain For Dummies, IBM Limited Edition. Wiley, Hoboken (2017)
19. Xu, X., et al.: A taxonomy of blockchain-based systems for architecture design. In: Proceedings of 2017 IEEE International Conference on Software Architecture, pp. 243–252 (2017). https://doi.org/10.1109/icsa.2017.33
20. Ellervee, A., Matulevicius, R., Mayer, N.: A comprehensive reference model for blockchain-based distributed ledger technology. In: Proceedings of 2017 in ER Forum/Demos (2017). http://ceur-ws.org/Vol-1979/paper-09.pdf
21. Wüst, K., Gervais, A.: Do you need a Blockchain? IACR Cryptology ePrint Archive (2017). https://eprint.iacr.org/2017/375.pdf
22. Damiani, E., et al.: Porting the pay with a (group) selfie (PGS) payment system to crypto currency. In: Belqasmi, F., Harroud, H., Agueh, M., Dssouli, R., Kamoun, F. (eds.) AFRICATEK 2017. LNICST, vol. 206, pp. 159–168. Springer, Cham (2018). https://doi.org/10.1007/978-3-319-67837-5_15
23. Keramati, A., Taeb, R., Larijani, A.M., Mojir, N.: A combinative model of behavioural and technical factors affecting 'Mobile'-payment services adoption: an empirical study. Serv. Ind. J. **32**(9), 1489–1504 (2012). https://doi.org/10.1080/02642069.2011.552716
24. Koenig-Lewis, N., Marquet, M., Palmer, A., Zhao, A.L.: Enjoyment and social influence: predicting mobile payment adoption. Serv. Ind. J. **35**(10), 537–554 (2015). https://doi.org/10.1080/02642069.2015.1043278
25. Srivastava, L.: Mobile phones and the evolution of social behaviour. Behav. Inf. Technol. **24**(2), 111–129 (2005). https://doi.org/10.1080/01449290512331321910
26. Wang, Y., Hahn, C., Sutrave, K.: Mobile payment security, threats, and challenges. In: Proceedings of 2016 Second International Conference on Mobile and Secure Services, pp. 1–5 (2016). https://doi.org/10.1109/mobisecserv.2016.7440226
27. O'Driscoll, K.: The agile data modelling and design thinking approach to information system requirements analysis. J. Decis. Syst. **25**, 632–638 (2016). https://doi.org/10.1080/12460125.2016.1189643
28. Brace, W., Cheutet, V.: A framework to support requirements analysis in engineering design. J. Eng. Des. **23**(12), 876–904 (2012). https://doi.org/10.1080/09544828.2011.636735

29. Mittal, P., Singh, N.: Speech based command and control system for mobile phones: issues and challenges. In: Proceedings of 2016 Second International Conference on Computational Intelligence and Communication Technology, pp. 729–732 (2016). https://doi.org/10.1109/cict.2016.150

30. Kam, A.C.S., Sung, J.K.K., Lee, T., Wong, T.K.C., van Hasselt, A.: Improving mobile phone speech recognition by personalized amplification: application in people with normal hearing and mild-to-moderate hearing loss. Ear Hear. **38**(2), e85–e92 (2017). https://doi.org/10.1097/aud.0000000000000371

31. Fouzan, A.: Voice Recognition Anatomy, Processing, Uses and Application in C#. SSRN (2017). https://doi.org/10.2139/ssrn.2968335

32. Damiani, E., et al.: Pay-with-a-Selfie, a human-centred digital payment system. arXiv Prepr arXiv:1706.07187 (2017). https://arxiv.org/abs/1706.07187

33. Ali, R., Barrdear, J., Clews, R., Southgate, J.: Innovations in payment technologies and the emergence of digital currencies. Bank Engl. Q. Bull. **54**(3), 262–275 (2014). https://EconPapers.repec.org/RePEc:boe:qbullt:0147

Practical Method for Evaluating the Performance of a Biometric Algorithm

Tahirou Djara[1,2]($\boxtimes$), Abdou-Aziz Sobabe[1,2],
Macaire Bienvenu Agbomahena[1,2], and Antoine Vianou[1,2]

[1] Laboratoire d'Electrotechnique de Télécommunication et d'Informatique
Appliquée (LETIA/EPAC), Université d'Abomey-Calavi (UAC),
Cotonou, Benin
csm.djara@gmail.com
[2] Institut d'Innovation Technologique (IITECH), Abomey-Calavi, Benin

Abstract. This paper presents a modality-independent method of evaluating the performance of an algorithm in biometrics. The operation mode is about developing a JAVA application that offers the user a graphical representation of the evaluation results. This application is interacting with a MySQL database containing the extracted signatures as well as the matching values of the modalities present in the evaluated biometric system. The evaluation system is used to generate the Genuine Matching and Impostor Matching score distribution curves, the False Match Rate and False Non Match Rate curves and the ROC curve. 1000 lines of code were used to develop the application. The method proposed is original and practical. Thus, an application of this method has been made in the case of a contactless fingerprint modality. We plan to improve the developed method by adding the representation of 4 main operating points (EER, WER, Fixed FMR, Fixed FNMR).

Keywords: Biometrics · Performance evaluation · Biometric algorithm
Genuine Matching (GM) · Impostor Matching (IM) · False Match Rate (FMR)
False Non Match Rate (FNMR) · Receiver Operating Characteristic (ROC)
Modality-independent

1 Introduction

Biometrics is a global technique aimed at establishing the identity of a person by measuring a morphological (such as face), biological (such as DNA, genetic inheritance) and/or behavioral (such as signature) characteristics. The usual techniques of access control are based on what we know (password, PIN code, etc.) and what we have (identity card, badge, etc.) [1]. But these methods pose problems of reliability such as falsification of document, forgetting one's code and decryption of password. Contrary to "what we know" or "what we have", biometrics is based on "what we are" or "how we behave" and thus avoids duplication, theft, forgetfulness or loss. A biometric system can operate either in authentication mode or in identification mode. Authentication is to answer the question: are you the one you claim to be? On the other hand, identifying comes down to answering the question: who are you? The

© ICST Institute for Computer Sciences, Social Informatics and Telecommunications Engineering 2019
Published by Springer Nature Switzerland AG 2019. All Rights Reserved
R. Zitouni and M. Agueh (Eds.): AFRICATEK 2018, LNICST 260, pp. 125–132, 2019.
https://doi.org/10.1007/978-3-030-05198-3_11

characteristics used must meet 5 modalities. They must be universal, unique, permanent, easy to collect and acceptable [2].

According to [3], two very basic questions often arise when dealing with biometric systems or components: how can the accuracy of a biometric system (or its components) be measured and how to compare different systems with each other? The answer to these two questions lies in the determination of a sixth modality, that of performance. This performance factor has a double advantage for the designer but also for the user of the system. For the designer of a biometric system, he has the obligation to produce information to assess the performance of his product in comparison with existing ones. On the user's side, the performance of a biometric system makes it easy for him to make a decision as to the choice to be made in the large array of existing biometrics. Contrary to what one could imagine, the evaluation of the performance of a biometric system is based on a very varied range of parameters with possibilities of combinations. Some parameters are quantitative (for example the processing time) while others are qualitative (for example the satisfaction of the user). The analysis of the performance of a biometric system takes into account the context of implementation. According to a study presented in [2], DNA and Iris show the best performances in terms of treatment algorithms (EER) but at the same time they are the most hated by users.

In this paper, we show how to obtain the curve of the GM (Genuine Matching) and IM (Impostor Matching) distributions, the False Match Rate (FMR) curve, the False Non-Match Rate (FNMR) curve and the Receiver Operating Characteristics (ROC) curve to evaluate the performance of any biometric identification algorithm. For the display of the characteristic curves, we used a database where the various extracted signatures are saved as well as the values of pairings. The evaluation method developed was tested on a practical example based on contactless fingerprint. In Sect. 2, we present the previous work in biometrics evaluation. The operating principle of the developed method is presented in Sect. 3 while Sect. 4 presents an application of the method to a biometric system using a contactless fingerprint. Section 5 concludes the paper.

2   Related Work

Biometric systems are designed and developed in laboratories with the purpose of being used in everyday life. But before deployment in a real situation, it is necessary to evaluate them in order to know their performances and their limits. Depending on the application, this evaluation can consider several parameters such as: ease of use for users, security, cost, data protection problems, reliability of the system or sensors, maintenance requirements, human control requirements in operational mode and of course recognition error rates [4].

Taking into account the opinion of the user, [5] presented an overview of existing evaluation aspects of biometric systems based on data quality, usability and security. Regarding the biometric systems tested, the robustness of a system against attacks, the computation time required during the verification phase and its ease of use were identified as important factors influencing user's opinion. Several studies have shown that the quality of biometric samples has a significant impact on the accuracy of a matcher. On the security aspects, [6] present 8 vulnerable points of attacks in a bio-metric system.

[2] have made a survey on international competitions and platforms that aims to evaluate the performance of biometric systems. All that works have been synthesized in the Table 1.

Table 1. International biometrics competitions and platforms

Category of competition	Name of competition	Year	Performance metrics used
Mono-modal competitions	FVC [7]	2000, 2002, 2004 and 2006	GMS and IMS, average and maximum template size, average enrolment and verification time, FTE and ROC curves
	FpVTE [8]	2003	ROC, DET, FAR and FRR
	SVC [9]	2004	EER
	CBT2006 [10]	2006	FNMR, FMR, Transactional-FNMR, Transactional-FMR, FTA, Transactional-FTA, and FTE
	ITIRT2005 [11]	2005	FNMR, FMR, T-FNMR, T-FMR, FTA, T-FTA, and FTE
Multi-modal competitions	BMEC	2007	ROC curves and their corresponding EERs
Platforms	BioSecure	2007	ROC curves and their corresponding EERs
	GREYC-Keystroke [12]	2009	GMS and IMS, ROC curves and the FTA rate
	FVC-OnGoing [13]	2009	FTE and FTA, FNMR for a fixed FMR and vice-versa, average enrolment and verification time, maximum template size, GMS and IMS, ROC curves and their corresponding EERs

Earlier studies devoted to estimating the performance of biometric systems, have specified three types of rating [14]. These are: technology evaluation, scenario evaluation and operational evaluation. The technology evaluation is responsible for testing only the performance of the algorithmic parts of the system (feature extraction, comparison and decision) using a pre-acquired database. The scenario evaluation covers a broader field of action that also includes the sensors, the environment and the specific population of the tested application. The operational evaluation for its part takes into account a global biometric system under real conditions of use.

We focused in this work on the technological evaluation, which will test only the algorithmic part of the system using a database that we built. The objective is to provide the research community with a detailed protocol that presents the code of the evaluation program in a transparent manner, regardless of the number and types of modalities used.

3 Presentation of the Operating Principle of the Developed Method

To implement our method of evaluating the performance of algorithms in biometrics, we first developed a graphical interface under JAVA using the NetBeans IDE 8.2 for the automatic generation of each of these curves (GM, IM, FMR, FNMR and ROC). The JAVA code structure and the excerpt of the graphical interface developed are available in the appendix document at https://refod.net/iitech/paper/Appendix.pdf. The metadata needed to generate the curves consists of the signatures of the biometric modality selected for the identification. These signatures and the different matching values will be stored in a MySQL database. A connection is established between the JAVA program and the created database.

3.1 Principle of Design of Different Charts

This paragraph provides the technical details of the design of the three evaluation graphs presented. For any given modality (fingerprint, hand geometry, face, iris, gait, DNA, etc.), the protocol used for the matching test is as follows:

Let S_{ij} be the jth signature extracted from the ith modality M_{ij} ($1 \leq i \leq n$; $1 \leq j \leq m$). The S_{ij} signature extracted from M_{ij} is stored in a MySQL database.

For signature matching, we do the following operations:

1. Genuine Matching (GM) study: each S_{ij} signature is compared with the set of S_{ik} signatures ($k \neq j$) from the same i, which provides the corresponding match value gms_{ijk} (Genuine Matching Score) saved in a table of the database.
2. Impostor Matching (IM) study: the first S_{kl} copy of each modality is compared with each copy of the remaining modalities S_{ij} ($i > k$) and provides the corresponding matching value ims_{ik} (Impostor Matching Score) saved in another table of the database.

The number of matches (NGRA: Number of Genuine Recognition Attempts and NIRA: Number of Impostor Recognition Attempts) is defined in each case by the following formula:

$$\text{Case 1}: \text{NGRA} = \left\|\{gms_{ijk}, i \in [1...n], 1 \leq j \neq k \leq m\}\right\| = n \times m \times (m-1) \tag{1}$$

$$\text{Case 2}: \text{NIRA} = \left\|\{ims_{ik}, i \in [1...n], 1 \leq j \neq k \leq m\}\right\|$$
$$= m\left[(n-1)+(n-2)+\cdots+1\right] \tag{2}$$

The Genuine Matching-Impostor Matching Chart. The graphical representation of GM and IM distributions shows how the algorithm differentiates the two classes. For each distribution (GM and IM), it is necessary to create a text file (txt format) which saves gradually after comparisons the value of pairing. Once these files are created, it is a question of counting the repetition of each value of pairing and thus the probability of appearance. The count result at each distribution is also stored in a text file. At the graph level, the match values will be represented on the x-axis while the number of repetitions (count) will be on the y-axis. The code used for this operation is available in the appendix document.

The FMR-FNMR Chart. The GM and IM distributions are used to calculate the FMR (t) and the FNMR (t) as functions of the t threshold that characterizes decision-making in the verification phase.

FMR(t) and FNMR(t) are defined as:

$$FMR\ (t) = \frac{card\{ims_{ik}/ims_{ik} \geq t\}}{NIRA} \tag{3}$$

$$FNMR\ (t) = \frac{card\{gms_{ik}/gms_{ijk} < t\}}{NGRA} \tag{4}$$

card denotes the cardinal of the set considered, FMR (t) corresponds to the percentage of users recognized by error ($ims_{ik} \geq t$) and FNMR (t) corresponds to the percentage of users rejected by error ($gms_{ijk} < t$).

The code used to generate the FMR-FNMR chart is available in the appendix document.

The ROC Chart. The ROC curve is the one that gives the FNMR as a function of the FMR. This curve is obtained by using the code available in the appendix document.

The Complementary Code. The complementary code consists of the two remaining code portions for the database connection and the JAVA main project. These codes are available in the appendix document.

3.2   Database Creation Principle

The database to be created will have as many tables as needed. Thus, for each signature sub-modality (for example the sub-signatures of bifurcations on the one hand and endings on the other hand for a fingerprint signature), a table is created for storing the metadata of the signature. This means that there will be as many tables as signature sub-modalities. In addition, the results of each pairing operation are also stored in tables. There will therefore be two tables for the genuine and impostor classes whose codes are available in the appendix document.

4   Application of the Method to a Biometric System Using a Contactless Fingerprint

4.1   Fingerprint Acquisition System

This is an application called Contactless Biometric Fingerprint Software (CBFS) developed by [15]. The launch of the CBFS automatically triggers the activation of the webcam connected to the computer and opens an intuitive graphical interface (see Fig. 3 in the appendix document) with 4 zones for interaction between the user and the application. The first area at the top left of the interface gives an instant snapshot of the image in the webcam field. This zone 1 is used to adjust the finger which one wants to recover the image of the fingerprint. The bottom left (zone 2) contains the command buttons used to capture the image of the fingerprint once the adjustments are judged satisfactory. As for the upper right (zone 3), it shows the user the image that has just been taken. Finally, the last part (zone 4) is at the lower right position of the interface. It consists of a message display space for the purpose of assisting the user throughout the process of acquisition of fingerprints.

For experimentation, we created a database of 420 fingerprints comprising 28 sets of different fingers (each finger representing an individual), each comprising 15 different acquisitions.

4.2   Protocol Used for the Matching Test

Note S_{ij} the jth signature extracted from the ith fingerprint E_{ij} ($1 \leq i \leq n$; $1 \leq j$ m). The signature S_{ij} extracted from E_{ij} is stored in a MySQL database called *"fingerprint"*. For each fingerprint, the extracted signature is represented as:

$$\begin{bmatrix} x_1 & y_1 & \theta_{11} & \theta_{21} & \theta_{31} & z_0 & z_1 & \cdots & z_n \\ x_2 & y_2 & \theta_{12} & \theta_{22} & \theta_{32} & z_0 & z_1 & \cdots & z_n \\ x_M & y_M & \theta_{1M} & \theta_{2M} & \theta_{3M} & z_0 & z_1 & \cdots & z_n \end{bmatrix} \quad (5)$$

for bifurcation points (first sub-modality for the fingerprint) and

$$\begin{bmatrix} x_1 & y_1 & \theta_1 & z_0 & z_1 & \cdots & z_n \\ x_2 & y_2 & \theta_2 & z_0 & z_1 & \cdots & z_n \\ \cdots & \cdots & \cdots & \cdots & \cdots & \cdots & \cdots \\ x_N & y_N & \theta_N & z_0 & z_1 & \cdots & z_n \end{bmatrix} \quad (6)$$

for endpoints (second sub-modality for fingerprint).

(xi, yi) denotes the position of the minutiae. θ_{ij} denote the relative angles between the branches of bifurcations and θ_i the termination angle as defined in [15]. z_i represent the characteristics extracted at the level of each minutia. Expression (5) represents a table called *"bifurcations"* in the fingerprint base while expression (6) represents a table called *"terminations"* in the same base. Figures 4 and 5 in the appendix document respectively show an illustration of each table.

For the test, we perform the following operations:

1. Genuine Matching (GM) study: each S_{ij} signature is compared with the set of S_{ik} signatures ($k \neq j$)) from the same finger i, which provides the corresponding match value gms_{ijk} (Genuine Matching Score) recorded in the "intraclasse" table of the "fingerprint" database. Figure 6 in the appendix document gives an illustration of this table.

2. Impostor Matching (IM) study: the first copy S_{k1} of each fingerprint is compared with each copy of the remaining fingerprints $S_{ij}(i > k)$ and provides the corresponding matching value ims_{ik} (Impostor Matching Score) recorded in the "interclasse" table of the "fingerprint" database. Figure 7 in the appendix document gives an illustration of this table.

According to Eqs. (1) and (2), NGRA = 5880 and NIRA = 5670 in our case.

Curves Construction. Let *msintra.txt* and *msinter.txt* be the files of the GM and IM matching values, then *countIntra.txt* and *countInter.txt* the corresponding count files. The application allows us to have the GM and IM distributions curve, the FMR and FNMR curve and the ROC curve (respectively Figs. 8, 9 and 10 in the appendix document).

5 Conclusion and Perspectives

In this article, we presented a practical modality-independent method for evaluating the performance of an algorithm in biometrics. This method was tested using a contactless fingerprint system. Our experimental protocol has two main phases: the curves construction and the database creation. At the curves construction phase (GM-IM, FMR-FNMR and ROC), the developed JAVA code was presented. At the database creation phase, we explained the test operations for attempted authenticity and imposture from extracted signatures. In each case, these signatures as well as their match values are stored in tables of a MySQL database. The originality of the approach we propose lies in the detailed presentation of the methodology and the JAVA and SQL codes that have been developed.

Our first perspective will be to represent the major operating points of our application case on a curve of error rates according to the decision threshold as well as on a ROC curve [4]. The 4 operating points that will be the subject of our future work are: EER, WER, Fixed FMR and Fixed FNMR.

We also plan to develop two complementary modules to measure the FTA (Failure To Acquire Rate) and FTE (Failure To Enroll Rate) characteristics [10]. In addition, we will adapt the developed method to a multimodal biometric system.

References

1. AlMahafzah, H., AlRwashdeh, M.Z.: A survey of multibiometric systems. Int. J. Comput. Appl. **43**(15), 36–43 (2012)
2. El-Abed, M., Charrier, C.: Evaluation of biometric systems, chapter 7. In: New Trends and Developments in Biometrics, pp. 149–169 (2012). https://doi.org/10.5772/52084. hal-00990617
3. Precise Biometrics: White-Paper, Understanding biometric performance evaluation. AB – SPA 133 1000 4160/wpbpe RA (2014)

4. Allano, L.: La Biométrie multimodale: stratégies de fusion de scores et mesures de dépendance appliquées aux bases de personnes virtuelles. Thèse de doctorat, Institut National des Télécommunications dans le cadre de l'école doctorale SITEVRY en co-accréditation avec l'Université d'Evry-Val d'Essonne (2009)
5. El-Abed, M., Giot, R., Hemery, B., Rosenberger C.: Evaluation of biometric systems: a study of users' acceptance and satisfaction. Inderscience Int. J. Biom. (IJBM), 1–27 (2012). https://doi.org/10.1504/ijbm.2012.047644. hal-00984024
6. Marasco, E., Ross, A.: A survey on anti-spoofing schemes for fingerprint recognition systems. ACM Comput. Surv. **47**(2), 1–36 (2014). Article A
7. Maltoni, D., Maio, D., Jain, A.K., Prabhakar, S.: Handbook of Fingerprint Recognition, 2nd edn. Springer Science+Business Media, New York (2003). © Springer-Verlag London Limited 2009
8. FpVTE: Fingerprint vendor technology evaluation 2003 (NISTIR 7123) (2003). http://fpvte. nist.gov/. Accessed 13 Jan 2018
9. Zhang, D., Jain, A.K. (eds.): ICBA 2004. LNCS, vol. 3072. Springer, Heidelberg (2004). https://doi.org/10.1007/b98225
10. IBG: International biometric group, comparative biometric testing. Round 6 Public Report (2006)
11. IBG: International biometric group, independent testing of iris recognition technology. Final report (2005)
12. Giot, R., El Abed, M., Rosenberger, C.: GREYC keystroke: a benchmark for keystroke dynamics biometric systems. In: IEEE Third International Conference on Biometrics: Theory, Applications and Systems (BTAS), pp. 1–6 (2009)
13. Dorizzi, B., et al.: Fingerprint and on-line signature verification competitions at ICB 2009. In: Tistarelli, M., Nixon, M.S. (eds.) ICB 2009. LNCS, vol. 5558, pp. 725–732. Springer, Heidelberg (2009). https://doi.org/10.1007/978-3-642-01793-3_74
14. Phillips, P.J., Martin, A., Wilson, C.L., Przybocki, M.: An introduction to evaluating biometric systems. Computer **33**(2), 56–63 (2000)
15. Djara, T., Assogba, M.K., Vianou, A.: A contactless fingerprint verification method using a minutiae matching technique. Int. J. Comput. Vis. Image Process. **6**(1), 12–27 (2016)

Software Defined Networking (SDN) for Universal Access

Adama Nantoume[✉], Benjamin Kone, Ahmed Dooguy Kora,
and Boudal Niang

Ecole Superieure Multinationale des Telecommunications,
Dakar BP10000, Senegal
{adama.nantoume, ahmed.kora, boudal.niang}@esmt.sn,
benjikone@yahoo.fr

Abstract. Ensuring Universal Access/Universal service to the populations of developing countries is up to now a big problem which can be explained by the fact that the telecommunication operators estimate certain areas unprofitable. The Universal access to the Technologies of Information and Communication being a non-discriminatory right for any citizen wherever he lives, different approaches are implemented to guarantee it. One of these approaches is to recourse on cheap equipment associated with innovating technologies. The aim of this article is to be able to study to what extent the Software Defined Networking could be a viable solution for the localities interested in Universal access. To reach this goal, we have been lead to study a typical Voice over IP traditional architecture and the architecture tooled with the Software Defined Networking technology.

When implemented the Software Defined Networking technology is supposed to guarantee a good quality of service. In our contribution we have set up a Voice over IP environment with Asterisk server as equipment of the network core, and affordable equipment such as the WIFI access points in the element entitled, ≪Collecting subscribers≫. The Quality of Service being our preoccupation, the comparison of all our results shows that the architectures with Software Defined Networking offer a better quality of services.

Keywords: OpenFlow · Quality of service (QoS)
Software Defined Networking (SDN) · Universal access/Universal service
Voice over IP (VoIP) · WIFI

1 Introduction

Universal access is a problem common to all the countries. The level of progression varies from one country to another. The poor profitability of certain areas arouses an a priori reluctance of operators who refuse to deploy their equipment in certain areas of the territory.

Being concerned only in gaining money, they actively look for ways to reduce their *capital expenditure* (CAPEX) and their *operational expenditure* (OPEX).

One of the most used approaches is the recourse on less costly equipment associated to a set of services matching the needs of the targeted localities.

© ICST Institute for Computer Sciences, Social Informatics and Telecommunications Engineering 2019
Published by Springer Nature Switzerland AG 2019. All Rights Reserved
R. Zitouni and M. Agueh (Eds.): AFRICATEK 2018, LNICST 260, pp. 133–144, 2019.
https://doi.org/10.1007/978-3-030-05198-3_12

The concern in this article is to be able to determine to what extent the Software Defined Networking (SDN) could be a viable solution for the areas interested in Universal access. To achieve this goal, a comparative study will be conducted between simple network architectures using SDN with the traditional architectures. The SDN architecture is supposed to guarantee an acceptable quality of service. Our contribution was partly about configuring different architectures with affordable equipment such as WIFI and a network core based on Asterisk. The quality of the service has been our preoccupation. We have chosen the most known cases of use which are the voice and the data to measure their Key performance Indicators (KPI) in a traditional environment, and in another one containing an SDN structure with OpenFlow. Both results will then be compared.

To do this work properly, we will proceed as follows:

- in the first part, we will give a general presentation of the SDN,
- in the second part, we will give a description of the OpenFlow protocol,
- in the third part, we will show our approaches
- in the fourth part, we will display our different results and will analyze them before concluding.

2   Generalities on the SDN

The SDN generality is a new paradigm in the network field. It is a technology in full growth. Due to its young age, it can take several meanings, according to the field. The most common meaning is the one given by Open Networking Foundation (ONF). ONF is a foundation which has much worked at the implementation of this technology. According to it, the SDN is defined as being an architecture in which the control plan and the data plan are uncoupled: the intelligence of network state is logically centralized, and the infrastructure abstracted from the applications [1].

The main idea of the SDN, as in the definition, consists in separating the function of transmission from the network, carried out by the control plan. Routers and switches are confined on the functions of packets switching. All the network services are implemented in only one controller common to several equipments. This separation allows to make the network much more flexible in its management, creates an ideal framework for the innovation as well as the progression of the network [2]. The SDN architecture presents three layers which are [3]:

- The **Infrastructure layer** is composed of physical and virtual peripherals of network. It is the lowest layer of the structure; it is composed of all the knots of the network, which communicate with the control layer through the OpenFlow Protocol,
- The **Control layer** centralizes the intelligence of the network. Composed of *Application Programming Interfaces* (APIs) in charge of ensuring the communication between the control layer and the upper and lower layers, it has a global view of the network. It registers the peripherals (users and network), the details of interconnection between them and administers a data base of the flows. These

pieces of information allow it to instruct the peripherals and implement rules (routing, sharing of responsibilities, etc.).

• The **Application layer** gathers the service networks, the orchestration platform and the business application. The application layer is in charge of the applications necessary to the customers and their requirements in terms of network, storing, calculation, safety and administration. In other words, it is the business layer. It is the layer that makes the two other layers function. At this level, the applications communicate with the controller through the APIs.

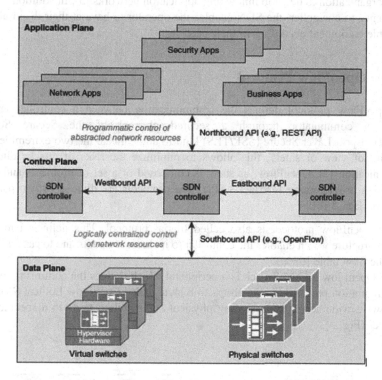

Fig. 1. SDN architecture [4]

2.1   The Interfaces

The south interface (southbound) provides the logical connection (signaling) necessary between the SDN controller and the commutators of the data plan. (see Fig. 1)

The north interface (northbound interface) provides the communication between the application level and the controller. Its aim is to define the needs of the application and to pass the commands to orchestrate the network with a good quality of service, appropriate safety and the required care.

2.2 The Abstractions

Scott Shenker, member of the board of the Open Networking Foundation and Open-Flow researcher, shows that the SDN can be defined by three fundamental abstractions [SHEN 1]: The forwarding, distribution and specification [4].

We note that one of the advantages of the decentralization of the controller is that the whole administration of the network is centralized and configurable. The modifications can dynamically be operated according to the needs. The SDN technology also allows flexibility to the network eliminates dependence on certain suppliers and allows a third organization to develop innovating application networks [5]. In addition to non-dependence to a supplier, the SDN enables the operator to have at their disposal very affordable equipment according to their need [6].

3 The OpenFlow Protocol

The OpenFlow protocol defines the communication between a controller and an OpenFlow commutator through a secured channel of the Secure Sockets Layer/Transport Layer Secure (SSL/TLS) kind to authenticate the two extremities. On the point of view of safety, this allows to minimize the risks of attacks during a communication [7]. OpenFlow, as such, is composed of a set of protocols and of an application programming interface (API). The protocols are divided in two parts, as shown on Fig. 2 [8].

- The OpenFlow protocol is also called filarial protocol. This defines a message infrastructure which enables the controller to include, to update and to cancel entries in the flow table [6],
- The OpenFlow logical Switch is a peripheral which defines the administration and configuration protocol via the abstraction layer called OpenFlow Logical Switch. It allows a wide access by assigning physical commutation ports to a specific controller (Fig. 3).

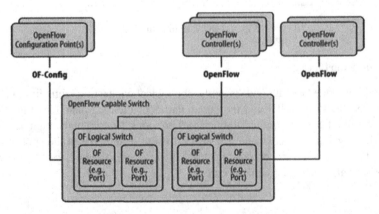

Fig. 2. Relationship between OF CONFIG and OpenFlow protocol [8]

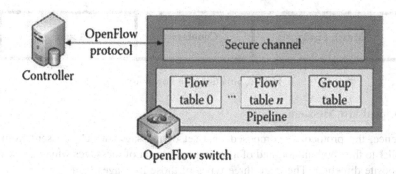

Fig. 3. OpenFlow general architecture

3.1   The OpenFlow Ports

With the OpenFlow protocol the ports are very important because it is through them that the packs get in and out. The connection of two OpenFlow switches is done with the ports. There are three types of ports in the OpenFlow protocol which are the physical ports, the logical ports and the reserved ports [10]. These ports can, at the same time be used as entry ports and exit ports for a pack.

- The physical ports for a pack are ports that can be seen on network equipment (e.g. Ethernet port),
- The logical ports are not linked to a physical port on the commutator. However the logical ports can be configured to correspond to a physical port on the commutator. When the packs are treated by the OpenFlow commutator, the physical and logical ports are treated the same way.

    The reserved ports are specific ports used to engage a specific action. This action is started by sending a pack to a reserved port. An OpenFlow commutator is conceived to take care of five types of reserved ports. There are three other types of optional reserved ports which can be in charge of the commutator.

3.2   Flow Table

An OpenFlow commutator is composed of one or more flow tables and of an Open-Flow group table. Each table is composed of a set of flow entries. A flow entry is composed of a set of match fields, counter and actions (or actions). A flow entry is composed of:

- **Match fields:** Correspondence fields which define the pattern of pack flows through the instantiation of the heading fields, from the Ethernet layer to the transport layer,
- **Counters:** counters on the packets,
- **Actions:** actions to apply on the packets which correspond to the flow entry (Fig. 4).

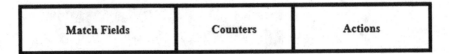

Match Fields	Counters	Actions

Fig. 4. Structure of a flow entry

3.3 OpenFlow Message

In essence, the protocol is composed of a set of messages which are sent from the controller to the commutator, and of a corresponding set of messages which are sent on the opposite direction. There are three types of those messages [10].

– Messages from the controller to the switch, messages sent from the switch to the controller to administer or inspect its state. It also administers the configuration of the switches, the configuration of the roles, the configuration of asynchronous messages and many others [10].
– The asynchronous messages are sent from the switch to the controller without the switch being solicited by the controller. For example, when the switch receives a new packet, it will send a packet-in message to the controller in order to ask what section must be applied on the packet.
– The symmetric messages are generated in both directions (either by the controller or the switch) without the switch being solicited by the controller. For example, Hello (used at the same time by the switch and the controller), Echo (used at the same time by the switch and the controller) and Error (used in the switch) are messages which are classified in the symmetric messages (Fig. 5).

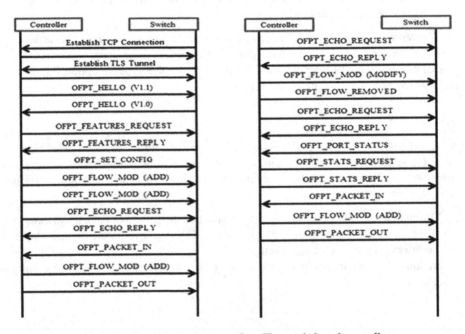

Fig. 5. Communication between OpenFlow switch and controller

4 SDN Implementation

We have realized SDN implementation in two steps in our approach.

4.1 First Step

The first one consisted in integrating the OpenFlow protocol on the different access points (the TP-link WR 1043nd). This integration has required the use of the Pantou method and OpenWrt.

In fact Pantou transforms an access point or a wireless router into compatible OpenFlow equipment [12]. Thus, fundamentally with Pantou, OpenFlow functions on OpenWrt as an application. OpenWrt is an Open source extensible exploitation system designed for the router, which is entirely customizable for the needs of the users and developers.

4.2 Second Step

A second process was about choosing an SDN router. In fact there are many of them on the market (license for sale or free license) [13], among which Opendaylight, POX, NOX, RYU....

We opted for the RYU controller which provides software components, with well-defined API, which allow the developers to create easily new management and network control applications [14]. This approach by components helps the companies personalize the deployments to meet their specific needs. Developers can rapidly and easily modify the existing components or implement their own to make sure that the underlying network can meet the changing requirements of their applications. The programing with RYU is done in Python language, which we used to control the access to the different access points.

In this first architecture, we have the classical case of an Asterisk environment. To accede to the server, we have used two access points (TP link wr1043nd).

The customer is placed on either side of the access points during the different tests. The links between different entities are ensured with the help of Ethernet cables.

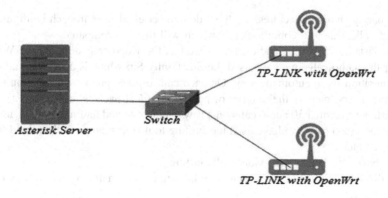

Fig. 6. Architecture without integration of SDN

We note that we are in a local environment, that means that server and access points are in a same network.

This case (Fig. 6) is without integration of the SDN. Like all access points, the screening policies, of fire guard and even the routings are configured at the level of the graphic interfaces of the access point. We can then say that the control part is at the level of the access points.

In the second case (Fig. 7) underneath, we have proceeded by the modification of the functionalities of the TP LINK router in order to integrate those of the SDN. First, we have changed the firmware of the two TP LINK access points into OpenWrt, and then we have installed the OpenFlow protocol as an application.

On the contrary of the first case, here the control part is centralized in a RUY controller. On the second, are programed the different access policies, the routing of the packets, etc. Python is the programming language which is used to implement these policies.

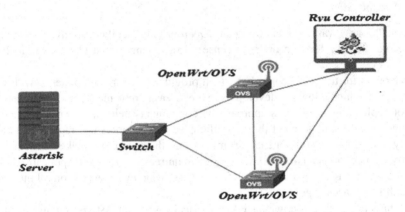

Fig. 7. Architecture with integration of SDN

5   Test and Analysis of Results

In comparing two architectures, we have done a series of tests in each configuration. We will collect the out coming results which will then be compared.

The tests are about the audio calls as well as the video calls done on the WIFI.

For the audio calls, we have used the StarTrinity Sip which is a software allowing call generation in an automatic way. On each call, it gives precise information on the QoS parameters, namely the number of packets, the lost packets, etc.

We have executed 50 audio calls on a row lasting one and half a minute (1 mn 30).

For the video calls, we have used the sniffing tool Wireshare to collect the different QoS parameters.

We have done thirty (30) video calls lasting 2 min.

In all cases graphs will be presented to highlight the variation of the latency on the customer's side.

The variation of the latency (simple WIFI and OpenFlow) of the fifty audio calls is presented in the graph below.

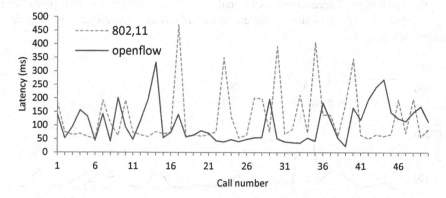

Fig. 8. Audio calls latency

On the Fig. 8 we notice a neat difference between the variation of the latency of the WIFI and OpenFlow, which does not present any correlation in terms of nature of the curves however. On the other hand, we notice that at the level of amplitudes, the 802.11 presents higher pikes widely exceeding the maximal amplitudes of the OpenFlow.

Synthesis:

In terms of voice quality (MOS) we have noticed that the two technologies (802.11 and OpenFlow) offer a good quality of perception to human ear.

No loss of packet is registered during the calls.

To appreciate the difference at the level of the latencies an average of 802.11 and OpenFlow latency seems to us necessary. The curve below represents the average of both latencies (Fig. 9).

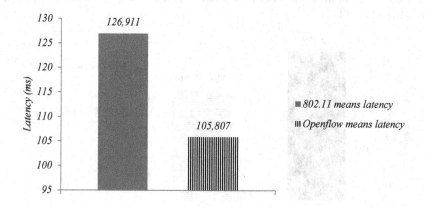

Fig. 9. Audio calls latency average

The curve enables us to notice a very good improvement of the latency with the integration of the OpenFlow protocol, although the average values of latency, according to ITU are considered very well (<150 ms).

The same type of measurements by making calls is used for the video calls. The variation of the latency of these different video calls is also represented on the graph underneath (Fig. 10):

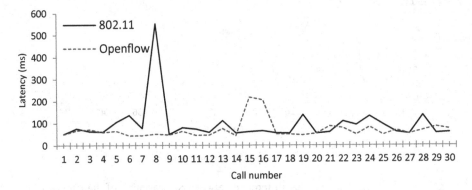

Fig. 10. Video call latency

We notice that at the level of the video calls, the latency curve 802.11 presents values higher than that of the OpenFlow on a great number of points (number of calls).

It is to be noted that the sequential of the values of the latency are due to the number call simulations operated on the server.

Synthesis
Just like the audio calls in terms of voice quality (MOS) we have noticed that the two technologies (802.11 and OpenFlow) offer a good quality of perception to human ear.

No loss of packet is registered during the calls.

Both technologies present a good value of latency; however the curve also enables us to notice a good improvement of the latency with the integration of the OpenFlow integration (Fig. 11).

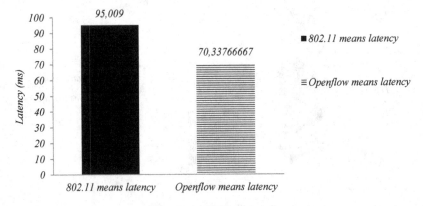

Fig. 11. Video call means latency

General Synthesis

We make all measurements in the conditions. The obtained results show that traditional VoIP network and network with SDN implementation offer different quality of service. By comparing results, we notice that with either video or audio calls, the integration of the SDN causes an increase of the network performance (reduction of the latency).

6 Conclusion

At the end of our work about the implementation of SDN solutions in order to facilitate, if not guarantee Universal Access, the different solutions that we have implemented were based on the use of very affordable equipment as well as on the advantages that the SDN technology offers, namely the use of Cloud. What motivated the experimentation of such solutions is to enable the handicapped areas (the rural areas) to benefit from the information and communication technologies (ICT) services. In fact, operators are very reluctant when it comes to serving those areas which are considered unprofitable (low population density) because the CAPEX and OPEX equipment cost is relatively high.

In one word, we can say that the SDN brings about not only an improvement in terms of quality of service (QoS) in the network, but also a decrease in CAPEX and OPEX. Thus, it is an ideal solution for the areas which are ready for Universal access and Global Service.

References

1. https://www.opennetworking.org/sdn-definition/. Accessed Oct 2017
2. Kreutz, D., Ramos, F.M.V., Verıssimo, P.E., Rothenberg, C.E., Azodolmolky, S., Uhlig, S.: Software-defined networking: a comprehensive survey. https://arxiv.org/pdf/1406.0440. Accessed Aug 2017
3. https://www.sdxcentral.com/sdn/definitions/inside-sdn-architecture/. Accessed Oct 2017
4. Foundations of Modern Networking SDN, NFV, QoE, IoT, and Cloud de William Stallings. Addison Wesley 2015-10-29
5. Nugroho, A.S., Safitri, Y.D., Setyawan, T.A.: Comparison analysis of software defined networking and OSPF protocol using virtual media. In: 2017 IEEE International Conference on Communication, Networks and Satellite (Comnetsat) (2017)
6. Mahesh, A., Chandrasekaran, A., ArunKumar, R., SivaKumar, K., Vigneshwaran, N.: Cloud based firewall on OpenFlow SDN network. http://ieeexplore.ieee.org/document/8186699/. Accessed Dec 2017
7. Pujolle, G.: Software Networks: Virtualization, SDN, 5G and Security, p. 84. Wiley-ISTE, Hoboken (2015)
8. Nadeau, T.D., Gray, K.: SDN: Software Defined Networkings, p. 237 (2013). books.google. com
9. Morreale, P.A., Anderson, J.M.: Software Defined Networking Design and Deployment, p. 110. CRC Press, Boca Raton (2015)
10. Hu, F.: Network Innovation through OpenFlow and SDN Principles and Design, p. 96. CRC Press, Boca Raton (2014)

11. International Journal of Advance Research in Computer Science and Management Studies Research Article/Paper/Case Study. www.ijarcsms.com
12. https://www.sdxcentral.com/projects/pantou-OpenWrt/. Accessed Nov 2017
13. Doherty, J.: SDN and NFV Simplified A visual Guide to Understanding Software Defined Networking and Network Function Virtualization, pp. 462–466. http://ptgmedia.pearsoncmg.com/images/9780134306407/samplepages/9780134306407.pdf
14. ryu Documentation Release 4.21 p 3. https://media.readthedocs.org/pdf/ryu/stable/ryu.pdf

Gaming and User Experience

Awale Game: Application Programming Interface and Augmented Reality Interface

Marie-Parisius Dorian Houessou[1,2], Vinasetan Ratheil Houndji[1,2(✉)],
Eugene C. Ezin[1], Manhougbé Probus A. F. Kiki[2,3], Harold Silvere Kiossou[2,3],
Jean-Baptiste Maureen Sossou[2,3], and Faizath Jedida Zoumarou Walis[2,3]

[1] Institut de Formation et de Recherche en Informatique (IFRI), UAC,
Abomey-Calavi, Benin
`parisius.houessou@gmail.com, ratheil.houndji@uac.bj`
[2] Machine Intelligence For You SARL, Abomey-Calavi, Benin
[3] Ecole Polytechnique d'Abomey-Calavi (EPAC), UAC, Abomey-Calavi, Benin

Abstract. Awale game is one of the famous board games from Africa
with many variants and is now played worldwide in various forms. In
this paper, we propose an open-source Application Programming Interface (`API`) for developers to allow an easy implementation of the various
variants of Awale as well as artificial intelligence based players. The `API`
is available online at https://github.com/Machine-Intelligence-For-You/
Awale. Based on this `API`, we propose a PC Awale game, a mobile Awale
game, and an Augmented Reality Game. The Awale `API`, PC game, and
mobile game are implemented in the programming language `Java` while
the game in Augmented Reality is realized with the `C#` programming
language, Unity 3D game engine and the `Vuforia` Augmented Reality
`SDK`. The various tests carried out show that the `API` and the different
games are totally functional. This `API` was also used for the first edition of
MAIC, an Artificial Intelligence contest https://mify-ai.com/maic2017/.

Keywords: Awale · `API` · Augmented Reality · Artificial Intelligence
Board game

1 Introduction

It is well known that games are an integral part of the human life. Among
the board and society games, Awale is one of the most famous African games.
It has several playable versions on electronic terminals. Awale itself exists in
several forms (Mancala, Oware, Ayo, Wari, etc.) according to specific ethnic
groups in which it is found. The existence of its different variants makes hard
the implementation of this game and causes a variation of the implementation
of an Artificial Intelligence (AI) for each of them. However, to the best of our
knowledge, there is no generic `API` Awale Game to ease the implementation of

© ICST Institute for Computer Sciences, Social Informatics and Telecommunications Engineering 2019
Published by Springer Nature Switzerland AG 2019. All Rights Reserved
R. Zitouni and M. Agueh (Eds.): AFRICATEK 2018, LNICST 260, pp. 147–154, 2019.
https://doi.org/10.1007/978-3-030-05198-3_13

the different variants of the game. Here we develop an API to ease this game implementation such that it would be possible to create various kinds of Awale games, which can use the latest technologies such as Augmented Reality. This paper proposes an open-source Application Programming Interface (API) for developers to allow an easy implementation of the various variants of Awale as well as artificial intelligence based players. Our goal is to make available to the scientific community a set of functionalities to easily implement software agents for the Awale game. The API is very generic and allows the modification of several values such as the game board's size, the number of holes, the number of seeds per hole when starting the game, the time of play per player, and the game's direction. To ensure that the API is functional, we develop (based on it):

- a graphical PC Awale game;
- a mobile Awale game;
- an Augmented Reality (AR) based on the mobile Awale game.

The paper is organized as follows: Sect. 2 gives a background of Awale game, API and AR technology; Sect. 3 describes the different tools used; Sect. 4 presents the class diagram; Sect. 5 shows some graphical interfaces obtained; and Sect. 6 concludes.

2   Background

Awale game is a board game from Africa. It seems to come exactly from Ethiopia and spread to the whole African continent [7]. It's a "count and capture" type game in which you distribute seeds in holes. Awale game requires abilities such as reflection, decision and strategy that ranks it at the same level as chess. A classical Awale game is played using a board containing two rows of six holes. In some variants of the game, one can find two bigger holes on the edges. The seeds played in this game usually come from the tree "Caesalpinia bonduc" and are called in the Fongbe language "Adjikouin". They can however, be replaced by balls or pebbles and must be forty-eight for a classic Awale. Games are played according to well-defined rules. Many video games exist today on several terminals in the Awale Game especially on smartphones and are available on the different mobile apps downloading platforms like PlayStore or AppStore. Below we define API and AR which are the two main contributions about Awale game in this paper.

API stands for Application Programming Interface and is a set of routines, protocols, and tools used to design applications [2]. An API specifies how the software components interact. APIs can also be used to create Graphical User Interface components. The goal of an API is to make easy the development of a computer program by giving developers access to pre-made and modifiable blocks of code. APIs offer to developers the simplification of tasks and standardization. There are many types of API which can be classified into seven categories [6]: Web Services, WebSockets API, Library based API, Class based API, Operating System functions and routines, Object Remoting APIs, and Hardware APIs. In the world of games, several API exists to help developers design games. For example, we have a Chess Game's API[1] that allows developers to embed a chess game on their website or develop a Chess Game for iPhone. We also have many similar examples for designing RPG[2] games such as League of Legends, Witcher or Kingdom Hearts II. One of them is Readgame available at https://pastebin.com/jgNes9j8.

Augmented Reality (AR) is a technology for adding virtual content to the real world [1]. Note that AR should not be confused with virtual reality that allows immersion in a totally virtual world. It is often associated with the addition of 3D content to an environment seen from a camera. AR is not very new because the first papers on the subject are from the end of the twentieth century. However, in recent years, this technology experienced a great democratization thanks to smartphones composed of several sensors. It has many applications in architecture, medicine, commerce, print media, etc. The main uses of AR today are, among others, QR code or bar code scanner, and video game development like Pokemon Go [8] that has a worldwide success. Augmented Reality comes in many forms. Many tools exist to help developers to create AR applications. Note that we have many games today using AR technology. For example:

– AR defender [9] is a commercial casual game that was released on the iPhone. It makes use of its proprietary marker pattern printed on a card so that the software can make use of the phones camera to detect the position and orientation to place a virtual tower. The goal of the game is to defend the tower by moving the camera and shooting various weapons at the enemy units that try to take down the tower. It is claimed to be the first complete and fun AR game on the iPhone [10];
– Ingress [11] is a location-based, AR mobile game developed by Niantic. This game has a science fiction back story with a continuous open narrative. Ingress is also considered to be a location-based exergame;
– Augmented Reality Chess [12] is a marker based AR Chess game on Android developed by Contra Labs Official. By using pattern printed on card and the phone camera to play chess game like the classical one.

3   Materials and Methods

The set of material used was divided in two main parts:

– the tools needed to implement the API and the different graphical interfaces;
– the material to design the game in Augmented Reality.

Figure 1 gives a general view of the different tools used. To implement the Awale API we used the following tools:

– Unified Modeling Language (UML) to model the system by mainly designing a class diagram and a sequence diagram [3];

---

[1] https://chess.gallery/api/gameref.
[2] Role-Playing Game.

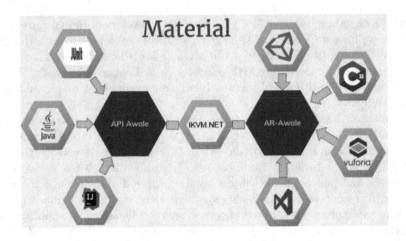

Fig. 1. Different tools used

- Java programming language to implement the different classes and the interaction between them and also the basic Artificial Intelligence algorithms [4];
- Junit as test framework for unit testing [13].

For the Awale AR Game we used:

- The game engine Unity for the game designing [14];
- C# as an object-oriented programming language to implement the game
  mechanics [5];
- IKVM.NET to convert the Awale API source code from Java to C# [15];
- the most popular SDK for Augmented Reality, Vuforia [16]. It is a set of tools
  to create AR applications for mobile terminals. Vuforia uses a computer vision
  technology to identify the targets (2D or 3D dimension objects) in real-time.

This work was lead using the scrum sgile methodology. It had two main
parts: the modeling part and the development part. The aim of the modeling
part is to give a specific view of the system using UML diagrams such as class
diagram, use-case diagram and sequence diagram. After the modeling we started
the development phase. This latter has two parts: the API development and the
AR game development. For the implementation of the Awale API we use the
results from the modeling, especially the class diagram to implement in Java all
the classes, the attributes, the methods, and the relations between the different
classes. This API allows an easy implementation of an AI based player. Note
that, thanks to this ease, the Awale API was used for an Artificial Intelligence
contest, MAIC 2017 (https://mify-ai.com/maic2017/).

To develop the AR Awale Game, first we convert the API Java code using
IKVM.NET [15]. Then we obtain a dll package from the Jar package. Thus the
API can be used in Unity with the C# language. After importing the model and
3D graphic object of the game, we add the different features from Vuforia to
enable AR mode of the game and then implement the game mechanics.

4 Modeling

Figure 2 shows the class diagram used to implement the Awale `API`.

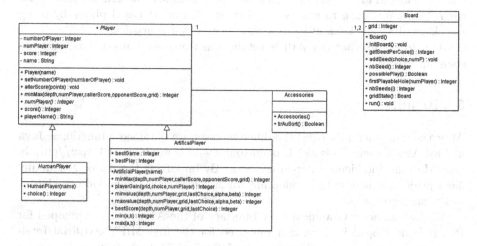

Fig. 2. UML class diagram

This `API` had two important classes: `Player` and `Board`.

First let us focus on the class `Board`. This class has the attribute `grid`, an array of integers, which contains the state of the board with the number of seed by hole. The class `Board` has some interesting methods such as:

- `initBoard()` initialize the board game with a given number of seeds by hole;
- `addSeed(choice, numP)` adds one seed in each hole during the playing move based on the hole *choice* chosen by the player *numP*;
- `firstPlayableHole(numPlayer)` gives the first playable hole (from 0) on the board with respect to the given player *numPlayer*;
- `possiblePlay(i)` is true the given hole *i* is playable and false otherwise;
- `gridState()` returns an object `Board` that represents the current state of the board game.

The class `Player` has currently four attributes:

- `numberOfPlayer`, a class variable that contains the number of players;
- `numPlayer`, the identifier of the player in the game;
- `score`, the score of the player;
- `name`, the name of the player.

We now describe some methods of the class `Player`.

- `alterScore(points)` sets the score of the player to *points*;
- `score()` returns the current score of the player;

– `playerName()` gives the name of the player.

Actually the class `Player` is an abstract class. In the game, one should instantiate one of its sub-classes `HumanPlayer` and `ArtificialPlayer`. Note that the class `ArtificialPlayer` has some methods such as `minMax`, `maxValue`, `minValue`, `bestScore` to ease an implementation of AI based player by using the classical `Alpha-beta` algorithm with customized heuristics.

Also to ensure that our API is totally functional we implemented and run some unit tests.

5   Results

After the implementation and the different tests, we obtained a functional `Java` API for Awale game. This `API` is open-source and is available at https://github. com/Machine-Intelligence-For-You/Awale. By importing the Awale `API` in any `Java` project, it is easy to develop any variant of Awale Game and associate it to an intelligent agent.

Figure 3 shows a Graphical User Interface of the Awale game developed for PC. It is developed in `Java` and was used for the first MIFY Artificial Intelligence Contest (https://mify-ai.com/maic2017/). The source-code as well as the best algorithms of the contest are available at https://github.com/Machine-Intelligence-For-You/MAIC2017.

Fig. 3. PC game

We also realized an `AR` Awale game playable on iPhone and Android smartphone. Figure 4 presents the interface of the AR Awale's Game. We use the features of `Vuforia` knows as virtual buttons to interact with the board. Only the

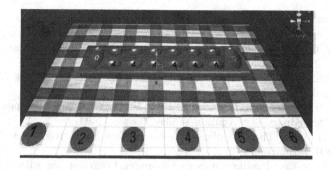

Fig. 4. AR game

mode Player vs AI is currently available. This AR Awale game is playable by using a classical virtual reality headset.

A mobile Awale game (see Fig. 5) is also developed for smartphone under Android OS. In its current version, the game supports Alpha-Beta algorithm and has an implementation of AI algorithms developed by the first three winners of the MAIC 2017.

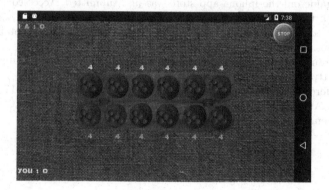

Fig. 5. Mobile game

6 Conclusion

In this paper, we have introduced an open-source Awale Game Application Programming Interface (API) for developers. The aim is to allow an easy implementation of the various variants of Awale. This API makes available to the scientific community a set of functionalities to allow an easy implementation of software agents for the Awale game. We also presented a PC Awale game, a mobile Awale game, and an augmented reality Awale game, developed based on this API. We do hope that the github repository of the Awale API (https://github.com/Machine-Intelligence-For-You/Awale) will have more contributors to improve its performance and functionalities.

References

1. Cushnan, D., El Habbak, H.: Developing AR Games for IOS and Android, p. 117. Packt Publishing, Birmingham (2013)
2. Mulloy, B.: Web API Design Crafting Interfaces that Developers Love, 38 p. Apigee (2012)
3. Rumbaugh, J., Jacobson, I., Booch, G.: The Unified Modeling Language Reference Manual, 2nd edn, p. 742. Addison-Wesley, Boston (2004)
4. Schildt, H.: Java The Complete Reference, 7th edn, p. 1057. New York City, McGraw-Hill Companies (2007)
5. Nakov, S., & Co.: Fundamentals of Computer Programming with C#, 1122 p. (2013)
6. API Types, Sarah Maddox Simple Classification of APIs. https://www.slideshare.net/sarahmaddox/api-types. Accessed 23 June 2017
7. Awale Game Background and Rules. http://www.myriad-online.com/resources/docs/awale/english/background.html. Accessed 04 June 2017
8. Pokemon Go: Official web site. http://www.pokemongo.com/. Accessed 12 Sept 2017
9. AR defender. http://www.ardefender.com/. Accessed 19 Apr 2018
10. ORI Inbar: The RST fun augmented reality game on the iphone app store was just submitted 2010. http://gamesalfresco.com/2010/09/23/the-first-fun-augmented-reality-game-on|-the-iphone-app-store-was-just-submitted. Accessed 19 Apr 2018
11. Ingress. https://www.ingress.com/. Accessed 19 Apr 2018
12. Augmented Reality Chess. https://play.google.com/store/apps/details?id=com.contralabs.game.archess. Accessed 19 Apr 2018
13. JUnit Framework by JUnit. http://junit.org/junit4/. Accessed 04 June 2017
14. Unity. https://unity3d.com. Accessed 04 June 2017
15. IKVM Jeroen Frijters. http://www.ikvm.net/. Accessed 04 June 2017
16. Vuforia Augmented Reality SDK Vuforia. https://www.vuforia.com/content/vuforia/en.html. Accessed 04 June 2017

Vector Space Model of Text Classification Based on Inertia Contribution of Document

Demba Kandé[1], Fodé Camara[2(✉)], Reine Marie Marone[1,2],
and Samba Ndiaye[1]

[1] Department of Mathematics, Cheikh Anta Diop University, Dakar, Senegal
demba4.kande@ucad.edu.sn
[2] Department of Mathematics, Alioune Diop University, Bambey, Senegal
fode.camara@uadb.edu.sn

Abstract. The use of textual data has increased exponentially in recent years due to the networking infrastructure such as Facebook, Twitter, Wikipedia, Blogs, and so one. Analysis of this massive textual data can help to automatically categorize and label new content. Before classification process, term weighting scheme is the crucial step for representing the documents in a way suitable for classification algorithms. In this paper, we are conducting a survey on the term weighting schemes and we propose an efficient term weighting scheme that provide a better classification accuracy than those obtening with the famous TF-IDF, the recent IF-IGM and the others term weighting schemes in the literature.

Keywords: Vector space model · Classification · Text mining
Term weighting scheme

1 Introduction

In the recent years, web users generated a large amount of various and useful text information. This textual data from Facebook, Twitter, Wikipedia, Blogs, and so one can be analyzed to identify most informative comments, to get users' opinions from comments, to recognize a potentially spam content, etc.

Before classification, text documents must be represented in a way suitable for data mining algorithms. Thus, several term weighting schemes (also called vector space models) have been developed in the literature to improve the performance of text classification algorithms. These techniques can be divided into two approaches, unsupervised and supervised term weighting methods, depending on the use of the class label in training corpus. The pioneer works are the unsupervised weighting scheme, binary and the popularly-used TF-IDF [3]. The binary method tells when a term appears in a document, and TF-IDF determines terms that are frequent in the document, but infrequent in the corpus.

However, the traditional unsupervised weighting scheme is not really useful for text classification tasks. As an alternative, various works have been done on weighting models based on the known class label, including, the recent TF-IGM scheme [9]. TF-IGM adopts a new statistical model to measure a term's class distinguishing power. To the best of our knowledge, it is the most efficient term weighting scheme.

R. Zitouni and M. Agueh (Eds.): AFRICATEK 2018, LNICST 260, pp. 155–165, 2019.
https://doi.org/10.1007/978-3-030-05198-3_14

This paper challenges TF-IGM [9], and introduce a new and efficient supervised term weighting scheme based on inertia contribution of document. Our weighting scheme has the benefit because it affects positively the classification performance. The experimental results show that our algorithm outperforms the famous TF-IDF, and the recent and efficient TF-IGM.

The rest of the paper is organized as follows. Section 2 discusses related works. In Sect. 3, we give the details of our proposition. In Sect. 4, we evaluate the performance of our algorithm. Section 5 concludes the paper and gives some future works.

2   Analyses of Current Term Weighting Schemes

In the literature, various term weighting schemes have been proposed for text categorization (TC), and thus for optimizing the classifier accuracy. We have focused on the limitations of TF-IDF [3] and TF-IGM [9] and others, which are respectively the most used and the most efficient term weighting schemes.

We can explore the literature, through a simple example. Let's consider the following corpus, denoted d:

Table 1. An simple example of corpus d

Id document	Document contain	Class
d_1	"The sky is blue"	Negeative
d_2	"The sun is bright today"	Positive
d_3	"The sun in the sky is bright"	Positive
d_4	"We can see the shining sun, the bright sun"	Positive

Then, its dictionary is {'blue', 'sky', 'bright', 'sun', 'today', 'can', 'see', 'shining'}.

2.1   Traditional Term Weighting Schemes

Traditional term weighting schemes are Binary (or Boolean), TF and TF-IDF weighting [2], which are originated from information retrieval. As the weight of a term, the term frequency (TF) in a document is obviously more precise and reasonable than the binary value, 1 or 0, denoting term presence or absence in the document because the topic terms or key words often appear in the document frequently and they should be assigned greater weights than the rare words. But term weighting by TF may assign large weights to the common words with weak text discriminating power.

To offset this shortcoming, a global factor, namely inverse document frequency (IDF), is introduced in the TF-IDF scheme.

$$w(t_j) = tf_{ij} \times log\left(\frac{N}{df_j}\right)$$

(1)

Where tf_{ij} denotes the frequency of term j in document i and N is the total number of documents and df_j is the number of documents that contains the term j.

The weight is composed of two factors: the local factor TF (for Term Frequency) metric that calculates the number of times a word appears in a document; and the global factor IDF (Inverse Document Frequency) term is computed as the logarithm of the number of the documents in the corpus divided by the number of documents that are specific to the term. The basic idea of TF-IDF is to determine term weight that are frequent in the document (using the TF metric), but infrequent in the corpus (using the IDF metric).

The term frequency (i.e., TF) for sky in d_1 is then 1. The word sky appears in two documents. Then, the inverse document frequency (i.e., IDF) is calculated as $\log\left(\frac{4}{2}\right) = 0.301$. Thus, the TF-IDF weight is the product of these quantities: $1 \times 0.301 = 0.301$.

The main drawback of TF-IDF is the fact that it unsupervised method; it does not take into account the distribution of class label.

Since the traditional TF-IDF (term frequency-inverse document frequency) is not fully effective for text classification. Several various of TF-IDF based on supervised methods have been proposed in the literature. These variants introduce a new statistic model: feature selection models to measure the term's distinguishing power in a class.

2.2 Supervised Methods Term Weighting

By considering the deficiencies of TF-IDF, researchers have proposed supervised term weighting schemes (STW) [4]. Otherwise, weighting a term by using an information known by the classes. The distribution of a term in different category is described with a contingency table shown in Table 2.

Table 2. The contingence table information

Class	c_k	$\bar{c}_k$
t_j	AA	B
$\bar{t}_j$	CC	D

A denotes the number of documents belonging to category c_k where the term t_j occurs at least once; B denotes the number of documents not belonging to category c_k where the term t_j occurs at least once; C denotes the number of documents belonging to category c_k where the term t_j does not occur; D denotes the number of documents not belonging to category $\bar{c}_k$ where the term t_j does not occur. The contigence table shows that:

- if term t_j is highly relevant to category c_k only, which basically indicates that it is a good feature to represent category c_k, then the value of $\frac{A}{B}$ tends to be higher.
- if the value of $\frac{A}{C}$ is larger, which means that the number of documents where term t_j occurs are greater than the documents where term t_j does not occur in class c_k.

- if term t_j is highly relevant to category $\bar{c}_k$ only, which basically indicates that it is a good feature to represent category $\bar{c}_k$, then the value of $\frac{B}{A}$: tends to be higher.
- if the value of $\frac{B}{D}$ tends to be higher, which means the number of documents where term t_j occurs are greater than the documents where term t_j does not occur in class $\bar{c}_k$.
- The product of $\frac{A}{B}$ and $\frac{A}{C}$ indicates terms t_j's relevance with respect to a specific category c_k. On the other hand, the product of $\frac{B}{A}$ and $\frac{B}{C}$ indicates terms t_j's relevance with respect to a specific category $\bar{c}_k$.

In [4], combining the term frequency and $\chi 2$ statistic, authors introduce the TF-Chi2 weight of term t_j:

$$w(t_j, c_k) = tf_{ij} \times \frac{N \times (A \times D - B \times C)^2}{(A+B) \times (C+D) \times (A+C) \times (B+D)} \tag{2}$$

In TF.Chi2, the weight of a term is specific to the c_k category, i.e. it depends on the contribution of the term in the c_k category. But, the size of the positive class is often smaller than that of the negative counterpart. The Chi2 statistic is limited in the case of multi-class classification, because it is a bi-class schema, hence causes performance loss of classifier. In addition to the drawbacks listed above, the terms informations in the corpus have not been considered [3].

The Measure of Relevance and Distinction with the AD metric [5] is frequently used as a criterion in the field of machine learning. It is based on the notion of relevance of characteristic from the distribution of terms in the category c_k. The more a term contributes to the distinction of category c_k, the higher its relevance is in c_k. AD of a feature t_j toward a category c_k can be defined as follows:

$$w(t_j, c_k) = \frac{A}{B} \times \frac{A}{C} \times \left(\frac{A}{B} \times \frac{A}{C} - \frac{B}{A} \times \frac{B}{C} \right) \tag{3}$$

In AD metric, only the known information of the category is considered, it ignores the contribution of the terms in the corpus [4] and constitutes a method to bi-class. In the case of multi-class classification some category may not be taken into account because are all group in c_k.

The work in [6], proposed a term frequency based on weighting scheme using naïve bayes (TF-RTF). It considered the binary text classification case (for a document, d, and its label, c_k, let $c_k = 1$ denote the positive class, and $\bar{c}_k = 0$ the negative one) and calculated the weight of a term from the posterior probability of each class:

$$w(t_j, c_k) = Nu * \left| log \frac{(M1u+1)}{(M0u+1)} + log \frac{(M0+p)}{(M1+p)} \right| \tag{4}$$

Where N_u is the term frequency of a word w_u in the document; M_{1u}, M_{0u} are the term frequencies of w_u respectively in the positive class and negative class; M_1, M_0 are respectively the total term frequencies in the positive class and negative class;

$\log \frac{(M_0+p)}{(M_1+p)}$, is the ratio of total term frequencies. Like all probability patterns, *TF-RTF* can cause a loss of information in multi-class categorization.

As others proposed metrics, the Information Gain [7] of a given feature t_j with respect to class c_k is the reduction in uncertainty about the value of t_j when we know the value of c_k. The more Information Gain is high for a feature, the more important a feature is for the text categorization. Information Gain of a feature t_j toward a category c_k can be defined as follows:

$$w(t_j, c_k) = \sum_{c\epsilon\{c_k\bar{c}_k\}} \sum_{t\epsilon\{t_j\bar{t}_j\}} P(t_j, c_k) \log \frac{P(t_j, c_k)}{P(c_k)P(t_j)} \tag{5}$$

Where $p(c_k)$ is the fraction of the documents in category cover the total number of documents, $p(t_j, c_k)$ is the fraction of documents in the category c_k that contain the word t over the total number of documents. $p(t_j)$ is the fraction of the documents containing the term t_j over the total number of documents.

The work presented in [8] (TF-BDC), the relevance of a term in a category is defined from the value of entropy. More the entropy is high, more it appears in several categories, and less discriminating they are. However, higher the concentration of the feature in a c_k category is, more important its discriminating power is. Conversely, a term with a more or less distribution uniform in the different categories has often-smaller entropy.

$$w(t_j, c_k) = 1 + \frac{\sum_{k=1}^{|c|} \frac{p(t_j|c_k)}{\sum_{k=1}^{|c|} p(t_j|c_k)} \log \frac{p(t_j|c_k)}{\sum_{k=1}^{|c|} p(t_j|c_k)}}{\log(|C|)} \tag{6}$$

With $p(t_j, c_k) = \frac{f(t_j, c_k)}{f(c_k)}$, where $f(t_j, c_k)$ denotes the frequency of term t_j in category c_k and $f(c_k)$ denotes the frequency sum of all terms in category c_k.

Example: *in Table 1, the term "sky" has an entropy more higher than the term "sun", but "sun" has a higher discriminant power because it is specific to the category "positive".*

Like all feature selection methods, TF-BDC ignores the contribution of terms in the document collection.

In order to overcome the shortcomings of the bi-class schemes, Chen and al. propose Inverse Gravity Moment –TF-IGM [9] in order to explore both the contribution of terms in the classification and the provision of information in corpus. It is defined by:

$$w(t_j, c_k) = tf_{ij} * (1 + \lambda \cdot igm(t_j)) \tag{7}$$

Where $1 + \lambda \cdot igm(t_j)$ denotes the igm based global weighting factor of term t_j in document d_i, and $\lambda \epsilon[5; 9]$ is an adjustable coefficient for keeping the relative balance between the global and the local factors in the weight of a term. The $igm(t_j)$ is defined as follows:

$$\frac{f_{j1}}{\sum_{r=1}^{m} f_{jr}} \tag{8}$$

Where the frequency f_{jr} ($r = 1, 2, ..., m$) usually refers to the class-specific document frequency of the term and f_{j1} the maximal frequency of the term of the class m (sort in descending order). TF-IGM is a supervised term weighting system (STW) because the global *IGM* weighting factor depends only on known class information, and the contribution of terms on the corpus is ignored.

Like all the supervised methods studied in this paper, only class information is used to determine the overall factor. However, the relevance of a document *di* depends on its position relative to the center of gravity *Gi*. Hence the importance of the terms that constitute it.

3   Our Proposed Term Weighting Scheme: TF-ICD

In this section, we propose a so-called *ICD* (inertia contribution document) model to measure the class distinguishing power of a term and then put forward a new term weighting scheme, TF-ICD, by combining term frequency (TF) with the ICD measure.

3.1   Problem Definition and Motivations

Let *d* be a set of labeled documents d_i, in which class is of a finite number of discrete symbols, each representing a class of the classification problem to be addressed. A document d_i is represented as a vector of terms $d_i = \{t_{1i}, ..., t_{ri}\}$ where r is the cardinality of the dictionary $\{t_1, ..., t_n\}$, and $0 < t_{ij} < 1$ represents the contribution of term t_j to the prediction of class. Thus, d_i is represented by a matrix t_{ij}. Non-zero t_{ij} indicates that term t_j is contained in d_i.

The aim of our proposition is to transform the initial corpus *d* into matrix t_{ij} such as t_{ij} outperforms the state-of-the-art term weighting scheme by giving better classifier accuracy:

$$tf - icd(d) = \text{matrix } t_{ij}/f : \{T_1, ..., T_n\} \rightarrow class\ is\ better.$$

Where *icd* represents our statistical model that measures the information quantity of a document, which reflects the term's class distinguishing power.

3.2   Analyzing the Discriminating Power of a Document

From the multidimensional statistical models a corpus can be presented as an individual-variable as described in the Fig. 1.

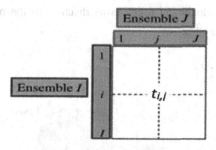

Fig. 1. Matrix t_{ij}/f: $\{T_1, .., T_n\}$

Where I is all individuals (documents), J is set of variables (terms), and t_{ij} is frequency of the term j in the document i.

By replacing the contingency table with the probability table, we obtain (Fig. 2):

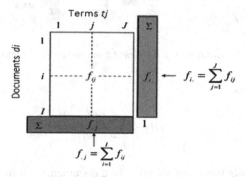

Fig. 2. Matrix f_{ij}/f: $\{T_1, .., T_n\}$

From its average conditional distribution ($\frac{f_{ij}}{n}$ likelihood of using the t_j term). The higher the independence gap, the lower its weight is and its high inertial contribution $\lambda_{(di)}$.

3.3 Inertial Contribution of a Document–ICD

The inertial contribution is the amount of information that a document provides in a corpus, it depends on the product of two measures: (i) the weight of a document d_i; (ii) and its difference to independence.

The weight of a document is the probability of obtaining the document d_i belonging to the category c_k and is defined by

$$\frac{f_i}{n}.$$

(9)

The relevance of a document relies to its distance to the origin of the center of gravity described in Fig. 3.

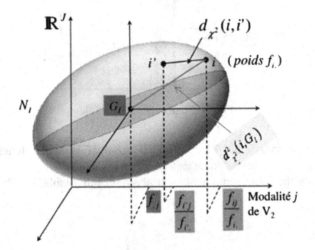

Fig. 3. Distance of a document from the center of gravity.

$$d_{\chi^2}^2(i, GI) = \sum_{j=1}^{j=J} \frac{(f_{ij} - f_j)^2}{f_j} \tag{10}$$

We thus obtain the inertia contribution of a document d_i in the corpus, defined by

$$\lambda(d_i) = \frac{f_{i.}}{n} \cdot \sum_{j=1}^{j=J} \frac{(f_{ij} - f_j)^2}{f_j} \tag{11}$$

The Table 3 presents the inertia distribution by categories and by term.

Table 3. Intrtia distribution by categories and by term

Class	c_1	c_2	...	c_k
$\lambda(c_k)$	$\sum_{d \in c1} \lambda(d_i)$	$\sum_{d \in c2} \lambda(d_i)$	...	$\sum_{d \in ck} \lambda(d_i)$
$\lambda(t_{ijed})$	$\sum_{\{d_i \in c_1\}} \lambda(d_i)$	$\sum_{\{d_i \in 2\}} \lambda(d_i)$	...	$\sum_{\{d_i \in k\}} \lambda(d_i)$

$$ICD(t_j, c_k) = log_2\left(1 + \frac{\sum_{\{d_i \in c_k\}\{t_{ij} \neq 0\}} \lambda(d_i)}{N_j}\right) \qquad (12)$$

Where $\sum_{\{d_i \in c_k\}\{t_{ij} \neq 0\}} \lambda(d_i)$ is the sum of the inertia of documents d_i of category c_k containing t_j and N_j is the number of documents d_i of category c_k containing t_j.

3.4   Term Weighting by TF-ICD

The weight of a term in a document should be determined by its importance in the corpus and its contribution to text classification, which correspond respectively to the local and global weighting factors in term weighting. A term's contribution to text classification depends on its class distinguishing power, which is reflected by its contribution of documents inertia. Higher the inertia is, greater term weighting is important. This last can be measured by the ICD metric.

Hence, instead of the traditional IDF factor, a new global factor in term weighting is defined based on the ICD metric of the term, as shown in (12). Therefore, the TF-ICD weight of term t_j in document d_i is the product of the TF-based local weighting factor and the ICD-based global weighting factor, i.e., $w(t_j, c_k) = tf_{ij} \times ICD(tj, c_k)$, which is expressed as (13).

$$w(t_j, c_k) = tf_{ij} \times log_2\left(1 + \frac{\sum_{\{d_i \in c_k\}\{t_{ij} \neq 0\}} \lambda(d_i)}{N_j}\right) \qquad (13)$$

4   Experiments

4.1   Datasets

In order to evaluate the performance of the proposed method, we used the Spam collection [10]. In data preprocessing, all words are converted to lower case, punctuation marks are removed and we used stop lists and no stemming algorithm.

The sms spam collection is composed by 4,827 legitimate messages and 747 mobile spam messages, a total of 5,574 short messages. Table 4 shows its basic statistics.

Table 4. Basic statistics.

Class	Amount	%
Hams	4,827	86.60
Spams	747	13.40
Total	5,574	100

4.2 Results

After applying our term weighting scheme, we have tested three well-known data mining algorithms on the transformed corpus. Table 5 shows the effectiveness of our term weighting algorithm for text classification. The classification accuracies obtained by successively applying SVM, DT and LR algorithms on our term weighting representation are better than those obtained on TF-IDF and TF-IGM.

Table 5. Basic statistics.

	Classification accuracy		
Algorithm	*tf-icd*	*tf-igm*	*tf-idf*
SVM	**0.8829**	0.8779	0.8756
DT	**0.9354**	0.9292	0.9297
LR	**0.8836**	0.8787	0.8763

5 Conclusion and Perspectives

In this paper, we studied the term weighting scheme issue. We proposed an efficient term weighting scheme based on inertia contribution of a document.

The test results of text classification show their convincible efficiency. We plan in our future work to conduct our algorithm on others benchmarks data sets.

Acknowledgment. We would like to express our sincere thanks to the CEA-MITIC ⊚CEA MITIC

(Centre d'Excellence Africain en Mathématiques, Informatique et Tic) who financed our research by paying the publication fees of the 2papiers that we published in Africatek2018. The CEA-MITIC, located at the UFR of Applied Sciences and Technology (UFR SAT) of the Gaston Berger University (UGB) of Saint-Louis in Senegal, is a consortium of university institutions in Senegal and subregion of Senegal, research institutions and national, regional and international companies involved in the ICT sector.

References

1. Dejun, X., Maosong, S.: Chinese text categorization based on the binary weighting model with non-binary smoothing. In: Sebastiani, F. (ed.) ECIR 2003. LNCS, vol. 2633, pp. 408–419. Springer, Heidelberg (2003). https://doi.org/10.1007/3-540-36618-0_29
2. Lan, M., Tan, C.L., Jian, S., Yue, L.: Supervised and traditional term weighting methods for automatic text categorization. IEEE Trans. Pattern Anal. Mach. Intell. **31**(4), 721–735 (2009)
3. Deng, Z.-H., Tang, S.-W., Yang, D.-Q., Zhang, M., Li, L.-Y., Xie, K.-Q.: A comparative study on feature weight in text categorization. In: Yu, J.X., Lin, X., Lu, H., Zhang, Y. (eds.) APWeb 2004. LNCS, vol. 3007, pp. 588–597. Springer, Heidelberg (2004). https://doi.org/10.1007/978-3-540-24655-8_64
4. Debole, F., Sebastiani, F.: Supervised term weighting for automated text categorization. In: Proceedings of the 2003 ACM Symposium on Applied Computing, pp. 784–788 (2003)

5. Yang, J., Wang, J., Liu, Z., Qu, Z.: A term weighting scheme based on the measure of relevance and distinction for text categorization. In: International Conference on Advanced Computing Technologies and Applications, ICACTA-2015, pp 13–22. https://doi.org/10.1016/j.procs.2015.03.074

6. Feng, G., Wang, H., Sun, T., Zhang, L.: A term frequency based weighting scheme using naïve bayes for text classification. J. Comput. Theor. Nanosci. 319–326 (2016). https://doi.org/10.1166/jctn.2016.4807

7. Wang, T., Cai, Y., Leung, H., Cai, Z., Min, H.: Entropy-based Term Weighting Schemes for Text Categorization in VSM. In: 2015 IEEE 27th International Conference on Tools with Artificial Intelligence, 12 p. https://doi.org/10.1109/ictai.2015.57

8. Yoshida, T.M.M.K.K.: Term weighting method based on information gain ratio for summarizing documents retrieved by IR systems. J. Nat. Lang. Process. 9(4), 3–32 (2001)

9. Chen, K., Zhang, Z., Long, J., Zhang, H.: Turning from TF-IDF to TF-IGM for term weighting in text classification. J. Expert Syst. Appl. 66(C), 245–260 (2016)

10. Cormack, G.V., Gómez Hidalgo, J.M., Puertas Sánz, E.: Spam filtering for short messages. In: Proceedings of the Sixteenth ACM Conference on Conference on information and Knowledge Management, Lisbon, Portugal, 06–10 November 2007, CIKM 2007, pp. 313–320. ACM, New York (2007). http://doi.acm.org/10.1145/1321440.1321486

11. Geng, J., Lu, Y., Chen, W., Qin, Z.: An improved text categorization algorithm based on VSM. In: 2014 IEEE 17th International Conference on Computational Science and Engineering. https://doi.org/10.1109/cse.2014.313

12. Wu, H., Gu, X., Gu, Y.: Balancing between over-weighting and under-weighting in supervised term weighting. Inf. Process. Manag. 53, 547–557 (2017). https://doi.org/10.1016/j.ipm.2016.10.003

13. Karisani, P., Rahgozar, M., Oroumchian, F.: A query term re-weighting approach using document similarity. Inf. Process. Manag. 52(3), 478–489 (2016). https://doi.org/10.1016/j.ipm.2015.09.002

14. Haddoud, M., Mokhtari, A., Lecroq, T., Abdeddaïm, S.: Combining supervised term-weighting metrics for SVM text classification with extended term representation. Knowl. Inf. Syst. (2016). https://doi.org/10.1007/s10115-016-0924-1

15. Pang, B., Lee, L.: A sentimental education: sentiment analysis using subjectivity summarization based on minimum cuts. In: Proceedings of the ACL 2004. http://www.cs.cornell.edu/people/pabo/movie-review-data

Mood and Personality Influence on Emotion

Tahirou Djara[1,2(✉)], Abdoul Matine Ousmane[1,2],
and Antoine Vianou[1,2]

[1] Laboratoire d'Electrotechnique de Télécommunication et d'Informatique
Appliquée (LETIA/EPAC), Université d'Abomey-Calavi (UAC),
Cotonou, Benin
csm.djara@gmail.com
[2] Institut d'Innovation Technologique (IITECH), Abomey-Calavi, Benin

Abstract. Animated conversational agents (ACA) are intended to be used to establish a relationship and communication between human and machine. In order to make credible interactions, one of important elements is to equip them with a personality that will be able to vary their behavior and social attitudes in the image of the human. This article presents the concepts and tools of personification of the machine for simulating mood and personality influence in other recognition systems of emotion.

Keywords: Emotion · Personality model · Recognition systems

1 Introduction

Nowadays the machines occupy a preponderant place in our daily lives. The study presented in [1] thus demonstrates that the social rules governing human-machine interactions are identical to those between two humans. While Bledsoe's dream [2] of seeing computers befriend individuals is still a long way off, many efforts are being made to give these machines around us a typically human look and feel. This phenomenon is called personification. There are two key elements to consider: emotion and personality. The role of emotions is no longer to be proven since Picard's founding book on Affective Computing [3]. Personality, for its part, can be defined as "the set of attributes, qualities and characteristic that distinguish the behaviour, thoughts and feelings of individuals" [4].

Miller et al. [5] show that the combination of personality and emotions, but also motivation and culture, plays an important role in behavior by influencing decisions.

In this article, we will attempt to propose a model for simulating the links between mood, personality and emotions. We present in Sect. 2, a survey about systems implementing personality models. Section 3 presents the personification of ACA by highlighting the modeling of emotions and personalities. An application of mood and personality impact on emotion using algebraic representation of emotional states and Five Factors Model (FFM) in Sect. 4. Section 5 concludes the paper.

© ICST Institute for Computer Sciences, Social Informatics and Telecommunications Engineering 2019
Published by Springer Nature Switzerland AG 2019. All Rights Reserved
R. Zitouni and M. Agueh (Eds.): AFRICATEK 2018, LNICST 260, pp. 166–174, 2019.
https://doi.org/10.1007/978-3-030-05198-3_15

2   Survey About Systems Implementing Personality Models

There are many computational models that simulate both emotions and personality. SCREAM [6] is one of those model where the personality will impact the regulation of emotions, especially the speed at which they decrease. André et al. [7] have various agents capable of expressing emotions and endowed with personality. This personality intervenes in the choice of the emotional responses of the agent, and the tone given to the speech. This impact on the agent's choices and decisions is also proven in a military scenario involving a team of two soldiers with distinct personalities. Their reactions to an identical event are then completely different: in the event of enemy fire, one will retreat while staying under cover while his teammate remains frozen [7].

The survey presented in [8] emphasizes that majority of existing models are based on the OCC model of emotions [9] and on the OCEAN model [10] to model personality. In this model, each individual is characterized by five distinct traits: Openness, Conscientiousness, Extraversion, Agreeableness and Neuroticism. In this same article, McCrae and Costa also apply to demonstrate the influence of these five traits on emotions, expressing for example the link between neuroticism trait and the propensity of an individual to feel negative emotions, such as anxiety, anger or depression.

Among computational models of emotions and personality that exist, two of them have particularly drawn our attention. The first, Alma [11], has the advantage of detailing the relationships between emotions, mood and personality. The proposed representation of emotions on a three-dimensional axis also makes it possible to observe evolution of emotional state and the dynamics implemented. The second computational model is FAtiMA [12]. FAtiMA is structured around a modular architecture to add or modify phenomenons such as culture or empathy in the process of triggering emotions of the agent. It also allows the management of goals and reaction strategies based on the intrinsic needs of the agent.

Regarding the conversational agent GRETA [13], works has already been done to try to model the personality. This research aims to improve the listening behavior of the agent [14] and more precisely the feedbacks made by the latter. A link is thus made between feedbacks frequency and extraversion trait but also between neuroticism trait and the feedbacks type made. An exuberant agent will thus act more often and will tend to imitate the gestures of the user with whom he is talking. Based on Eysenck's PEN model [15], this work focuses more specifically on the expressiveness of the virtual agent and not on the influence of the personality on the triggering of emotions.

In summary, although many models demonstrate personality influence on specific points, there is not, to our knowledge that models both the impact of personality on emotions, mood and the needs of an agent.

3   ACA Personification

We first present the way in which emotion is modeled and triggered in order to highlight the points of personality influence.

3.1 Survey About Emotion Modeling

Numerous studies have shown that modelling and sensing emotions can improve human-machine dialogue systems. Indeed, to study emotions in real contexts, a lot of research has been done to propose an annotation and validation protocol. So far there is not a unified model for representing emotions. "The richness of these data makes their classification extremely complex," according to Laurence Devillers. In fact the annotation is to find robust indices at different language levels: prosodic, lexical and dialogical, to identify emotions in verbal exchanges.

EARL (Emotion Annotation and Representation Language)
The Emotion Representation and Annotation Language EARL [16] has been proposed to allow the exchange of emotional data and the reuse of resources. it is a language for the representation of emotions based on XML. This language uses a variety of representations to describe the emotions, one finds the categorical description, the dimensional description and the description cognitive evaluation which allows the user to choose the suitable representation. Also The possibility of linking one representation to another makes the format usable in heterogeneous environments or there is a variety of representation of emotions.

However, this language does not allow to express the semantic and pragmatic nuances of emotions, and does not take into account elements that can have a significant impact on emotions, information that concerns the person in question (his social environment, his culture, his objectives …).

Emotion Markup Language EmotionML
Established by the World Wide Web Consortium (W3C) Emotion Markup Language Working Group (EmotionML) 1.0, released its first report describing a language designed to be usable in a wide variety of technological contexts all in taking into account concepts from the human sciences [17]. The purpose of this language is to allow the expression of emotions via the XML language. Indeed tag language can represent and process the emotional data. Thus, it allows to annotation of different emotional states. Which allows interoperability between the different components of a multimodal system.

This language is not specific to a model and an approach, it is quite simple, and it defines the tags (<category>, <dimensions>, <appraisals>), since it uses the vocabulary defined in the literature of emotions for the representation of emotional states.

EMMA (Multimodal Annotation Markup Language)
EMMA is a mark-up language for multimodal annotation. It is part of the W3C standards for multimodal interactions [18]. It is used by the systems to make the semantic representations of the varieties of information collected in input (speech, gestures, link …) to integrate them within a multimodal application. On the other hand EMMA does not standardize the representation of the incoming data of interpretations of the users and does not make it possible to define the annotated notions. Also this language is mono devices and more oriented towards the entries than towards the outlets.

Algebraic Representation of Emotional States

This is a multidimensional model based on the algebraic representation of emotions in a vector space [11]. Each emotional state corresponds to a vector in a space with n dimensions, each of which represents a basic emotion. Thus each emotion is described by a vector formed of n components expressed in a base with n axes where each axis represents a base emotion. This allows both to represent an infinity of emotions because the model is a continuous model and secondly to offer high-performance mathematical tools for the analysis and treatment of these emotions. It is this representation that we use in this article.

3.2   Personality Modeling

The personality psychology covers a broad field of study because the concept of personality can be approached on different levels: the level of the human species, the level of inter individual differences and that of the behaviors peculiar to an individual [19]. By focusing on the last two levels, two approaches stand out: "trait" approaches and "socio-cognitive" approaches. Personality traits describe a person. Several models of behavior are based on personality and its description as an interactive and dynamic system bringing together some psychological factors. A personality model must be as complete as possible in order to consider the complexity and dynamics of the human personality, emotions, cognitive abilities, etc. For example, Eysenck's PEN model characterizes personality by only 3 dimensions: extraversion (E), neuroticism (N) and psychoticism (P) (Eysenck and Eysenck, 1985). As for Silvermann, he characterizes the personality of Leaderships by 7 traits inspired by Hermann's model. The PERSEED model is a self-based personality model for artificial companions. The PERSEED model is based on various works in psychology dealing, on the one hand, with the socio-cognitive approach of personality and, on the other hand, with models of self-regulation. A full description of the model and its theoretical foundations can be found in Faur et al. But the most used model in the field of individual differences, in psychology as in affective computing, is the Five Factors Model (FFM) [10]. The FFM model is based on five personality factors, which are also called the Big Five. These five factors are: Openness to Experience, Consciousness, Extraversion, Amenability, and Neuroticism. These traits, as a whole or in particular, are very often used to computerize personalities. Big Five are used to influence motivation and goal selection [6]. They are also used to influence the emotional behavior of virtual entities [7] as well as verbal or non-verbal behaviors during conversation [8].

To determine these affective terms, we rely on the work of Gebhard [20] who defines eight "attitudes" (see Table 1) according to their positions on a three-dimensional axis PAD (Pleasure, Arousal, Dominance) [21]. Our model therefore takes these eight attitudes and automatically calculates their correspondence with the personality traits of OCEAN model according to the Mehrabian mapping cited in [10].

Table 1. Correspondence attitudes/OCEAN model

	P	A	D
anxious	-0.5	0.49	-0.5
Disdainful	-0.49	-0.49	0.5
Dependent	0.49	0.5	-0.5
docile	0.5	-0.49	-0.5
Bored	-0.51	-0.5	-0.5
Exuberant	0.49	0.5	0.51
Hostile	-0.5	0.48	0.5
relaxed	0.5	-0.49	0.5

O	C	E	A	N
2.8	3	1.2	2.6	1
1.2	5	3.8	1	3.2
4.2	1.2	2.4	5	2.6
1.6	2.8	2.6	4.2	5
1	4.8	1	1.8	3.6
4.2	2.4	5	4.2	2.2
5	3	3.2	1.8	1.2
3.2	3	4.8	3.4	5

4   Personality Impact on Emotion

4.1   Personality Impact on Mood

We have seen that mood represents an overall emotional state that is distinguished from emotions by its lower intensity and longer duration [20]. It can be represented by a valence whose value ranges from −10 for a negative mood to 10 for a positive mood. However, the initial mood of the agent is neutral. To model the influence of personality p on this initial mood, we are therefore inspired by the work of Russell et al. presented in [20]. These authors have indeed shown that the dimension of pleasure but also of dominance and arousal (arousal) determines the mood of an individual. The article also reports a greater influence of pleasure compared to excitement, dominance playing only a minor role. To represent this phenomenon in a model, the following formula is used:

$$Mood(p) = \alpha * valence(p) + \beta * arousal(p) + \gamma * dominance(p) \quad (1)$$

$$\alpha > \beta > \gamma$$

In order to obtain the moods indicated in Table 2, we have fixed the following values (The weighting given to the pleasure dimension is greater than that of excitation, itself greater than that of dominance): $\alpha = 8$, $\beta = 4$ and $\gamma = 21$ (these values were chosen heuristically, other values might be appropriate to specify different moods). An exuberant agent is therefore endowed with a strongly positive initial mood, unlike a disdainful agent. The mood will then fluctuate during the interaction depending on the emotional charge of the events perceived by agent.

Table 2. Correspondence personality/default mood

Attitude	Mood
Anxious	-3
Disdainful	-4.9
Dependent	4.9
Docile	1
Bored	-7.1
Exuberant	6.9
Hostile	-1.1
Relaxed	3

We propose moreover in the model to modify the function of decay of the mood so that it returns naturally to its value by default if no event coming to modify the emotional state does not appear in the environment. For this, we relied on the ALMA model by proposing a similar decay function [11].

4.2   Mood Impact on Emotion

In order to determine the true impact of mood, our model represents the emotions studied by a set of categories. Let $E = \{e_1, e_2, ..., e_m\}$ be the set of emotional categories studied by the system. The emotional state in our model at time t is represented by the vector e (t):

$$e(t) = \begin{pmatrix} e_1(t) \\ e_2(t) \\ \vdots \\ \vdots \\ e_m(t) \end{pmatrix} \quad \forall j \in [1, m], \quad e_j \in [0, 1] \qquad (2)$$

$e_j = 1$ maximum intensity of emotion; $e_j = 0$ absence of emotion.

Emotions are characterized by the following elements: - *stable state*: emotional intensity of the agent under no influence - *Activation threshold*: minimum intensity from which the agent feels the emotion - *Function of weakening*: evolution of the emotional intensity of the agent to reach its stable state.

The mood mainly affects the weakening of emotion. When it is positive, it accelerates the weakening of emotions, and slows them in the opposite case. The formula used in our model is as follows:

Is e (t') the emotional state calculated at instant t'.

Weakening of ej(t') at instant t (t > t'):

$$d_j(\Delta) = \begin{cases} e_j(t') & \text{if } \Delta = 0 \\ g_j(t' + \Delta) & \text{if } \quad T_j > \Delta > 0 \\ \text{stable state} & \text{if } \Delta \geq T_j \end{cases}$$

$$\Delta = t - t'$$

Tj: weakening time to reach steady state

gj is defined so that $d_j(\Delta)$ to be continuous and decreasing monotonous

We speak of linear weakening when mood is negative and exponential in the opposite case. The following formulas allow to implement them in our model.

Exponential weakening

$$d_j(\Delta) = \begin{cases} ej(t') * e^{-b*\Delta} & \text{if } T_j > \Delta \geq 0 \\ \text{stablestate} & \text{if } \Delta \geq T_j \end{cases} \qquad (3)$$

Linear weakening

$$d_j(\Delta) = \begin{cases} -b * \Delta + e_j(t') & if \ T_j > \Delta \geq 0 \\ stablestate & if \ \Delta \geq T_j \end{cases} \tag{4}$$

b is defined according to personality and emotional category e_j.

4.3 Personality Influence on Emotion

Our model is based on OCC theory [9] to calculate emotions. These are defined and characterized by threshold values (threshold) ranging from 0 to 10. The threshold value characterizes the minimum intensity that an emotion must reach to be felt.

In order to visualize this impact of personality on emotions, we define the personality by n dimensions represented by variables whose value is in interval $[-1, 1]$. The personality is represented by a vector with n factors with two opposite poles (positive and negative)

$$p = \begin{pmatrix} p_1 \\ p_2 \\ : \\ : \\ p_n \end{pmatrix} \forall i \in [1, n], \quad p_i \in [-1, 1] \tag{5}$$

pi = 1 maximum presence of positive pole of the factor
pi = 0 absence of the factor
pi = −1 maximum presence of negative pole of the factor.

The impact of personality is defined by the product of personality factors and emotional categories considered. In our model, this makes it possible to obtain the following matrix M.

Mn * m: influence of personality factor on emotional categories

$$M = \begin{pmatrix} f(p_1, e_1) & \cdots & f(p_1, e_m) \\ \cdot & \cdot & \cdot \\ \cdot & \cdot & \cdot \\ f(p_n, e_1) & \cdots & f(p_n, e_m) \end{pmatrix} \tag{6}$$

$\forall i \in [1, n]$ et $j \in [1, m]$, f $(p_i, e_j) \in [0, 1]$ $\forall$ $p_i \in [-1, 1]$
f (p_i, e_j): influence of factor p_i on categories e_j.

Let Sj the sensitivity of personality factors studied by recognition system on a given emotional category. It is expressed by the following formula

$$S_j = \frac{\sum_{i=1}^{n} f(p_i, e_j)}{card\{f(p_i, e_j)\}_{i=1,n}}$$

5 Conclusion and Perspectives

In this article, we have proposed a computational model to simulate personality influence on emotions and the impact of mood on the weakening of emotions. This model was developed to allow non-experts to simply determine the personality of an agent in a recognition system implementing OCEAN personality model. Many improvements can however be envisaged. For example, adding an emotional intelligence module to the architecture would allow the agent to express positive emotion while being in a bad mood to comply with sociocultural norms. The continuation of the work beginning in [20] is also envisaged, in order to model the impact of the personality on the different expressivity parameters.

References

1. Nass, C., Moon, Y., Fogg, B., Reeves, B., Dryer, D.: Can computer personalities be human personalities. Int. J. Hum.-Comput. Stud. **43**(2), 223–239 (1995)
2. Bledsoe, W.: I had a dream: AAAI presidential address. AI Mag. **7**(1), 57–61 (1986)
3. Picard, R.: Affective computing. Technical report no. 321, M.I.T Media Laboratory Perceptual Computing Section (1995)
4. Saucier, G., Goldberg, L.: Personnalité, caractère et tempérament: la structure translinguistique des traits. Psychol. Fr. **51**, 265–284 (2006)
5. Miller, L.C., Read, S.J., Zachary, W., Rosoff, A.: Modeling the impact of motivation, personality, and emotion on social behavior. In: Chai, S.-K., Salerno, J.J., Mabry, P.L. (eds.) SBP 2010. LNCS, vol. 6007, pp. 298–305. Springer, Heidelberg (2010). https://doi.org/10.1007/978-3-642-12079-4_37
6. Marsella, S.C., Pynadath, D.V., Read, S.J.: Psychsim: agent-based modeling of social interactions and influence. In: Proceedings of the International Conference on Cognitive Modeling, pp. 243–248. Citeseer (2004)
7. André, E., Klesen, M., Gebhard, P., Allen, S., Rist, T.: Integrating models of personality and emotions into lifelike characters. In: Paiva, A. (ed.) IWAI 1999. LNCS (LNAI), vol. 1814, pp. 150–165. Springer, Heidelberg (2000). https://doi.org/10.1007/10720296_11
8. Kasap, Z., Magnenat-Thalmann, N.: Intelligent virtual humans with autonomy and personality: state-of-the- art. Intell. Decis. Technol. **1**, 3–15 (2007)
9. Ortony, A., Clore, G.L., Collins, A.: The Cognitive Structure of Emotions. Cambridge University Press, Cambridge (1988)
10. McCrae, R., Costa, P.: Validation of the five factor model of personality across instruments and observers. J. Pers. Soc. Psychol. **52**(1), 81–90 (1987)
11. Gebhard, P.: ALMA - a layered model of affect. In: Proceedings of the Fourth International Joint Conference on Autonomous Agents and Multiagent Systems (AAMAS 2005), Utrecht (2005)
12. Dias, J., Mascarenhas, J., Paiva, A.: FAtiMA modular: towards an agent architecture with a generic appraisal framework (2011)
13. Asendorpf, J.B., Wilpers, S.: Personality effects on social relationships. J. Pers. Soc. Psychol. **74**(6), 1531 (1998)
14. Bevacqua, E., de Sevin, E., Pelachaud, C., McRorie, M., Sneddon, I.: Building credible agents: behavior influenced by personality and emotional traits. In: Proceedings of the International Conference on Kansei Engineering and Emotion Research, Paris, France (2010)

15. Mischel, W., Shoda, Y., Smith, R.: Introduction to Personality: Towards an Integration, 7th edn. Wiley, Hoboken (2004)
16. Extensible MultiModal Annotation markup language, We3C, W3C Recommendation, 10 February 2009. http://www.w3.org/TR/emma/
17. Tayari, I., Le Thanh, N., Ben Amar, C.: Modélisation des états émotionnels par un espace vectoriel multidimensionnel (2009)
18. Bates, J.: The role of emotion in believable agents. In: Communications of the ACM, Special Issue on Agents (1994)
19. Mehrabian, A.: Pleasure-arousal-dominance: a general framework for describing and measuring individual differences in temperament. Curr. Psychol. **14**(4), 261–292 (1996)
20. Scherer, K.: Emotion. In: Introduction to Social Psychology: A European Perspective, 3rd edn. pp. 151–191. Blackwell (2000)
21. Mancini, M., Pelachaud, C.: Generating distinctive behavior for embodied conversational agents. J. Multimodal User Interfaces **3**(4), 249–261 (2009). https://doi.org/10.1007/s12193-010-0048-y

Two Parallelized Filter Methods for Feature Selection Based on Spark

Reine Marie Ndéla Marone[1]([⊠]), Fodé Camara[2], Samba Ndiaye[1],
and Demba Kande[1]

[1] Department of Mathematics, Cheikh Anta Diop University, Dakar, Senegal
reine.marie.marone@ucad.edu.sn
[2] Department of Mathematics, Alioune Diop University, Bambey, Senegal
fode.camara@uadb.edu.sn

Abstract. The goal of feature selection is to reduce computation time, improve prediction performance, build simpler and more comprehensive models and allow a better understanding of the data in machine learning or data mining problems. But the major problem nowadays is that the size of datasets grows larger and larger, both vertically and horizontally. That constitutes challenges to the feature selection, as there is an increasing need for scalable and yet efficient feature selection methods. As an answer to those problems, we present here two effective parallel algorithms developed on Apache Spark, a unified analytics engine for big data processing. One of them is a parallelized algorithm based on the famous feature selection method called mRMR. In the second algorithm we propose a totally novel metric to select the more relevant and less redundant features. To show the superiority of that algorithm we have created its centralized version that we have called CNFS_Spark.

Experimental results demonstrate that our algorithms achieve a great performance improvement in scaling well and take less time than classical feature selection methods.

Keywords: Feature selection · Parallel computing · Apache spark
mRMR · Novel method · Big data · Large scale · High dimensional

1 Introduction

Feature selection has been successfully applied for years as a preprocessing step and has become an active research field in pattern recognition, statistics, and data mining communities.

In supervised learning, the main goal of feature selection is to choose a subset of input variables that produces higher classification accuracy by eliminating features with little or no predictive information. Feature selection can also significantly reduce the learning time of classification.

Feature selection methods are commonly categorized into filter, wrapper and embedded approaches [1].

© ICST Institute for Computer Sciences, Social Informatics and Telecommunications Engineering 2019
Published by Springer Nature Switzerland AG 2019. All Rights Reserved
R. Zitouni and M. Agueh (Eds.): AFRICATEK 2018, LNICST 260, pp. 175–192, 2019.
https://doi.org/10.1007/978-3-030-05198-3_16

In the wrapper methods a subset of features is ranked by the prediction performance of a classifier on the given subset [1]. The Wrapper methods are computationally expensive and over fit on small training sets.

Embedded methods perform feature selection during the modeling algorithm's execution [1]. These methods are thus embedded in the algorithm either as its normal or extended functionality. Embedded methods select features based on criterions that are generated during the modeling algorithm's execution. The chosen features are sensitive to the structures of the underlying classifiers.

Filter methods rely on in various statistical tests to evaluate and select features without involving any mining algorithm [1, 2]. The subset selection procedure is generally a pre-processing step. In our studies we have focused on the filters methods because they offer better computational complexity for datasets having large number of features.

But generally, classical feature selection algorithms are designed to run on a single machine and are not adapted for big-data problems [3]. In fact, algorithms do not scale well when dealing with very large datasets and their efficiency significantly downgrades.

Distributed computing techniques such as MapReduce [3] along with its open-source implementation Apache Hadoop can be a solution to solve this problem.

But the MapReduce parallel programming with Apache Hadoop is not suited for the feature selection because MapReduce programming model reads and writes from disk [4]. As a result, it slows down the processing speed. Spark is lightning fast cluster computing tool because of reducing the number of read/write cycle to disk and storing intermediate data in memory. That explains our preference for apache spark.

On that basis we have developed two novel, parallel and scalable feature selection algorithms named respectively PSFS-mRMR (for Parallel Spark Feature Selection method based on mRMR) and PNFS_Spark (Parallel Neighbor Feature Selection based on Spark) on the Spark framework.

The results that we obtained show that the parallelized methods outperform the centralized ones, in terms of scalability and efficiency which shows that parallelization is better than centralization.

The remainder of this paper is organized as follows:

Section 2 discusses related works.
Section 3 consists of defining the problem.
Section 4 presents the classical mRMR feature selection method.
Section 5 gives the metrics we used in our proposal.
Section 6 deals with the presentation of our methods.
Section 7 describes the experiments.
Section 8 consists of analyzing the experiment results.
Section 9 concludes the paper and gives some future works.

2 Related Works

Filter methods are kind of feature selection methods that attempt to assess the importance of features statically according to a heuristic scoring criteria without any particular classifier. Many filter methods are based on information theory specifically mutual Information but are centralized and do not scale well when dealing with big data. They must be parallelized to gracefully scale with larger datasets [5]. So, in this section we will discuss parallel approach of filter methods that have been proposed to decrease the training time and produce better accuracy.

In [6] authors implement on Apache Spark, a generic feature selection framework that includes a broad group of well-known information theory-based methods like mRMR. The experimental results demonstrate that this framework handles efficiently large-scale data and outperforms the sequential version.

Authors in [7] propose a package named mRMRe that extends mRMR by using an approach to better explore the feature space and build more robust predictors. In mRMRe, the main functions are implemented and parallelized in C using the openMP Application Programming Interface. mRMRe provides less learning time and can identify genes more relevant to the biological context and may lead to richer biological interpretations.

The work in [8] is a combinaison of ReliefF and mRMR consisting on two-steps: apply ReliefF on the first stage to find a candidate subset of gene and then use mRMR method for reducing redundancy and selecting an effective set of gene from the candidate subset. The experimental evaluation demonstrates the effectiveness of this algorithm.

In [9], a parallel version of mRMR called fast-mRMR is proposed to overcome the computationally expensive of mRMR. Authors provide a package with three implementations of this algorithm in several platforms, namely, CPU for sequential execution, GPU (graphics processing units) for parallel computing, and Apache Spark for distributed computing. The experimental results show that fast-mRMR outperforms the original version of mRMR and show a clear improvement when using the parallel and distributed versions over the sequential one.

In [10], authors reimplement four popular feature selection algorithms including RELIEF-F, InfoGain, CFS and SVM-RFE in Weka. Multithreaded implementations previously not included in Weka as well as parallel Spark implementations were developed for each algorithm. Experimental results obtained from tests on real-world datasets show that the new versions offer significant reductions in processing times.

In [11], authors, present a completely redesigned distributed version of the popular ReliefF algorithm based on the novel Spark cluster computing model called DiReliefF.

But the proposed algorithms in the related work include iteratively one or many features into the feature's subset to return. So the number of onward and backwards movements between the workers and the driver increases according to the number of features to select. This can lead to high communication and synchronization costs between the workers and the driver.

In what we propose, the score of each feature is calculated by the workers and sent once to the driver that selects the best features in one pass. That leads to less learning time while keeping a good accuracy.

3 Problem Definition

Our work concerns the binary classification problems. $c \in \{0, 1\}$ denotes the class label. Let F be the input set of attributes $\{f_1, .., f_n\}$ and I an instance represented by a n-dimensional vector $(v_1, .., v_n)$, where v_j represents the value of the attribute f_j in I and n the number of features which can be large. $J(S', D)$ is the objective function that measuring the quality of a subset S' of S using the data D. If $J(S'_1, D) > J(S'_2, D)$, it means that the subset S'_1 is better than S'_2.

So in this work, we proposed a high-dimensional filter method: PSFS-mRMR for Parallel Spark Feature Selection method based on mRMR (Minimum Redundancy and Maximum Relevancy) and another one called PNFS_Spark (Parallel Neighbor Feature Selection based on Spark) using the unified analytics engine for big data processing Apache Spark to implement them.

4 The Classical MRMR

mRMR (minimum Redundancy and Maximum Relevance) is an algorithm frequently used to rank features based on their relevance to the label class, and, at the same time, the redundancy of features is also penalized. The goal is to find the maximum dependency between a subset F' of features, and the class label l, using mutual information (MI) [12].

Let f_i and f_j be two features in F. $MI(f_i, f_j)$ is the mutual information between f_i and f_j. $MI(l, f_i)$ stands for the mutual information between the class label l and f_i.

The redundancy between features in F, is determined by

$$Q_I(F) \frac{1}{|F|^2} \sum_{f_i, f_j \in F} MI(f_i, f_j) \tag{1}$$

The relevance of the features in F with the class label l is given by

$$R_I(F) \frac{1}{|F|} \sum_{f_i \in F} MI(l, f_i) \tag{2}$$

Determine the best subset of features F^* in F, which contains maximally relevant and minimally redundant features consist of optimizing (1) and (2) as follows:

$$F^* = \arg \max_{F' \subseteq F} [R_I(F) - Q_I(F)] \tag{3}$$

5   Ours Proposals

- **PSFS-mRMR**

Many authors demonstrate that [13] SVMs (support vector machines) with simple feature rankings are effective on datasets. That's why, in our proposal PSFS-mRMR, we rank the features using a combination of [14] SVM and mRMR for better results. Let $\beta \in [0, 1]$ determines the tradeoff between SVM ranking and mRMR ranking. The relevancy $R_{F,i}$ of feature f_i in the F set in classification is given by

$$R_{F,i} \frac{1}{|F|} \sum_l MI(l, f_i) \tag{4}$$

And $Q_{F,i}$ the redundancy of feature f_i in the set F in classification is computed as follows

$$Q_{F,i} \frac{1}{|F|^2} \sum_{f_i, f_j \in F} MI(f_i, f_j) \tag{5}$$

Let ω_i represents the SVM weight of the attribute f_i.
For i-th feature, the ranking measure d_i is calculated as follows

$$d_i = \beta |\omega_i| + (1 - \beta) \frac{R_{F,i}}{Q_{F,i}} \tag{6}$$

- **PNFS_Spark**

In the PNFS_Spark we propose a novel metric called m_e that represents the median value of the relevance with the class label l. In fact, the median gives a satisfactory idea of the general tendency of a statistical serie (F set in our case). The outliers of the variable that might be in the series do not influence it.

Let n be the number of features in F and e a number given by applying the formula below if n is pair:

$$e = (n + 1)/2$$

or

$$e = (n/2 + n/2 + 1)/2$$

if n is impair.

m_e is obtained by:

$$m_e = R_{F,e} \tag{7}$$

where $R_{F,e}$ represents the relevance of e-th feature.

If the mutual information between 2 features f_i and f_j is greater than the median then f_i is considered a neighbor of f_j. The score of the feature f_i is given by multiplying its relevance $R_{F,i}$ with its number of neighbors.

6 Our Algorithms

Our proposed algorithms, called respectively PSFS_mRMR and PNFS_Spark are feature selection methods that we base on Spark, an open-source distributed cluster-computing framework.

In this section we describe how our algorithms perform.

Let S be the input dataset (composed of n attributes and m instances) and K the number of attributes that must be returned. Let β be a ratio between SVM ranking and mRMR ranking (in the case of PSFS_mRMR), and x the number of partitions for the dataset. F represents the space of attributes. The output S' is the subset of S constituted of K features that have the maximal d_i scores.

PSFS_mRMR method follows seven steps:

■ **Step 1: create x partitions of features**

1.   Construct $labels = \{l_1, \ldots, l_m\}$ the set of the class label in each instance.

2.   Construct $vals = \{\{v_i^1, \ldots, v_i^m\}$, i=1 to n $\}$

$vals$ represents the values v_i^j of each attribute f_i of instance I_j:

3.   Construct x subspaces of features SF_t, $t = 1..x$ from the space of feature F.

4.   Construct x subspaces sub_t of $\{\{v_i^1, \ldots, v_i^m\}$, i$\in$ SF$\}$

5.   Send each sub_t to a worker (between the x workers).

■ **Step 2: Combine features by two with class labels**

On each worker t:

6.   Map each attribute f_i with each other attribute f_j in F as follows:

$$f_i => \{ f_i, \{v_i^1, \ldots, v_i^m\}, \{v_j^1, \ldots, v_j^m\} , \{l_1, \ldots, l_m\}\}$$

We call the set $\{f_i, \{v_i^1, .., v_i^m\}, \{v_j^1, .., v_j^m\}, \{l_1, .., l_m\}$, i=1 to n, j=1 to n and $j \neq i\}$ $rdd2$.

- **Step 3: calculate the mutual information among the features and the relevance of each feature**
In this step, we use each element of rdd2 to calculate mutual information M_{ij} between each feature f_i and another feature f_j of F. We compute also the relevance R_i (mutual information with the class label) of f_i. We proceed as follows:
  For each element e $\subset$ *rdd2*

  7. *rdd* $[(f_i, M_{ij}, R_i)]$ = *mapToPair* (e=>{ f_i, M_{ij}, R_i })

  M_{ij} = *MutualInformation* ($\{v_i^1, .., v_i^m\}, \{v_j^1, .., v_j^m\}$)

  R_i= *MutualInformation* ($\{v_i^1, .., v_i^m\}, \{l_1, .., l_m\}$) /n

where $l_{k \in 1..m}$ is the class label in the instance I_k.
  End For each
The set constituted of each attribute f_i, mutual information between f_i and another attribute f_j and the relevance R_i between the class label and f_i will be called rdd3.

- **Step 4 : aggregate the mutual information for each feature by summing them.**
Calculate the redundancy of each feature f_i by summing its mutual information with other features. A set constituted of $\{f_i, sumM_{ij}, R_i\}$, where f_i is the feature, $sumM_{ij}$ the sum of mutual information between f_i and the other features and R_i the mutual information between f_i and the class label, is then obtained. This set is called $rdd4$.
This is done as follows:
  For each element (f_i, M_{ij}, R_i) $\in rdd3$

  8. *rdd* $[(f_i, sumM_{ij}, R_i)]$= *reduceByKey* $(\_+\_)$

  $$sumM_{ij} = \sum_{i=1}^{n} M_{ij}$$

End Foreach
- **Step 5: for each feature, compute the SVM weight**
In this step compute for each feature f_i its SVM weight ω_i as follows:
For each $f_i \subseteq F$

9. $rdd\ [(f_i,\ \omega_i)]=\ map\ (f_i\ =>\{\ f_i,\ \omega_i\})$

$\omega_i\ \subset\omega\ where\ \omega=SVMWeight(F)$

$End\ For\ each$

- **Step 6: for each feature, compute the rapport d_i between relevance and redundancy**

Determine for each feature f_i its score d_i, which represents a tradeoff between the redundancy and the relevance of f_i. Send d_i scores to the master.

This is done as follows:

$For\ each\ element\ (f_i,\ sumM_{ij},\ R_i)\ \subset rdd4$

10. $rdd\ [(f_i,d_i)]=\ mapToPair\ (\{f_i,\ sumM_{ij},\ R_i\ \}\ =>\{f_i,\ d_i\})$

$Q_i=\ sumM_{ij}\ /\ (n*n);$

$d_i\ =\beta\ +\ \omega_i+((1-\beta)*\ (R_i\ /Q_i));$

$/*\ \omega_i\ is\ the\ SVM\ weight\ of\ attribute\ f_i*/$

$End\ For\ each$

11. $Workers\ send\ d_i\ scores\ to\ the\ master$

- **Step 7: Choose the best features in F**

Master collects, orders and returns the K attributes that obtained the highest d_i scores. This is done as follows:

$On\ the\ master:$

12. $Collect\ and\ take\ ordered$

13. $Return\ S':\ optimal\ subset\ of\ K\ features\ in\ S\ with\ highest\ scores\ d_i.$

For PNFS_Spark:

PNFS_Spark algorithm follows seven steps:

- **Step 1: create x partitions of features**

1. Construct $labels=\{l_1,..,l_m\}$ the set of the class label of the different instance in S.

2. Construct $vals=\{\{v_i^1,..,v_i^m\},\ i=1\ to\ n\ \}$

vals represents the values v_i^j of each feature f_i in each instance I_j:

3. Construct x subspaces of features SF_t, $t = 1..x$ from the feature space F.

4. Construct x subspaces sub_t of $\{\{v_i^1, .., v_i^m\}, \quad i \in SF\}$

5. Send each sub_t to a worker.

- **Step 2: Combine features by two with labels**

On each worker x:

6. Map each attribute f_i with each other attribute f_j in F as follows:

$$f_i => \{ f_i, \{v_i^1, .., v_i^m\}, \{v_j^1, .., v_j^m\}, \{l_1, .., l_m\}\}$$

We call the set $\{f_i, \{v_i^1, .., v_i^m\}, \{v_j^1, .., v_j^m\}, \{l_1, .., l_m\}$, i=1 to n, j=1 to n and $j \neq i$ \} obtained $rdd2$.

- **Step 3: calculate the mutual information between features and the relevance of each feature**

In this step, we use each element of rdd2 to calculate mutual information M_{ij} between each feature f_i and another feature f_j of F. We compute also the relevance R_i (mutual information with the class label) of f_i. We proceed as follows:

For each element e ⊂ rdd2

7. rdd $[(f_i, M_{ij}, R_i)]$ = mapToPair (e=>{ f_i, M_{ij}, R_i })

M_{ij} = MutualInformation ($\{v_i^1, .., v_i^m\}, \{v_j^1, .., v_j^m\}$)

R_i= MutualInformation ($\{v_i^1, .., v_i^m\}, \{l_1, .., l_m\}$) /n

where $l_{k \in 1..m}$ *is the class label in different instances.*
End For each

The set constituted of each attribute f_i, mutual information between f_i and another attribute f_j and the relevance R_i between the class label and f_i will be called rdd3.

- **Step 4 : calculer la valeur medianne de la relevance des attributs avec l'etiquette de classe.**

Calculate R_{fe} the median value of the set of values of relevance R_i.

Let f_e be the index of the median value in the list of relevance values between features and class labels.

If (n%2==0)

$$f_e = (n+1)/2$$

else

$$f_e = (n/2 +n/2+1)/2$$

R_{fe}= rdd3 $[f_e]$. R_e

■ **Step 5: for each feature, determine the list of his neighbor**

In this step calculate for each feature f_i the ranking measure d_i that represents a tradeoff between the redundancy and the relevance of f_i. Then send all d_i values to the master.

This is done as follows:

On each worker x:

For each $f_i \subset sub_x$

    For each $f_j \subset F$

    /* M_{ij} represents the mutual information between f_i and f_j */

      If $(M_{ij} > R_{fe})$

          rdd $[(f_i, Vois_{ij})] =$ mapToPair $(\{f_i\} => \{f_i, f_j\})$

    EndForeach

EndForeach

  8. All workers send d_i to the master

■ **Step 6: for each feature, compute the ranking measure d_i which represents the score of the feature**

Determine for each feature f_i its score d_i , which represents a tradeoff between the redundancy and the relevance of f_i. Send d_i scores to the master.

This is done as follows:

For each element $f_i \subset$ rdd $[(f_i, Vois_i)]$

    For each element $f_j \subset$ rdd $[f_i].Vois_i)$

        rdd $[(f_i, d_i)] =$ mapToPair $(\{f_i\} => \{f_i, d_i\})$

        /* determines nV number of neighbor of f_i */

        nV=$Vois_i$.length

        /* the score d_i of f_i is obtained by multiplying its relevance R_i with its number of neighbor nV */

$$d_i = \sum_{i=1}^{nV} R_i$$

    End For each

  End For each

  9. Workers send d_i scores to the master

■ **Step 7: Choose the best features in F**

Master collects, orders and returns the *K* attributes that obtained the highest d_i scores. This is done as follows:
On the master:
  10.Collect and take ordered

Return S': optimal subset of K features in S with highest
   d_i **scores.**

7 Experiment Setup

The classifier that we used in our experiments is support vector machine.

The datasets used are from mldata.org [15] and are in LibSVM format. Table 1 describes those datasets.

Table 1. Characteristics of datasets

Name	Number of Features	Number of Instances
Colon-cancer	2000	62
Colon-Tumor	2000	60

We perform ours experiments on a cluster of 4 nodes, then on a cluster of 6 nodes. Each node runs at the linux and consists of 8 cores. Each core runs at 2.60 GHz and has 56 GB of memory and 382 GB of disk.

8 Experimental Results

We conducted the experiment with different number of selected features and number of nodes to measure the scalability of our propositions and compare the running time of ours methods in comparison with the centralized ones.

Figures 1, 2 and 3 show respectively the running time of PSFS_mRMR method and classical mRMR algorithm for selecting 25%, 50% or 75% of the colon-cancer dataset with various numbers of nodes.

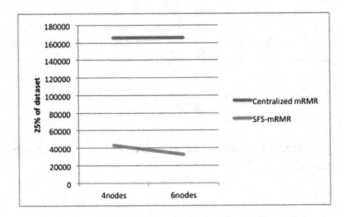

Fig. 1. Scalability of PSFS_mRMR and classical **mRMR** with 25%.

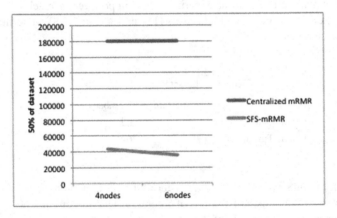

Fig. 2. Scalability of PSFS_mRMR and classical **mRMR** with 50%.

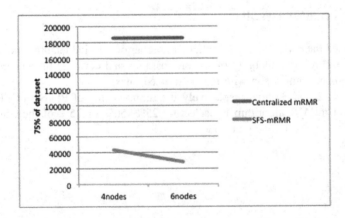

Fig. 3. Scalability of PSFS_mRMR and classical **mRMR** with 75%.

Figures 4, 5 and 6 show respectively the running time of **PNFS_Spark** method and its centralized version for selecting 25%, 50% or 75% of the colon-cancer dataset various numbers of nodes.

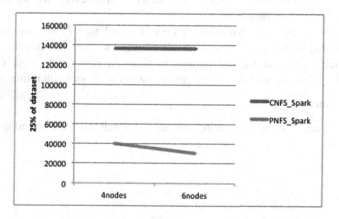

Fig. 4. Scalability of **PNFS_Spark** and **CNFS_Spark** with 25%.

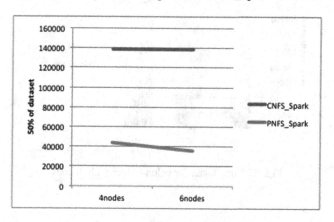

Fig. 5. Scalability of **PNFS_Spark** and **CNFS_Spark** with 50%.

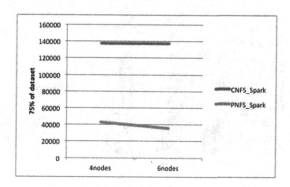

Fig. 6. Scalability of **PNFS_Spark** and **CNFS_Spark** with 75%.

From the figure, when we add more nodes, the running time of **PSFS_mRMR** and **PNFS_Spark** considerably decreases, whereas the time taken by **classical mRMR** and **CNFS_Spark** remains the same.

We have used 4 then 6 nodes for the scalability. And for every case we have run the tests using the same environment.

For every dataset we first select 25% then 50% and after 75% of features.

After having studied the scalability of our propositions we will study the time taken by the feature selection for our parallel methods in comparison with the central methods. We start first with the colon-cancer dataset then with colon-tumor.

- **Colon-cancer**

Figures 7 and 8 show the running time of PSFS_mRMR method and the classical mRMR.

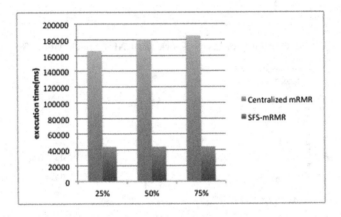

Fig. 7. Time taken for colon-cancer with 4nodes

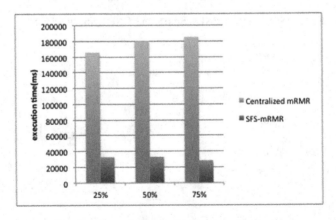

Fig. 8. Time taken for colon-cancer with 6nodes

Figures 9 and 10 show the running time of PNFS_Spark method in comparison with its centralized one for respectively 4 and 6 nodes.

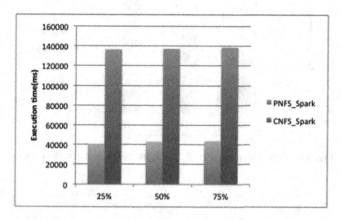

Fig. 9. Time taken for colon-cancer with 4nodes

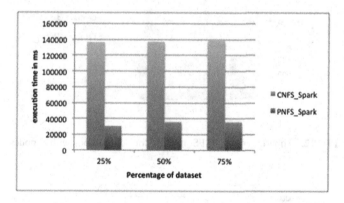

Fig. 10. Time taken for colon-cancer with 6nodes

From the results, we can see that, the running time of ours parallel methods is at least 4 times shorter than the classical **mRMR** and **CNFS_Spark** algorithm.

- **Colon-Tumor**

Results obtained for colon-tumor with 4 nodes are shown in Figs. 11 and 12: For a cluster of 6 nodes the running time is stated in Figs. 13 and 14.

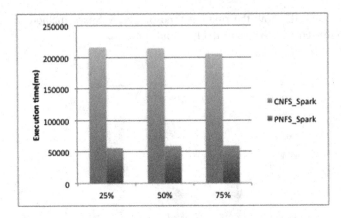

Fig. 11. Time taken per PNFS_Spark for colon-tumor with 4 nodes

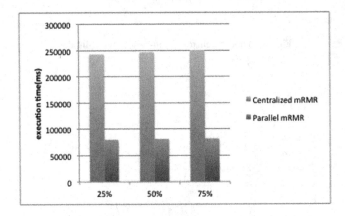

Fig. 12. Time taken per PSFS_mRMR for colon-tumor with 4 nodes

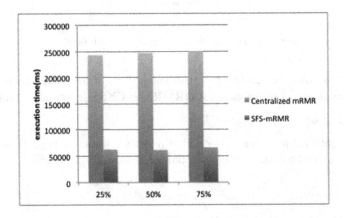

Fig. 13. Time taken per PSFS_mRMR for colon-tumor with 6 nodes

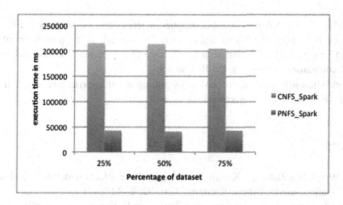

Fig. 14. Time taken per **PNFS_Spark** for colon-tumor with 6 nodes

As for the colon-cancer we can notice that the execution time of PSFS-mRMR and PNFS_Spark is also 4 times shorter at least.

Therefore, the conclusion of ours experiments is that parallel solutions outperform centralized methods in terms of running time. Moreover, when we add more nodes, the running time of ours methods becomes shorter, whereas the time taken by the centralized one remains constant.

Our empirical analysis confirms the scalability of ours algorithms with respect to the number of features and processing cores.

Our experiment is limited to the datasets up to 2000 features since beyond that number, the centralized algorithms takes too much time to run.

9   Conclusion

In this paper we have proposed two feature selection methods, which are capable of scaling feature selection to large datasets. One of them is a parallel version of a famous feature selection method called mRMR. Our proposal was developed on Spark, a unified analytics engine for large datasets processing.

Our methods consist of computing the score of each feature relatively to its redundancy with the others features and its relevance with the class label. Then return the features with the best scores.

Experimental results demonstrate that our parallel algorithms achieve a great performance improvement in scaling well and reducing the running time. In the case of mRMR our parallel method PSFS_mRMR have led to better performance in terms of selecting relevant and non redundant features.

In the future, we plan to parallelize many other classical feature selection methods like RELIEF or RFE-SVM.

Acknowledgment. We would like to express our sincere thanks to the CEA-MITIC (African Center of Excellence in Mathematics, Computer Science and **Tic**) who financed our research by paying the publication fees of the 2 papers that we published in Africatek2018.

The CEA-MITIC, located at the UFR of Applied Sciences and Technology (UFR SAT) of the Gaston Berger University (UGB) of Saint-Louis in Senegal, is a consortium of university institutions in Senegal and subregion of Senegal, research institutions and national, regional and international companies involved in the ICT sector.

In this work Microsoft Azure sponsored us by putting at our disposal a cluster of machines for the tests and we send them our warm thanks as well.

References

1. Liu, C., Wang, W., Zhao, Q., Konan, M.: A new feature selection method based on a validity index of feature subset. Pattern Recognit. Lett. **92**, 1–8 (2017)
2. Wenyan, Z., Xuewen, L., Jingjing, W.: Feature selection for cancer classification using microarray gene expression data. Biostat. Biom. Open Acc. J. **1**(2), 555557 (2017)
3. Zhao, Z., Cox, J., Duling, D., Sarle, W.: Massively parallel feature selection: an approach based on variance preservation. In: Flach, Peter A., De Bie, T., Cristianini, N. (eds.) ECML PKDD 2012. LNCS (LNAI), vol. 7523, pp. 237–252. Springer, Heidelberg (2012). https://doi.org/10.1007/978-3-642-33460-3_21
4. Singh, D., Reddy, C.K.: A survey on platforms for big data analytics. J. Big Data **2**(1), 8 (2015). Published online 9 October 2014
5. Jaseena, K.U., David, J.M.: Issues, challenges, and solutions: big data mining. In: Sixth International Conference on Networks and Communications (2014). https://doi.org/10.5121/csit.2014.41311
6. Ramırez-Gallego, S., et al.: An information theory-based feature selection framework for big data under apache spark. J. Latex Class Files **13**(9) (2014)
7. De Jay, N., Papillon, S., Olsen, C., El-Hachem, N., Bontempi, G., Haibe-Kains, B.: mRMRe: an R package for parallelized mRMR ensemble feature selection. Bioinformatics **29**, 2365–2368 (2013). https://doi.org/10.1093/bioinformatics/btt383
8. Zhang, Y., Ding, C., Li, T.: Gene selection algorithm by combining reliefF and mRMR. BMC Genom. **9**(Suppl 2), S27 (2008). https://doi.org/10.1186/1471-2164-9-S2-S27
9. Ramírez-Gallego, S., et al.: Fast-mRMR: fast minimum redundancy maximum relevance algorithm for high-dimensional big data: FAST-mRMR ALGORITHM FOR BIG DATA. Int. J. Intell. Syst. **32**, 134–152 (2016). https://doi.org/10.1002/int.21833
10. Eiras-Franco, C., Bolón-Canedo, V., Ramos, S., González-Domínguez, J., Alonso-Betanzos, A., Touriño, J.: Multithreaded and spark parallelization of feature selection filters. Journal of Computational Science **17**(Part 3), 609–619 (2016)
11. Palma-Mendoza, R.J., Rodriguez, D., de-Marcos, L.: Distributed ReliefF-based feature selection in spark. Knowl. Inf. Syst. **57**, 1–20 (2018)
12. Mandal, M., Mukhopadhyay, A.: An improved minimum redundancy maximum relevance approach for feature selection in gene expression data. In: IEEE/ACM Transactions on Computational Biology and Bioinformatics, July 2016
13. Chang, Y.-W., Lin, C.-J.: Feature ranking using linear SVM. In: Proceedings of the Workshop on the Causation and Prediction Challenge at WCCI 2008 (2008). PMLR **3**, 53–64
14. Mundra, P.A., Rajapakse, J.C.: SVM-RFE with MRMR filter for gene selection. IEEE Trans. Nanobiosci. **9**(1), 31–37 (2010)
15. http://mldata.org/repository/data/viewslug/ovarian-cancer-nci-pbsii-data/

Author Index

Printed in the United States
By Bookmasters